If Only
I Could Sleep

'2015
Jennifer—
Thank you for being
a strong force in empowering
our girls of tomorrow. I look
forward to working together—
I'm here for anything you
and your team need! Interact
Blessings—
Stephanie

If Only I Could Sleep

a survivor's memoir

STEPHANIE HENRY

EMERALD
BOOK CO.

The names and identifying characteristics of persons referenced in this book, as well as identifying events and places, have been changed to protect the privacy of the individuals and their families.

The freedom and well-being of children is at the heart of *If Only I Could Sleep*. The author has taken every safeguard to ensure that no child labor was used in the printing and/or distribution of this book. The author upholds, supports, and recognizes the right of the child to be protected from economic exploitation and from performing any work that is likely to be hazardous, interfere with the child's education, or to be harmful to the child's health or physical, mental, spiritual, moral, or social development.

Published by Emerald Book Company
Austin, TX
www.emeraldbookcompany.com

Distributed by Emerald Book Company

For ordering information or special discounts for bulk purchases, please contact Emerald Book Company at PO Box 91869, Austin, TX 78709, 512.891.6100.

Design and composition by Greenleaf Book Group LLC
Cover design by Greenleaf Book Group LLC
Illustration by Darren Heath

Publisher's Cataloging-In-Publication Data
(Prepared by The Donohue Group, Inc.)
Henry, Stephanie.
    If only I could sleep : a survivor's memoir / Stephanie Henry.—1st ed.

    p. ; cm.

    Issued also as an ebook.
    ISBN: 978-1-937110-46-8

    1. Henry, Stephanie. 2. Adult child sexual abuse victims—Biography. 3. Child sexual abuse.
4. Bulimia. 5. Drug abuse. 6. Autobiography. I. Title.

RC569.5.A28 H46 2013
616.85/83690092   2013938056

Part of the Tree Neutral® program, which offsets the number of trees consumed in the production and printing of this book by taking proactive steps, such as planting trees in direct proportion to the number of trees used: www.treeneutral.com

Printed in the United States of America on acid-free paper

    14 15 16 17 18   10 9 8 7 6 5 4 3 2

First Edition

TreeNeutral®

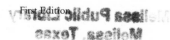

For my children—Miranda, Mary,
and John—for giving me life in return.

"Have courage for the great sorrows of life
and patience for the small ones; and when you
have laboriously accomplished your daily task,
go to sleep in peace. God is awake."

—VICTOR HUGO

When sleep was effortless

CONTENTS

Introduction

├─────────────┤

DEAR READER, WHAT GOOD AM I if I am quiet? I may be afraid to reveal who "Steph" is, but I am one who finds strength in my own fear.

So I am actually going to go through with it. Telling my story and getting it out into the world restores balance to mine.

"Steph," my friend Sandy told me, "life is like a compost bucket. It's full of disgusting, rotten, smelly, shitty, and repulsive things. Compost by nature is gross, yet it makes the best soil for growing beautiful, strong plants."

Throughout my journey I have found not only my truth but also the truth about others.

And I learned about emotional truth, spiritual truth, physical truth, and literal truth. Some of these truths I got to decide for myself; others, well, I had no choice in them. The *only* choice I have had is to tell it. These may be things you have never had to experience. Things that I pray to God you haven't. But if you do, know I am one of you.

While studying for my online writing class through Gotham Writer's Workshop, I stumbled upon a quote that would further confirm my will not to be silenced. Writer and teacher Molly Peacock wrote this about revealing the truth: "To bring a secret to life is not the same as destroying privacy. A so-called confession fosters a sense of the personal boundaries that are requisite for a zone of privacy. There is a way in which *not* speaking about a secret subject comes to feel dishonest."

My intentions for this book are to show that you have the ability and right to speak up, and to let you know, if you cannot, that there are those of us who can speak on your behalf. Not everyone can talk about a painful past. Not everyone *wants* to. I respect that. This is my burden to carry. I will carry it with dignity.

I've asked myself, tearfully, "Why? Why am I supposed to do this?"

I realized that, for one thing, I want my children to know their mother, all of me, and why I am who I am. I want to make sense out of confusion and to stop questioning why things happened as they did. Using the power I get from exposing the real me helps to make sense of all those unanswered questions.

I also decided I would take a long drive in search of someone who could answer a few of my questions. This professor in writing, a guru of sorts, was also a childhood friend. After Eric and I sat for what seemed like an eternity, he guided me to the closure I needed to finally make peace with the end of this portion of my life, hence the end of the book.

As we laughed and cried, recalling childhood memories, Eric reassured me that with some of his students, he would teach them to find a good stopping point while writing a paper. There is always more to write, but as he said, "Stephanie, writing is never done, it is only due." Smiling and getting up for another beer to quench our overtalked mouths I said, "You're absolutely right, professor. And this story is long and it is due." As we sat in silence a while, I knew it was time to drive home and sit here with you, the reader, and finish what I started. I cannot make this a short story, because as I told Professor Eric, "There's no way to make a long story short."

Loving children in Rwanda

Prologue

AS I BOUNCED IN THE back of a red pickup truck down bumpy dirt roads in Rwanda, my friend Peggy at my side, I couldn't help but think back a few months to a morning she and I were sitting on my front porch in Texas. That was the day I explained to Peggy that I believed that she was supposed to go with me on a journey to Rwanda to learn more about the orphan-empowering program of a group called Zoe Ministry, which I had learned about two years earlier.

Peggy wasn't sure she wanted to go. There was the issue of the country's troubled history and perhaps a little fear of the unknown. But I knew that in a matter of days she'd realize that, yes, she was supposed to be with me, partly for her own spiritual growth but also to reassure me that I was safe and not alone.

One of the things we would witness would be the aftereffect of the Rwandan Genocide, the terrible mass murder in 1994 of an estimated one million people. I had learned that it took place over 100 days— April 6 through mid-July—and was the culmination of years of ethnic tension between Rwanda's Tutsi and Hutu peoples. Peggy and I also had watched movies about the assassinations of president Juvénal Habyarimana and another political figure, which had set off a hideously violent reaction during which Hutu groups murdered members of the Tutsi minority, as well as pro-peace Hutus.

The facts and figures of what happened in those three months are horrific. No film or television documentary could remotely convey the reality. Seeing the country for myself, I feel I have a grasp of how tragic that time was.

I was wishing I could read the mind of the Rwandan lady next to me. Her name was Beata, and when she looked my way, she simply smiled, and I was sorry I couldn't speak her language. The one word I could make out was "genocide." Its meaning was all too obvious.

When you travel through Rwanda from Kigali to Butare, you pass many memorials along the way. Our destination was a former school that was now called the Murambi Genocide Memorial Centre. A place where 60,000 men, women, and children had been told they'd be safe. The school had been turned into a memorial to the victims of the massacre.

How easy it is to trust the untrustworthy and suffer the consequences. That's a lesson many of us have learned through devastating circumstances.

Inside this memorial, members of our group fell silent as they read the informational posters and watched the videos about the genocide. It was clear from the looks that passed among us that we couldn't imagine the hell the Rwandan people suffered. From time to time I covered my eyes and peered through my fingers, as my heart raced and I felt sick. All around us were classrooms with doors missing, empty schoolyards, and the musty smell of the clothes and shoes of the victims, which were on display. Taking in the photos and reading the stories of the deceased was hard, and I admit I sighed with relief when it was over—when I thought it was over.

I followed Beata, who wordlessly led me outside, toward the place where I assumed the truck was waiting to leave. But our group headed in the opposite direction, led by a local woman named Epiphanie, who was a genocide survivor and was now responsible for the orphan-empowerment program here. Abruptly Epiphanie stopped, but the group continued, and I could see Peggy up ahead, with her arms crossed protectively, walking slowly toward another building.

Beate pointed to crypts that were covered by clean slabs of cement with names etched in rows. There, I closed my eyes, trying to process the enormity of what had happened. I was sure I felt the ground moving, as if everyone below was crying for help.

Beata motioned for me to go with her, but for some reason I simply followed the crowd. I still find it amazing that she, a stranger, knew my heart and soul would not be able to stomach what I was about to see.

Picking up my pace—and wondering why I had chosen to wear flip-flops that day—I entered another building. My head was down, making sure I didn't trip on the stony path. The only time I looked up was when Peggy gave a sound that I later realized was probably a warning for me to turn back.

To my left was a doorless classroom. I could imagine tiny tables and chairs, reading circles with bookshelves lined with cardboard books, and posters teaching the alphabet, time, and measurements. But that was not what I saw.

In front of me were corpses, covered with a chalky white substance that apparently was used to leave them intact as a memorial. I use the word "intact" loosely, because these people had been mutilated in many horrifying ways. Confronted by such graphic evil, I fell to the ground, my tears flowing uncontrollably.

I thought then of a pathetic saying etched on my walls at home in Texas: "Pain is inevitable, suffering is optional." How badly I wanted to cross that out and write "Bullshit!!!!!!" beside it! These victims had no option!

Fear, sadness, and utter disgust overwhelmed me, along with incomprehension as to why things like this have happened in our world.

I forced myself up off the ground with the help of Beata, who had come to my rescue and put her arms around me. "It's okay, Ms. Stephanie. It's okay," she said in clear English, which I had assumed she didn't know.

I told myself, "Steph, get your ass up and walk! Respect this time, these grounds, and these souls!" I had no right to feel weak seventeen years after the suffering they endured. Beata herself had lost loved ones in this war.

After that, with each and every door I passed, I prayed for the souls that used to inhabit those bodies. The images of those children will never leave my sleepless nights. Did I have to see the body of a child, its mouth still wide open as if to scream? Was it necessary to see their suffering?

Well, knowledge is power, right? To my mind, suffering in silence is what causes more sickness and more abuse. Only when we speak up can we have the safety that we all deserve. I've heard that there is safety in numbers, but if that were true here, then I would not have been standing there looking into the face of a child of three or four years old who had screamed in the face of evil. Rather, I would have been walking by each classroom, listening to the sounds of reading and laughter, not the faint voices of ghosts telling me what happened. Numbers had nothing to do with it. There was no safety here.

If you take anything away from this experience I am sharing, remember that many of us have suffered different kinds of abuse at the hands of others. There on the ground that day in Rwanda, I realized that I not only felt responsible for everything that had ever happened to me but also that I felt responsible for not having prevented the genocidal hell. But there are lots of things that happen to us that are beyond our control.

It was then that I remembered another sick, twisted, and frequently whispered comment I had heard as a child: "Steph, don't tell anyone. If you do, it will be your fault that they're crying. It's your fault that you are so cute."

Suffering in silence, I felt alone.

Safe in Daddy's arms

Rocking the bib overalls
in fourth grade

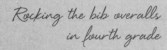

Photographs

SITTING ON THE FLOOR OF my library one evening, surrounded
by photos spanning my life and before, I felt as if I were floating in a pool
of memories. As I allowed those images to circle in my head, I could
almost hear each person's voice.

Looking at a tattered old picture, I see three people sitting in a
wooden restaurant booth. There's a man in a suit, his tie firmly tight-
ened and his arm draped around a lady. The man isn't looking at the
camera or smiling. He's looking at the woman in his grip, who's not
smiling either. But it's the third person in the photo I'm fixated on. He
has propped his elbow on the table, and he has a cigarette in his hand.
The photo was taken in 1957, long before smoking was banned from
restaurants. Though he's sitting, I can tell that his leather jacket is too
short for his body.

His head is full of hair, something I will never see in any other photo
of this man. In a mere five years from the time the photo was taken, he
and my mother met and married, moved to Denver, Colorado, had my
brother, Carl, and less than two years later had me.

My mother is hard to describe. But I'll try. In all the photos of her in
the early stages of her marriage to my dad she is never smiling. Not even
in her wedding photo. The pictures of her seem empty of happiness. You
can see her beauty, but she seems hollow. My mother was a middle child.
They're said to be the most troubled ones, like little lost sheep. Mom
was born between a hardhearted older sister and a fun-loving, somewhat
mysterious younger brother. After my grandmother's sister-in-law died
and due to her brother's inability to raise his own children, my grandmother added their two children to her family. Mom wasn't a troubled

child, I often heard people say. But they must not have been paying attention, because she was troubled—deeply.

Timing is everything. If my mother were in the market for love when a flamboyant, larger-than-life man appeared, claiming he could give her the world, well, she would be toast! I know she fell pretty hard for my dad, and I don't think she ever got back up.

It makes me think about those crazy, overadvertised dating services. Why shouldn't we all look at the profile of the person we are about to give our soul to? What would my father's profile look like? Would it say things like, "I am fun and loving but have just recently gone AWOL from the service, so I might have a few issues"? And mom? Hers might read, "I have been so sheltered from what looks fun and inviting that I am probably pretty desperate for love."

If my parents had exchanged their own personal stories prior to holy matrimony, would I even be here? That's like all the questions in life that just stump the human psyche, I guess. Like why is the Texas flower, the bluebonnet, actually purple? Or why do we drive in parkways and park in driveways?

Or why couldn't these two people, my mom and dad, be normal and provide a safe haven, something I never had until I found it on my own forty-plus years later? Then there is the question of my very existence. How did I get there? I discovered much later in life that I wasn't exactly a welcome package. Mom and Dad somehow got from Denver, Colorado, to Blackwell, Oklahoma, before my arrival, and then they put me in my grandma's care, which is why my bond with her was so powerful.

This picture of the father I barely recognize was probably taken about the time he was figuring out what to do with his life. His lost and angry look is like the one I sometimes see on my brother's manly face. Between 1957 and 1963 my dad gained 100 pounds and lost his hair. Later, he drank and stayed away from home for long stretches—and from playing with my brother and me.

Between his absences, Dad would surface fat and happy, and we'd be a family. When Dad did show up—I can't remember him being around too often—he always seemed to have a new dog with him. And when he left again, the dog would go, too. Mom wasn't a pet-loving woman. Dogs seemed to annoy her, and she didn't want to deal with them. Sometimes Dad brought home a bunch of stray dogs, all of which would follow him around like some kind of entourage. I bet the neighbors talked endlessly about the giant man walking the neighborhood with all those dogs.

I know Mom tried to create a home. I see photos of swing sets, birthday parties, and dolls tucked in beside me while I'm sleeping. She repeatedly said, "When you were born, we were very poor. That's why there are few photos of you and why I made your clothes out of the same material I used for my own." But to this day, I will never understand why she had to make the dresses *exactly* like the ones she wore. Talk about a way to cause a daughter to lose her identity early on—put clothes on her exactly like her mother's and call her "Sis." It was almost as if she had to make sure that the world knew I was only a tiny extension of her.

Photos of me as a baby? From this point it becomes clear that a lot of answers would come later in life.

Starved for Attention

IN MY EARLY TWENTIES, WHILE I was sitting by the ocean in Virginia Beach reading *My Mother/My Self* and trying to get away from a boyfriend who liked to push me into walls when he was angry, I finally connected the dots. In one photo of my mother and me, she has her arms wrapped around me, and I am looking off, expressionless. I look like I'm her possession, like something she took from the shelf, dusted off, and decided to play with a bit. Maybe in my mother's world she was able to control only a few things, and I was one of them. Dressing me in the exact same clothes she wore made it easier for her not to lose me in a crowd, I suppose.

I have several memories of Mom cooking from scratch. The comfort food that my grandma taught her to prepare was so good and always worked its magic. I can remember black, cast-iron skillets filled with Crisco and frying chicken that I was only allowed to watch from a distance because of my accident-prone nature. My favorite part of the fried chicken was the crunchy skin that had soaked up the Crisco and the sound it made in the back of my mouth when I'd bite down. There were mashed potatoes so creamy smooth that running my fingers through them was absolutely irresistible. My family always shamed me for eating potatoes with my fingers, but that was the only way I could truly enjoy them. A fork or spoon interrupted the sensation.

As I describe the food now, it is easy to see how it became my drug. Food filled me up on an emotional level I had never experienced. Mom did *that* right—cooking meals, that is. She never fathomed that I would take it to a whole other level, to an addiction. Mom was too wrapped up in her own sadness to do anything as a mother beyond providing the basics. But I watched her try.

One of my strongest memories is having tea with Daddy. In one photo, my massive father is sitting with me at a play dining table, holding a tiny, plastic teacup in one of his huge hands, his pinky up to look sophisticated, while I pour imaginary tea from the matching pot. My hair is pixie cut and straight, and I'm sure I'm wearing the dress for the special occasion. Dad's size didn't matter, you see, because I never felt afraid of him, ever. We were in a time and space that no one could interrupt.

Mom may have taken the photo. I'm not sure. But I know one thing for sure: She was anything but playful with me. Because of how she *wasn't* with me, I learned to be the kind of connected parent I always longed for.

I promised I'd be a playful mother, someday. But at the time, I focused on trying to get her attention in any way I could.

Pink Sponge Rollers

"HELLO, STEPHANIE, WHAT ARE YOU doing here? Your house is down the road a way," my neighbor said with a very concerned look on her face.

"I ran away from home, and I wanna be here," I answered with a certainty that I am sure made my neighbor think that, at the age of five or so, I actually believed it was a possibility. "I brought my pink bag." I had apparently taken off down the street in search of a new home. At least that is how the story went. Of course, I cannot say I remember exactly. After hearing a few different stories about my family's stint living in Arlington, Texas, I get a bit confused. But as I piece the stories together, it is easy to see we were having a tumultuous time, which is the relevant point here.

Memories from childhood seem to come to us in dreams, scents, or the words of a song. Sadly, they also come in the form of nightmares, and those are the ones we need hand-holding to get through. And get through, I will!

On some Saturday nights, we had a ritual. My mom would come out from the kitchen and say, "Go get the sponge rollers, Sis. We need to get your hair up before you go to sleep."

On one occasion, forgetting which bathroom drawer held the pink, spongy curlers with their pink plastic clips, I opened the one that held my dad's old-fashioned straight razor, and seeing it brought back a painful memory. I was the kid you couldn't leave alone for a second, because, sure enough, I'd get into some kind of mischief. I'd watched Dad shave, and I wanted that connection with him, not knowing that girls were not supposed to shave their delicate faces.

So I went for it, leaving a V-shaped scar on my cheek. These days I say the "V" is for "victory." More accurate would be "vulnerable, victimized, but vindicated," because the things that were done to me were not to be blamed on a little girl. Children are never the cause, never the reason for a cruel person to act on his sickness.

I closed the drawer and opened the one with the curlers and hollered back at my mother, "Here they are!" Then I sat between my mother's long legs, and she wrapped my wet hair so tightly around the pink plastic curlers that on Sunday morning I'd wake up with a look that could only be referred to as "Shirley Temple." Poor mom, once my curly locks hit the outside air they'd flatten out and return to my natural straight, baby-fine blonde hair.

Mom seemed to manage to find time to cook, clean, and have Carl and me looking perfectly put together for Sunday service. I wore plaid dresses, knee-high socks, and black patent-leather shoes as I squirmed in the church pew and tried to carry on conversations with those around me. That's where I first remember the smiles of strangers as I entertained them with my funny faces. "She is so cute and funny," the old lady in the pew behind us said, till the music stopped and mom pulled my dress to let me know it was time to be quiet and listen. I've never been able to sit still, and I'd slide my butt back and forth on the pew. I'm sure it was maddening to my mother.

Dad Will Save Me

"PISSED-OFF DADDY NIGHT" WHEN WE lived in Arlington is a very vivid memory, because after that my dad was around a lot. This was something I remember, because generally he wasn't there. Most of the time it was just Mom, Carl, and me at home, except when I was sent to Grandma's.

That night my brother grabbed my wrist and pulled me to the front door, yelling, "Pudge, hurry!" I never said a word, but I remember feeling warm pee run down my legs as we passed the place where I'd seen my dad's fist go into the cheap sheetrock wall. I wasn't afraid of Dad at all, even when I saw him yelling and hitting the wall. His fury was not directed at my brother or me, but at my mom and some other person, I'm not sure who. For most of my life, I've always felt his outbursts were directed at my creepy uncle—a great-uncle—who had finally made Dad so mad that he was ready to knock some respect into him. I was comforted by that. Dad must have finally found out what that man had done to me.

Carl pulled me to the neighbor's front porch and asked the little boy with the dark-framed glasses who lived there to get a towel. My brother always cleaned me up without shame, and he probably did so more than I recall. He was my first hero, the one who was there when Dad was not.

We went home the next morning to find Dad patching the hole in the wall and Mom sitting at the kitchen table with a cup of coffee in her hands as if nothing had happened. It seems like whenever hell broke loose in our home, it was followed the next morning by a hearty meal of eggs, bacon, and toast. The rule of the house was definitely hear no evil, see no evil, and sure as hell don't speak any evil.

Through the window, I saw the sun hitting our aluminum swing set that Dad had put up the Christmas before, and I looked at my brother. No words were needed. We bundled up on that cool October morning and went out to take turns swing-jumping. We'd see who could land on their feet after jumping from the swing in midair. He usually won, and I'd set off chasing butterflies around the yard.

It was in this home, I remember, that my dad came into my bedroom one night because I was crying. He turned the closet light on, looked under the bed, and said, "No monsters, little one," with a big smile.

But the recurring nightmare was as real as the pain I felt "down there." It was so real that it sent me into a quiet terror and made me hide under my many stuffed animals. I asked Dad to leave the light on, and I wondered if what I thought I remembered was only something I'd imagined. Something not real.

The reoccurring nightmare was difficult to describe. I thought I had done something wrong and I was being punished for it, and I was ashamed even though I had no idea what I had done. Abuse equaled punishment for me, as it does with all children. It is fairly easy at a young age to conclude that if you're being punished you must have certainly done something wrong. There wasn't anyone telling me that *I* wasn't the one who was doing wrong.

I am allowing my children to know how badly I was hurt because this knowledge, although very painful, also heals at the same time. I'm sacrificing my silence here to prove that sometimes there is, in fact, a monster under the bed, in the closet or, in my case, in the bathroom.

"Your mom and dad need me to watch you and your brother for a while," my great-uncle said that night with a syrupy, no-nonsense tone to his country drawl. "So why don't you go take your bath young 'un?"

I said nothing and did what I was asked. I was sitting in the tub, pouring bubble bath from a pink plastic bottle into the water when he came into the bathroom, shut the door, and said, "I'm going to help you in here."

That's all I remembered until I was in my thirties, when many of the lost details resurfaced during a session with an amazing counselor, "Dr. S," who saved my life by listening. Finding the words to define things is the first step—although a terrifying one—to healing.

With the counselor, I closed my eyes to allow the scene to surface. I began with what I could remember. "He was sitting in the corner of our small bathroom, which is basically a long, skinny stretch of space. Pushing his huge, wrinkled hand from my cheek, all I wanted was to get out of the tub. I didn't want to play with my bubbles. He kept touching me."

The tears poured out of me until I was sobbing. I felt angry and was clenching my teeth so tightly they hurt. Dr. S motioned for me to go on. "I felt limp and couldn't kick, scream, or anything. I sat there as he pushed me around on the slippery surface of the tub." For the first time, I'd described a scene that had haunted me for most of my life. I had to stop the regression so I could be in my thirties again and feel safe.

"Stephanie, you did amazing work!" Dr. S said. "As you continue to talk about what happened, it will lose power over you."

So many of us who have survived traumatic acts grew up thinking that silence was our only option. The abuser understands the minds of children and knows how to convince them that they are the reason for the abuse. For a long time, I was certain that I had caused this great-uncle, this old man, to hurt me. But then I realized that I wasn't the cause at all. No child is ever the cause of an adult's abuse. We survivors need to find someone to speak to and speak loud enough so that they hear what we are saying.

For me as a child, I had a one-two-three mentality that made sense of things. "One" was that there was an old, scary man who would show up at our home occasionally and hurt me. "Two," that Dad punched the wall that night out of anger at that man. And "three," that my dad was my protector, and I was safe. In my mind, the idea that my dad acted like a playground hero and beat up the old uncle gave me comfort.

I feel bad that when Dad was absent, my brother, only twenty months older than I, felt he was responsible for protecting me. He wasn't. He was only supposed to be concerned with things like his comics and building model airplanes.

My Savior, Grandma

MY OTHER COMFORT WAS GRANDMA Smith, my mother's mother, my rock and stability. She was a beacon of light that would constantly steer me toward safety when I was left drifting out in the middle of the sea of my life. Carl and I stayed with Grandma and Grandpa quite a lot, and I was always glad when that happened. More often than not, it was only me, while Carl had to stay home with Mom.

"Grandma is coming today, isn't she?" Carl asked Mom as we sat watching TV.

"Yes, she is," Mom said.

My grandma and my cousin Melody were the rescuers of my life. More times than I can recall, they boarded a Greyhound bus or jumped into a car to collect me and take me back home with them. It seemed as if every time the world caved in with Dad, Mom would have an overpowering need to rid herself of me as well. When he left, I had to go, too.

Cousin Melody was tall and loving. She was one of the two children my grandmother took in when Melody's mother died. Her dad was my grandmother's brother, and he wouldn't have been able to give up his drinking long enough to care for both her and her brother. He also would have been too consumed by the evil he carried around with him. This was the man who became my nightmare as a little girl, and I always hoped that Grandma had saved Melody from him.

At that time we were living in a place called Grand Junction. When Grandma was in our home, it was filled with the feeling that things were good. I don't mean it was full of gifts and jokes and laughter. Grandma just had a real stability about her. The odd thing is that no matter her age, she always looked the same. Grandma's ultimate goal in life was to "get home to the Father in Heaven." Ever since she was forty, she had her eyes set heavenward. But the universe seemed to need her here for a good long time.

"Grandma will stay here with you, Sis," my mother said, "while we all go to Six Flags tomorrow."

"Why can't I go, Mom? I'm big enough."

"Not this time. But when you're bigger, we'll take you."

So I watched the truck with my brother and cousins ride off to Six Flags, but Mom wasn't in it, and I have no idea where Dad was. I was left at home.

After Grandma arrived and got settled, I knew the first thing she would provide was something good to eat. Visiting her home in Missouri was best, but I was happy for her short visits to our house.

"Fried bologna sandwiches with mustard coming up, Stephanie," Grandma said.

I loved this treat because she would let me cut four slits in each piece of bologna to create little triangles and keep the processed "whatever meat" from bubbling up in the middle.

"You get the plates, and we will sit at the kitchen table," she said. I knew that if we were at Grandma's house I would be sitting in her kitchen, watching her grind ham in a heavy, metal contraption. As she turned the crank handle, chunks of ham would be transformed into tiny, wormlike pieces that she'd add stuff to for ham salad.

My family seemed to be obsessed with salads of all kinds. Dad's parents even owned a restaurant called The Salad Bowl. If you look up "salad" in the dictionary, you will find that it has to do with leafy mixtures and other combinations of food held together with mayo or other ingredients. But I love this quote found at the end of one definition: "The Declaration of Independence was . . . a salad of illusion." What a great metaphor for life! We take all the mixed-up ingredients of lies, secrets, and dysfunction, throw them into a bowl, paste them together with what appears to be normality, and call the mixture good. At the very least, it would fill you up for a while with the idea that you were satisfied.

Watching my five-foot-ten-inch grandmother fry the bologna, I wondered how someone as nice and sweet as she was could have a brother so mean and gross. Grandma was so wonderful, and he was so evil. It made no sense to me.

Tea With Daddy

WHEN I PUT TOGETHER CHILDHOOD memories, Christmas seems to be the easiest time to recall, especially when you have a dad who not only acts like Santa but also looks like him. Having my father on Christmas and birthdays at least gave me two times of the year that I could relish. Though I knew that each was just a twenty-four-hour thing, I loved every hour of our days together.

When the holidays came around, Dad would sit in my tiny chair at the tiny table Santa had brought me and have tea with me. He would move the toy plastic phone that Santa had also left and show me how when you turned the rotary dial, it would jingle. I adored this gift, especially when Dad picked up the receiver and said, "It's Santa! He wants to talk to you!"

I grabbed the phone and screamed, "Santa! It's Stephanie. Thank you for my presents! Dad, I can't hear him. Is he there?"

"Oh, he probably had to go back to work at the North Pole, but he heard you, don't worry."

I was sure Dad was telling me the truth, and I went right back to pouring make-believe tea into his cup.

Some of my favorite memories happened on Christmas morning. After the excitement of unwrapping presents was over, I'd fall asleep next to my mom on the couch. I felt there was never a better time in life. I could lie there with my head on her soft, floral robe, look up at her in her tight pin rollers, and know that all was well. Dad would be sitting in a recliner, while Carl would be lying on the floor, rolling a big plastic truck back and forth, catching the wheels in the shag carpet. The next day the world would be back to whatever passed as normal for us.

During these times, though, Dad was my safety, Mom was my

caretaker, and Carl, well, he was my friend and playmate. It was as if we all knew our characters in the play of our family of four. I just had no idea that the characters could have many personalities and demons to deal with. My character was the funny little girl who made people laugh. But all the while that tiny person was absorbing the personality of every person in her world. Later she'd take on so many personalities that she would have no idea what her own really was.

One morning I woke up and went looking for Mom.

"Good morning, Sis. Are you ready for your birthday?" My mother was standing in the kitchen, stirring the chocolate batter that would become the base for six candles at my birthday party. Peering at me through the horn-rimmed glasses she wore, my mom even had a smile that day—until the giant man behind me picked me up in the air and sang "Happy Birthday." His jovial laughter seemed only to annoy her.

"Steven, be careful! You are going to run her into the wall." I didn't care if he did. I was laughing and enjoying that moment of bliss a child has when she has captured the attention of two people most important to her.

Then the balloon popped: "Did you wet the bed again?" Mom asked. I squirmed out of Daddy's grasp and went to pull the wet sheets off my bed. To my shame, there was a dark yellow stain on the mattress, causing Mom to have to flip it day after day due to my inability to stop peeing in the bed.

As a child does, though, I just as quickly forgot about my accident and returned to helping Mom put the paper tablecloth on our dining room table. I pulled the plastic off the paper cups that had a Flintstones motif and asked, "Mom, can I set out the plates that match?"

Much later, my brother walked in with sleep still in his eyes and his button-up pj's wrinkled from what I am sure was a fitful night. He always had a smile for me. "Happy Birthday, Pudge!" he said. I'd acquired the nickname from Melody, and I wondered why I was so "pudgy." Only later in life did I discover that Melody called me that because of my pushed-up nose.

I really don't know how long we lived in that house or why the memories of it come easier than those of other homes we had. Maybe because I was actually here in this home, unlike other places we lived. In those days we seemed to move yearly, sometimes monthly, depending on the geographical cure needed to wipe the slate clean for my parents. As Dad tried and failed to make my mother happy, he'd find a different job, find us a different home, and most times find us a different town to live in. If one thing didn't work, well, both parents were experts at trying something new. Drinking kept Dad away, and sobriety kept him home. And the idea of a new place to live kept one thing very alive for them both—hope.

The year I celebrated my Flintstones-themed birthday is a fond memory. My mother spent that day baking chocolate cake for me and my friends. She tried to make our life as normal as possible as she struggled with finding the life and love she longed for. That did not make her a bad mother, only a mother who was preoccupied with how to fix the multitude of problems that walked through our door day after day.

Great-uncle was one of those problems, yet no one seemed to realize its severity. He'd show up—an evil drinking buddy with a taste for his own gratifying and sick needs—and then Dad would set off to the bar with him and the vicious cycle would start again. How could Dad not know? Or Mom? And how much more of his molesting did I have to endure?

Mr. Bubble

"HEY, YOU TWO, COME SAY hi to your great-uncle," my dad said, filling the doorway with his 300-pound, six-foot-five-inch frame.

I stood up, wiping the dirt off my knees and dropping my head as I got a huge sick feeling in the pit of my stomach. "You win, Carl. I landed on my face," I told my brother. Little did I know I'd keep falling on my face for years to come.

"Give me a hug, little girl," my great-uncle said in the creepy voice that made me shiver. I reluctantly walked over to him, and he placed his huge, bony hand on top of my blonde head. "Well, birthday girl, you gonna share some of that there cake with your uncle today?"

"I guess," I said, pulling myself closer to my dad, who had no idea how scared I was right then. Once I was in the arms of my dad or my big brother, I felt safe.

In that house, the walls of my bedroom had wood paneling. The smell of mothballs that my mother told me would protect the blankets from insects chewing holes in them lingered heavily. I remember that smell as vividly as another nightmare memory I finally allowed to resurface later in life so that I could heal.

There, the bathroom was long and narrow, and I was sitting in the tub, thinking back to another house and another time when I was in a shallow bathtub full of bubbles. I looked over my shoulder to find this disgusting man staring at me with a look that I'll never be able to erase from my mind. I still don't understand why my great-uncle was in the bathroom as I bathed. Where was my mom?

I picked up the pink Mr. Bubble bottle and started splashing it around. Suddenly he was sitting on the floor next to the tub. I pushed his hands off of me, I'm sure, but it would be years later, and only with professional help, that I could recall more than that. The next thing I remember is the pain as I lay in bed.

"Why is he in my bed?" I wondered. And when would Mom make that pain go away?

It baffles me how our body goes into survival mode in the face of a trauma. When I walked into the living room and saw my mom, dad, and this monster laughing, I was simply confused. This person had hurt me badly, but apparently it was nothing to worry too much about, if Mom and Dad were not concerned. I am sure now that neither knew what had happened. If they had, then surely that man would not have lived as long as he did.

Years later, I watched him die in a veterans' hospital while his sister—my grandmother—prayed for his forgiveness and hoped he'd make it to Heaven. I wasn't sure where he ended up, and I didn't care.

Thumbelina

ⵜ

"AAHHH!" I WAS SITTING ON the cement carport of our small home outside Salem, Missouri, crying my eyes out. I cradled Thumbelina in my arms, unable to inspect the damage the neighbor's dog had left. Finally I looked down and saw that the familiar, worn body of my tiny doll had been through torture. Her arms and legs were amputated, and the place where the pull string used to be was only a tiny hole. I would no longer be able to watch her move around as I pulled the string.

"Baby, what's wrong?" my dad asked as he opened the screen door from the kitchen.

I turned around and handed him Thumbelina as my tears fell. He took her tiny body in his massive hands and seemed as sad as I was. "Oh, honey, I am so sorry, but you can carry her just like this. She doesn't have to be perfect," he said softly. "Let's clean her a up a bit and let her sleep. She'll be fine."

Dad scooped me up, but my legs were getting too long to curl up in his arms, so I wrapped them around him, and into the house we went. He sat Thumbelina and me on the gold-colored, crushed-velvet couch and walked away to get me a wet washcloth.

My tears stopped, and my mothering instincts kicked in. I needed to make my baby better. No matter what, she was still my baby, and she needed love.

"Use this," Dad said, handing me a dishrag with soapy water on it.

I washed the dirt from the doll's eyes and face and stuffed the silky cotton that filled her body back in through the holes. Mom must have taken her when I fell asleep that night, because in the morning Thumbelina's holes were mended. I wish Mom had let me know when she did things like this; maybe she was afraid I'd think she loved me.

By fall, when I had turned a year older, I was presented with a new Thumbelina that looked exactly like the original one did years before. A perfect little pull-string baby with two arms and two legs. I wasn't warm to the idea of having something I loved replaced—that was impossible to do—but I happily accepted that the new, perfect Thumbelina was only given to me to help me protect the *real* one.

I didn't mistreat her at all. I was happy for the help. It's a lot of hard work to keep your children safe, and extra eyes are always welcome. Plus when I'd put all my toys to bed at night, I'd give perfect Thumbelina a very important job: I had decided, because her eyes always stayed open, that she could watch out for me, too, while I slept. I gained a respect for her, because in this house on a quiet dirt road in Missouri, my dad was always home with us, and everyone was happy. For a while, anyway.

"Gypsies, Tramps, and Thieves"

———————

"BUBBA, HURRY! IT'S TIME TO start!" I shouted. My brother raced into the living room, sliding on the wooden floor. Then he swung around to mess with the metal antenna on the TV to get a better picture.

Before I hit the divan, ready for our favorite show, I could already hear the song "I Got You Babe" coming from the tiny TV.

To try to describe my favorite part of *The Sonny & Cher Show* would be impossible, because every segment was etched in my mind forever. I was mesmerized by Cher's flowing, black hair, which nearly hit the floor of the stage. My brother and I sat, laughing and singing, as if we were right there with the two people I thought were so unique and in love.

When a commercial came on, I ran to potty, so I wouldn't miss my favorite part. Jumping back onto the couch, I stared at the piano on the screen and watched Cher slide onto it as she sang "Gypsies, Tramps, and Thieves." Someday I was going to move like that.

The show introduced me to the idea that being different was always best. My whole life I've been walking in the opposite direction of the rest of the world—but not on purpose. I'd always find myself going right when the crowd was going left.

I think that my dad was the one who ingrained in me the concept that imperfection was the way to peace. But for other reasons, my need to be perfect was set in motion anyway, along with my inability to achieve it.

Before *Sonny & Cher* came to an end, the two stars stood center stage, reading fan letters and looking at the screen. "Write in and tell us your thoughts," they said. "As always, we love our fans."

Carl and I looked at each other and knew exactly what we should do. He disappeared and then resurfaced to meet me in the kitchen.

"Bubba, scoot the table a little," I said, so I could fit into the chair, which was squashed against the fridge in our extremely small kitchen.

Carl set a piece of notebook paper on the table and wrote as I dictated. He wrote fast, and although I cannot recall our conversation, I know we decided it made perfect sense to end our fan letter by inviting them to our house for a visit.

Carl went off to find an envelope and then sealed the letter inside. Then we set it on the kitchen table and agreed we'd walk it to the mailbox together in the morning when we woke up.

The next day, as we wiped the sleep from our eyes, we filled our bowls with Super Sugar Smacks and milk and sat with our breakfast as Mom ran the vacuum cleaner.

I watched her turn off the machine, roll the cord around the clip that kept it in place, and put it in a skinny closet off the living room. I remember looking at her that morning: She was tall and had long, dark brown hair that she pulled back with a red handkerchief folded in a triangle and tied in a tiny knot at the nape of her neck. She looked pretty in shorts and a button-up shirt that looked like a work shirt a man would wear. Her horn-rimmed glasses had long been out of date, but even in the early seventies she could pull it off. She looked good.

The only thing missing from my mother was a smile. When I was older I used to think she didn't smile because of her crooked teeth, but I doubt that was the cause of her frown.

"Stephanie, go make your bed," she said. "And, Carl, take the trash out when you are done eating your cereal."

When Mom stuck in the purple-colored eight-track tape of Henry Mancini's instrumental music we knew it was clean-the-house day. Mom would hum to the music as she sprayed Pledge over the dusty coffee table, probably dreaming that the handsome man was dedicating the tunes to her. She was a hopeless romantic.

Our letter to Sonny and Cher still lay on the table. Now that Carl and I were both awake, we put our spoons down in unison, picked up our cereal bowls, and drank the rest of the milk, which had been colored and sweetened by the sugary cereal.

Bubba grabbed the envelope, and we raced to the mailbox at the end of our long driveway. My brother and dad had turned it into a tractor with wheels and painted it yellow for everyone who drove by to see.

With ear-to-ear smiles, we put in the letter we'd addressed "TO: Sonny and Cher Bono. FROM: Carl and Stephanie Henry." No street name. Nothing else.

But we knew they'd get it, and we knew beyond a shadow of a doubt that Sonny and Cher were coming to visit. So we waited . . . and waited . . . and waited.

Barbie Birthday Cakes

WE MOVED AGAIN, BUT THIS time Dad found us a farm outside the same town. He was huge that year, a consequence of having given up smoking and booze. The house was cozy, with low ceilings and a room I shared with my brother. The kitchen had Formica-topped counters along with the dinette set that had followed us from Colorado and Texas to here. It had been a while since Carl or I had spent time living with our grandparents, which meant things were somewhat normal in our home.

"Mom, where's Carl?" I asked, while Mom decorated a birthday cake. Her creative side seemed to surface around birthdays. It was time for another of mine.

"He's at the shed with the new puppies," she said.

I ran out the back screen door to find them, and I saw Dad working on an electric fence that I think he was trying to install himself. He waved and made a funny face at me, and I stopped to take in the scene: Mom baking, Dad working outside, and my brother playing with newborn puppies. In that moment I was entranced by this scene of family life. I watched squirrels race up and down a tree until I remembered how gross it was that dad had grilled one of those poor creatures for dinner!

"How many are there?" I asked Carl as I came up behind him.

"A lot, Pudge. Look!"

"Mom is making my Barbie cake," I told him. "It's almost time!" Mom had stuck a Barbie in the middle of a Bundt cake and made an icing dress to cover the poor naked girl. I came back inside to check on my cake and was stopped in my tracks. *He* was back. Creepy uncle was sitting at the kitchen table. He got up, walked over to the counter, and used his long, bony fingers to wipe the icing off Barbie's boobs in a single swoop. Then he stared at me as he licked the goo off his fingers.

Suddenly I felt ill and terrified, and I wondered why no one made him stop being so gross. Why someone didn't stop him from visiting our home at all.

The stone walls we put up in our minds in order to survive are very strong, and it seems as if for each scary moment I added more mortar to reinforce mine. I wouldn't recall these moments in the kitchen for a very long time. But this man would enter our lives, and my dad would eventually exit. The false camaraderie between the two men would take precedence in our family.

In those days it didn't take much to make Mom angry: my arguing with Carl, for example. One swipe of a switch torn from a tree across my legs should have been enough to teach me not to argue with him on our car rides between home and Grandma's house. Because when Mom got angry, I got scared.

Fortunately, Carl was the sweetest brother a girl could ask for, so our arguments were few and far between. We shared a room with twin beds. A window took up an entire wall. It looked directly out into the barn-yard area where I would sit for hours watching the chickens run around and naming them all.

Grandma and Mom had apparently decided that was the summer that chickens would run around with their heads cut off. Grandma came to visit, and I was mortified to look out the window and see my named pets running in circles without their heads.

"Grandma, stop!" I cried as I banged on the window, shouting that I hated her.

"I still remember that day, Stephanie," my grandma would later remind me. "I felt awful that you hated me for killing those poor chickens."

"It's okay, Grandma. I'm sure I calmed down when you served those delicious fried chicken meals. But you also told me that the ones I ate were from the local market, not my pets."

I would have believed anything I was told. Just as I believed that our family was exactly how families were supposed to be, that the people who came and went in our home were supposed to be there. Even the great-uncle who always scared me during his visits. He continued to make his way to our doorstep and to me, wherever we lived.

The year I watched him die in a VA hospital was one of relief, though when I saw my grandma cry, I cared less what he had done to me and instead wondered what in the hell he had inflicted upon her and others. She'd make me go with her to visit him, and the odor of that green-walled institutional room still haunts me.

There was a man in the bed next to him, and he always smelled as if he had crapped his pants, and no one came to clean him up. I would sit in the corner in a cold metal chair and look at my decrepit, old uncle, a lonely, smelly man. I convinced myself that he was being punished for what he'd done to me.

"Grandma?" I sheepishly called out when the deathwatch was finally over.

"Yes, sweetheart?"

I got up from the chair, put my hand in hers, and said, "I'm sorry he died." Then I quickly added to myself, "But I'm not, really."

On our quiet ride home from the hospital, I said to her, "Grandma, I'm sorry about wetting the bed all the time." I thought this was a good time to apologize for that. She squeezed my knee, and we both knew that it didn't need to be talked about. Or the time that she changed my sheets in the middle of the night and there was blood. That had to have been such a difficult night for her. Especially because I was only nine years old.

I knew she'd take care of me. But who did Grandma get to talk to?

Perhaps you wonder why I'm telling all this. Maybe there are people who hate the abused for exposing secrets, but believe me, my good intentions far outweigh my need for everyone to like me. I just wish I didn't have to go through more abuse as I grew older. I thought after he died, the nightmare would be over. I couldn't have been more wrong.

Spinning Vinyl

MY DAD LEFT MISSOURI AHEAD of us to get a new house in a town called Siloam Springs, somewhere in Arkansas. He called on the phone when he got there and told me there was a flood, and the water was so high that he was watching theater seats float out into the road. That made me terrified to move there, but I knew I'd be okay if I had Dad, so I let go of the fear.

Carl and I were happy in Arkansas. He loved making forts, and we'd spend hours sitting under them with pillows and my stuffed animals. It was a little haven that was cozy and safe. We played school and office on our old back porch with its crooked floor, and Carl would prop up the dinner table to level it out so our papers wouldn't fly off. Carl was the boss, and I was the secretary, of course, because that's how it was supposed to be. But I didn't mind. It was the seventies.

This was also the year I met someone who'd never leave my life again. One day, while Carl and I were painting our white picket fence, a tiny, redheaded girl rode into our driveway on a blue bicycle. She sat there with self-assurance and said, "Whatcha doin'?"

Carl smiled at me, then at her, and from then on, we'd love our visits with Nesey. We'd listen to a turntable spin Donny Osmond's "I'm Your Puppet" or Janis Joplin's *Pearl* album. Dad would ask to borrow the record player to take to his office. He loved music.

"Spinning vinyl," he'd say, "there's nothing like it!"

Sometimes he'd take me to the local Pizza Hut or to his favorite Mexican restaurant on the other side of town. We'd listen to Herb Alpert and the Tijuana Brass play "Green Peppers," and Dad would use music to teach me things of the utmost importance—like how the song "Lucy in the Sky With Diamonds" was about LSD and how I should not do drugs. I wish now I had a sort of punch list of what Dad advised me to do and not to do. Like how ketchup is good on everything under the sun, and the grease from a steak is best when "sopped up by the bread."

"Steph, always ask if you aren't sure about something," he told me once. That was it. Only a vague comment, and I had no idea what he was talking about. I was always too busy devouring my food to focus on the conversations.

Music—that's an element of life that I will always need. Music gives us memories both good and bad, and it can take us back so far that we feel as if we've been time-warped into our past.

Dad ran a mobile-home lot on the west side of Siloam Springs, which sat conveniently on the state line of Oklahoma and Arkansas. Growing up, we called the west side the wet side; the east was the dry side. The church we went to was exactly next to the state line, on the dry side, of course. The place where I got busted for buying beer at age sixteen was right across the street from my youth-group building. You could see the powerful balance between the two places. Or, more accurately, the division between right and wrong. With the bar on one side and church on the other, there I was, trying to figure out how to get to one side without the other side knowing.

One of the greatest things about Dad's trailers was playing house in those that were set up for showing. My father would argue that trailers were for cows and mobile homes were for people. So I always tried to say, "Dad, can we play in the cow trailer?" just to get him to follow with his traditional answer: "Sure, if you are a cow."

Laughing, Carl and I would take off down the lot with friends and go inside the show homes and play house. We'd serve the plastic fruit and veggies on the CorningWare plates. And if the water was hooked up, we'd serve make-believe wine in the matching glasses.

During those times when Dad was happy and sober, we'd find him in his office—yet another trailer—singing and drumming on his desk. He usually had Freddy Fender or Glen Campbell playing. Our record player went from house to work, and as the times changed from vinyl to clunky eight-track tapes, so did Dad.

Stop Sucking Your Thumb

MR. ELLIS'S FOURTH-GRADE CLASS WOULD teach me the Pledge of Allegiance, the Bible verse John 3:16—which we were to recite every morning—and about falling in love!

"Ahhh, Steph, are you in love?" my friend Rhonda asked as she leaned over the aisle to squeeze my kneecap, which apparently was a way to test if you were boy crazy or not. Whether it tickled me or just plain bugged the crap out of me, I jumped, which showed, yes, that I was crazy. If she only knew!

Being a woman at the age of ten would prove difficult, since I didn't have a clue what this meant. But I quickly realized that having absolutely no boobs wasn't going to help. In 1974, finding out what being a woman meant was impossible for me. Even today, some of the writing out there about women is astounding. From my research, I found that we—women, that is—have what are referred to as "secondary characteristics that make them distinct from men." At ten years old, if I had had this information, I would have known that someday I'd have a few "secondary" features that I could use to woo my first love. As it was, I got a few tips here and there, thanks to the mom of one of my girlfriends and her extracurricular activity of being a belly dancer. She'd pass along many ideas of how to get a man. I'd then take on her role with my other girlfriends and become the one they'd ask for advice. Along with making sure we couldn't get pregnant when a guy touched our boobs (no matter our boob size), we would spend hours talking about what we thought we knew.

The days of running down from school to my house for TV and peanut-butter-and-honey sandwiches were over. Now we all made a beeline for Barnett's Dairette or the Dairy Queen, which was only a block away, but was where the "hoods" hung out. It was at Barnett's that I learned the art of seduction, but not until I devoured my crinkle fries, which left so much grease on my lips I used it for lip gloss. One afternoon, when I discovered that a boy I liked, Louie, was hanging out at the Dairy Queen, I felt I had to venture over a couple of times. He was the cool guy in his crowd.

I decided to make my move the following day in Mr. Ellis's class. I could see it. I would proclaim my love for Louie, who sat in front of me, and he would turn around and do the same. With my heart racing, I put my pencil down, and without regard to the teacher, I tapped Louie on the shoulder, ever so lightly.

"Huh?"

That was his first word of affection to me. Honestly, that would have been enough. I could have created my own illusion, a vision of home, children, and a white picket fence. But, no, I had to do more. "Louie, I think . . . I mean . . . I . . . love you," I blurted out.

Louie looked like he had either a gas bubble in his stomach or had eaten something very bad. He said, "What!? Stop being stupid. You still suck your thumb, we're in the fourth grade, dummy!"

I sat there in my dark blue overalls that had a tractor neatly stitched on the bib and started to cry. I cried like any self-respecting woman would when rejected by the love of her life. The rest of the day, I watched my girlfriends sing "Mr. Postman" on the playground while I pushed dirt around with my feet, wondering if I'd ever find love. Then I realized exactly what I needed to do; it was time to become a woman. When I got home that day after school I had a plan. First I took my thumb out of my mouth and proclaimed myself a woman. After I wolfed down my peanut-butter-and-honey sandwich, I went to my room and threw the silky nightgown of my mom's that I slept with onto the top shelf of the closet. The garment gave me one of my only close connections to Mom, something that I was always desperate for, but now I realized there were other people who could fill my empty places. And it would have started with Louie, if only he had felt the same about me.

I'm Confused—
How Are Babies Made?

———————

IF YOU DON'T HAVE ANYONE who guides you into womanhood, you have to figure things out on your own. Soon enough I'd have more information about the obligations of womanhood, but it would only confuse me in a whole new way.

"Girls," one of our female teachers said, "we are going to see a film tomorrow about our bodies. So tell your parents tonight when you go home, please."

Of course I didn't.

The next day they lined us up against the wall in the hallway after lunch, and all the boys walked by and snickered. How did they find out what was happening? As we single-filed into the old gym and slid down the long wooden bleacher one at a time, I suddenly felt a sharp pain in my butt.

"Is something wrong, Steph?" a friend next to me asked.

I shook my head no, because I couldn't even speak. A huge splinter had come loose and jammed itself into my skin through my white pants. Gritting my teeth and not moving, I just sat there, miserable. I was praying that the film would soon be over so I could say I had to go to the bathroom, where I'd pull out the splinter.

The film started. "Girls, today we will learn about the changes that your body will be making," the narrator of the film said. Finally my butt went numb enough so I could focus on the screen, which showed swimming sperm that seemed to force themselves upon a poor egg. The movie continued with information about pads and tampons, and it talked about the consequences of having sex.

When the movie was over and we started to exit, to my horror a girl behind me said rather loudly, "Stephanie started her period. It's on her pants."

Number one, I hadn't. The blood was from my butt wound. And number two, who says something like that?

I was wearing white, and until I pulled the giant piece of lumber out of my aching ass the blood wasn't going to stop! My friend saved me by wrapping her sweater around my waist for the remainder of the day, and she never mentioned anything about it to me. But she did say, "Shut up, Carla," to the idiot girl who wanted to ruin my already feeble self-esteem, adding, "You have bad breath, and we all know it!"

Girl power—nothing like it!

Always in Trouble

AFTER FOURTH GRADE, WE STOPPED moving, and we lived in the same place until I graduated high school. Same Arkansas town, that is. We kept changing houses, but I was getting to know people and finding a "hometown."

I spent most of my days throughout the next year perfecting the arts of tetherball, dodge ball, and watching boys kiss girls in the corner of the schoolyard. I stayed pretty much out of trouble, except for the occasional trip to Dr. Walker's office. The tall, dark-haired principal was new to our town, and the mere sight of him made most students shudder, but apparently I wanted his attention.

"Stephanie, did you call Mr. Ellis a pervert?" Dr. Walker asked me one morning in his office.

With tears rolling down my face, because I knew he was going to have to tell my mom, I nodded. He smiled and said, "You don't even know what that is, do you, honey?"

"No, but everyone told me to say it."

"Stephanie," he continued kindly, "you can't keep doing everything everyone wants you to do just to be liked."

I turned my head to look for the electric paddle I had heard he had in his office. And I saw it! Maybe it wasn't really electric, but it was connected to some plug-in thing, and it made me think of the boys on the playground who got caught kissing girls. Did they get paddled by that thing?

Dang! If only I had been like my daughter Mary. One day when I picked her up from elementary school her teacher pulled me aside. "Mrs. Henry," she said, "there was a boy chasing the girls today on the playground and trying to kiss them."

Smiling, I thought she was about to tell me Mary had been kissed and was upset. But that wasn't it.

"Your Mary threw her hand up at the boy and said, 'Stop! It's flu season!'"

What a smart girl! Me, on the other hand . . . if a boy had wanted to kiss me, I'd have chanced getting the bubonic plague.

Sixth grade was a year I really felt happy. It was the beginning of the end of my being a little girl. Soon we'd all be off to junior high. At school I loved the walk from the sixth grade building to the band room. We had to pass by the elementary kids, and I remembered how Mr. Ellis had brought us all into this area to see my first solar eclipse. Passing the cafeteria, I could smell the fish sticks, and I couldn't wait to glob tartar sauce all over them and gobble them down.

"Steph, hurry, or Mr. B is gonna be pissed!" my bandmate Roy said, trying to move me along.

As we filed into the band room at the top of the walkway, I smiled and joked with my friends. We all sat in our assigned spots and got our instruments out of their cases, wiping them off and prepping for an hour of musical harmony. Or so we all hoped. But as Roy got situated, he started to laugh and motioned me to look, though I had no idea at what.

"Hey, Steph, Mr. B's zipper is afraid of heights," Roy joked.

His eyes were looking to the front of the class where the teacher was standing, and by this time about ten others had noticed what Roy was laughing at. As my eyes focused, I was staring straight at Mr. B's zipper because I was the closest to him. I started to laugh, too. My laughs are anything but quiet, and when I get tickled I cannot control the volume.

When Mr. B glared at me, it only made it worse, though I was trying with all my might to stop. *Look down,* I said to myself, but with Mr. B's serious look stretched across his face and his fly open so wide that I could see the design on his boxers, I wasn't having much success.

Finally the whole room broke out laughing, which caused Mr. B to point his stubby finger at me and direct his eyes to his office. Without any verbal order, I knew exactly what I was supposed to do.

I got up, and with the entire class watching, it hit me: Wait, I didn't start this! "Why am I in trouble?" I asked. But I had no choice. I stepped into his soundproof office, and after telling the class he would be right back after he dealt with "Henry," the teacher followed me.

Mr. B was a short, squat man, with black hair slicked back and glasses that rested on his chubby cheeks. Now don't misunderstand me; I was not a malicious child, nor did I make fun of anyone. But his zipper being down was funny to all of us, and I was singled out to try to explain things to our teacher.

"Now, Stephanie Henry," Mr. B said, "do you want to tell me why you were disrupting our class?"

"Not really," I said, looking at my Keds tennis shoes and wishing I hadn't written all over them. The entire class was trying to read our lips and faces to see how bad the punishment was going to be.

"This is your last chance," he went on, "to tell me what was so funny, or you'll be suspended from band for two weeks, and I'll send a note home to your parents."

I wondered if he knew that my parents were divorced, and how he would send a note to my dad because he lived in a trailer, and I never saw a mailbox near it.

"Also, you will tell me who started this little show, Stephanie, and anyone else responsible."

By now I had tears in my eyes, and I knew that saving face for my friends was going to win out over dropping Roy or anyone else into the proverbial grease.

"I don't know," I said.

"I am sure you do know, young lady," Mr. B insisted, "but if this is how it is, then go out and pack up your flute case, and head to your next classroom. For two weeks you will have to sit in the library."

"Okay," I mumbled, and with my head low, I walked out of his office. For some reason, though, I found it necessary to turn around as he tinkered with something on his desk.

"Mr. B?"

"What, Stephanie?"

"Your zipper is down."

And I left with a strange sense of pride about what I was doing for my fellow man. It would be the topic of conversation in our tiny sixth-grade circle for weeks.

Later, though, when my dog was killed over Halloween and some other bad things happened, I had to wonder if I was being punished for everything—even something as simple as causing the band teacher shame and embarrassment.

The year ended with a roller-skating party that wonderful Ms. Jensen gave us, and I felt excited about the summer and what it would bring. I didn't know it would be the last one I'd have with my dad.

Forever Friends

GROWING UP, I HAD A sisterhood—including a few guys—with an unspoken pact. I now know that part of my strong attachment to the people in this group was that I longed to be a part of their families. Joanne had it all—beautiful hair and a bedroom like something out of a fairytale. Her house was huge, and her mom always had snacks for us after school. And it's where I first heard that ELO stood for Electric Light Orchestra. Joanne's dad put a jukebox in the basement, and everyone loved hanging out at her house. It was where we had boy-girl parties and secret kissing games. Even though Joanne's mom was quiet as a church mouse, I knew she was home when all of us were there. It was comforting.

LaDonna was tall, with a mane of dark hair and eyes of ocean blue. Her house had huge closets that held outfits with the tags still on them. LaDonna was my rescuer in more ways than one. She got a car early on and was everyone's driver, poor girl. It was great for after-school trips to Sonic for cheese-covered tater tots and Cokes. I'll never forget when Darren, the love of LaDonna's life, entered the scene. Darren cherished her, and they are still together today. Tall and committed, this guy was so different from the guys I dated, boys who'd forget my name and toss me out like yesterday's garbage when they were done with me.

Dana, who ended up marrying Joanne's brother, came into our group a bit later and fit in just fine. Her light green sports car was also a popular ride in high school, and her mom always gave me a listening ear. Dana's mom was someone I felt connected to even though I wasn't sure why. She left her door open for me, and although I hadn't known Dana as long as my other girlfriends, we were just as close.

Brietta was a tiny girl with a quiet spirit, one of the best listeners

I have ever known. With her there was an unspoken agreement that I could be at her home anytime. The only thing remotely "wrong" she did was to drive her parents' car straight through the garage when her dad was trying to teach her to drive. Instead of hitting the brake, she hit the gas and ended up at the clothesline out back. Brietta's parents were always a team. I had a secret crush on an older brother of hers who was off to college before I was barely out of diapers. Toward the end of our high school days, Brietta, LaDonna, and I were like the Three Muske-teers. We did everything together. Later, in my first marriage, they got me down the aisle.

Tami's home was right on the way to every school function we had. Our gang—both girls and boys—always stopped there as a meeting point. Then we either paired off or caravanned to whatever game we were cheering at.

Tami's dad put a trampoline in that huge yard of theirs, and it was a hit. I could never jump on it, though, because every time I did, I'd pee my pants. And even if I acted like I never got embarrassed, I did. Especially if the boys were there. Giving into peer pressure to jump like the others one afternoon, I ended up running off and crying silently because Kurt, the one boy I liked—who I knew wasn't interested in me—was right next to me when in fact I did pee my pants! He became Joanne's boyfriend.

That year everyone was getting "dropped," which meant that you wore a three-tier necklace with your boyfriend's initials on it. For about a week, when Joanne dumped him, Kurt let me be his girlfriend, and I had no problem wearing the hand-me-down drop. But that didn't last long. Kurt was one of those guys every girl wanted to be with, and even though my stay was short, sweet, and sort of an afterthought, I can still say I was one of his girls. But Joanne's friendship meant more than finally being the girl that got to hang off the arm of good-looking Kurt.

The best thing about the gang was that I was completely comfortable with them, but I kept my secrets to myself about the abuse at home. I was the master of hiding behind a funny mask, just wanting all my friends to feel happy and loved. One friend, Eric, once he was old enough, got a really cool motorcycle and would often show up at the city pool in the nick of time, right before I did something very stupid, like ride off in the car with a boy who thought I was pretty or kiss a boy under the swinging bridge, which was a notorious make-out spot. When he and I started doing stand-up comedy for our friends, we had a blast. It seemed we could make just about anything funny, even if it got me in serious trouble at school. (I had bad timing when it came to knowing when to talk and when to shut up!)

There was Robert with his serious look; his thick-rimmed glasses and dark eyes always comforted me in times most needed. When he met Annette, they were like Darren and LaDonna—mates for life.

There are lots of others, too, who helped mold the person I became. Even now, reaching back into my past, I can see the blessings that were hidden and recognize what these friends did for me at the time. Angie was the country girl who taught me about farming, horse riding, and counting the kittens before I drove off to make sure one hadn't hidden on a tire.

Tracy sang like an angel. When I heard her, I could escape the hell I dealt with in my head and at home.

Carla never knew that I would have given anything for her to be my real sister, to live with her and her brothers and sisters in their house. The chaos of so many people under one roof felt comfortable.

Martha was a fascinating girl who had more sweaters than one person ever needed in winter and a choice of perfumes to play dress-up with while we shared secrets. She had her own private room off the house, which her dad shared with her stepmother and their family. When Martha's mom would visit, she'd drive into town in a bohemian-looking Pacer, like something straight out of Woodstock. Martha's mom was colorful and vibrant, and I never understood why Martha wasn't living with her. But I loved Martha's ability to have answers for everything, as if she knew she'd be our legal counsel when we were adults.

Celebrating birthdays and collaborating on our efforts to have the best time, best reputation, and best laugh was our mission. Even if Kurt didn't love me that year, I could set my sights on Brian, the quietest guy, I think, known to man but absolutely wonderful to look at. Brian, Jon, and I shared many birthdays together, attempts, I think, by Jon's and Brian's mothers to get all of our friends under one roof every year to inspect our goings on. I found security and fun with these girls and guys, and I loved them all very much. I still do.

The Man in the Blue Chrysler

HE DROVE UP THE DRIVEWAY in an obnoxious blue Chrysler with a makeshift bar in the trunk and parking tickets spilling out of the opened glove box. The music pouring through the open windows was loud enough for the neighbors to enjoy. I was in Dad's apartment, where tattered and yellowed Beetle Bailey comic strips were taped to the fridge, where Gaston Leroux's *Phantom of the Opera* topped a tower of books, and where my mom had allowed me to have the joint boy-girl birthday party that year when I turned twelve. I rarely did the friend get-togethers at my home. I was embarrassed most of the time that our home was uncomfortable. Mom had apparently asked Dad to leave so we could use the space. Maybe she left too, because I don't remember seeing her there either.

We played spin the bottle and other kissing games while Captain and Tennille sang "Muskrat Love" over and over in the background. And I had my real first kiss with a boy named Mark. I remember thinking at the time how much Mom must trust me. It wasn't until later that I realized her leaving me alone wasn't so much an issue of trust as it was her being able to escape from me for a few hours.

The next morning I peeked out the window blinds and watched Dad open the door of the Chrysler and reenter my world. The car was large, as was the man, and I couldn't help but stare at him as I never really had before. My dad was always one for a dramatic entrance, and I hope I have been able to have the passion he had for life. When he was happy, the whole world was happy. But this day he was just as sad and broken as he was big. It was as if he were carrying a huge wooden cross on his back. I've often wondered if he'd somehow known that in a few short months he would be dead.

I'd always dreamed about how my daddy was supposed to keep the evils of the world from me. With his size and power, I thought he was more than capable of that job. He came up the walk and knocked, as if he were a stranger. When I opened the door, he asked me, without even a hug, if I had time for him and told me that he had a birthday gift for me. A moment later we were sitting on the couch, and he handed me a tiny box with turtle earrings inside. I have them to this day, though I don't think I've ever worn them. The silence was as awkward as any that a preteen girl would have with her father, but our family drama made it that much more strange.

Then Dad asked if I had heard his Bee Gees album. He got it from his bedroom and put it on the turntable, and we sat there listening to the sounds of these brothers, as he strummed on the acoustic guitar he had recently acquired. That was all the bonding he was capable of, and I can appreciate now how much it took for him to give me that moment. We were just a father and daughter on a cold fall day in October, listening to music and not even looking each other in the eye. We occasionally exchanged a faint smile of appreciation. I'm sure we were only there for an hour, but it seemed like a whole day to me.

Bless his heart; life and all its expectations were just too much for my dad to bear. He had so much self-loathing. His inability to sober up long enough to feel the pain and get through it finally got the better of him. He gave up. But giving up and giving in are quite different. I see now that he believed that my mother, brother, and I would be better off in his absence.

Some days I feel his presence so strongly that it's like he's standing right next to me. I can almost hear him say, "Baby, I am so sorry, but please try to learn more about my life and my death. I had some qualities you would have been proud of."

Church Pews

THAT YEAR THE CHRISTMAS CANTATA was held the day after Christmas, and Mom, Carl, and I got into our clunky car to head for church. We'd been attending what was referred to as a Bible church, which I found confusing. Didn't all churches read from the same Bible? Religion was one of the most confusing things to me as a child. As an adult, well, I am finding my way in and around it. I was at least hopeful that my baptism at age nine had secured my place in Heaven, like Grandma had said it would.

"Bye, Dad!" I yelled out the window as Mom backed out of the driveway. I remember asking her if Dad could move back into the house since it was Christmas. Carl just sat there, quiet as usual, looking at me as if I had just asked Mom where babies came from. Mom was humming to prepare herself for her trio, the "Three Anns." This was always a kid's favorite time, even if sitting in a boring church service was part of the ritual. Mom stood there on that small, raised platform in front of the church, singing with her eyes closed, in her religious trance, and Carl and I waited impatiently to get out of there and back to our new toys.

After she was done she sat by us in the pew, and I started my normal church routine. I played a game that I created to block out the all-too-boring message of how I would probably end up going to hell unless I did all the things taught by the people who would likely be standing next to me in purgatory. The game I'd made up involved giving names to the regulars at the service. Like the Flag Sisters, three elderly women who must have spent the entire week preparing their hair color for Sunday. I liked to imagine them strolling the aisles of the Five & Dime to find the perfect colors.

No matter our age, we women allow our hairstyles to speak for us before we ever open our mouths. It declares who we are inside and how we feel. Which is why, as soon as I was allowed to, I colored the mousey hair I had. I was sure I had pissed off the hair gods, who had turned my soft, blonde baby hair to a color that referred to a disgusting rodent. Sometimes I used to imagine that when my childhood was ended because of what people did to me, I also lost my childhood-colored hair. A punishment of sorts.

The Flag Sisters found a trio of shades that turned their hair—you guessed it—red, white, and blue. They also sat in that order. It was all very patriotic.

There were other regulars, too. To my right and back a few seats was Babbling Betty, who would start talking in some strange language during the sermon. After a new pastor came and decided that she was speaking devil talk, she'd be quickly escorted out the door of the church as soon as she started babbling. My grandmother explained Betty was speaking in tongues, which only confused me more. I thought all humans used their tongues to speak. (Okay, adults, what can we learn from this? When explaining things to children, be specific; they can handle it better than you can most of the time.)

Sitting right in front of me was a boy whom I stared at all through the service. He was beautiful, with dark, curly hair and eyes that would drive me insane for many years to come. As the pastor was preaching on the sins of the flesh, there I was, allowing my flesh to melt at the sight of that boy. I would sit there and wonder what it would feel like to kiss him. We were always very good friends but nothing more. When he turned to look at me, his eyes pierced me and I'd melt, even if he was just my "friend."

That evening while I played my mental game a police officer walked up the aisle and whispered something into my mom's ear. She quickly gave my brother a look that said, "We're leaving—now!" She gave me an aggressive yank by the arm to force me to my feet, which seemed to be cemented to the floor. Instantly I felt fear that caused me to feel so ill that I thought I would vomit. But I was afraid that if I did, some of the other church members might also be playing my name game, and they would forever remember me as Vomit Girl. I held it in until I was alone, the beginnings of what would soon become a ritual for me.

Mom drove us to the local hospital, and there sat the Chrysler in the parking lot of the emergency room entrance. One of the car doors was wide open, but there was no sign of Dad. After that, it is impossible to tell what happened chronologically. Mom probably realized I would begin crying so uncontrollably that neither she nor I could stop it, so she sat me in another damn pew—in the hospital chapel.

Good grief! What is the obsession with church pews, anyway? All I knew is that when I was in one, I had to remain quiet for a length of time that seemed humanly impossible. Or that I was about to hear bad news about my impending doom as a sinner. And there I was again, in a pew waiting for bad things to happen.

No one explained my dad's death to me. I just found myself back at school, hoping that my homeroom teacher wouldn't make us go around the room and tell what we did on our Christmas break. I'd have to say, "I buried my dad." Once back at school, I'd hear farfetched stories of how he was killed by the Mafia. My dad had just opened a BBQ place called none other than Fat Daddy's BBQ. Since he was known for his giant presence and love for food, it was a perfect name. Kids would talk around me like I wasn't even there, telling stories of how he owed money and couldn't pay. All I knew was that things felt very different. I felt stranded.

Dear Santa,
Can I Have My Dad Back

MOTHER SPENT THE LAST FEW hours of Dad's life in his hospital room. I think he must have asked for forgiveness from her and from God, and that was it: "Oh, God, so sorry for all I did. I know that my ex-wife and kids will be better off without me, so I am going to leave now and come be with You." I assume that was his prayer that day. Everything was such a secret in our home; I couldn't even tell you when their divorce had taken place. I know that all I wondered was why I didn't get to see my Dad before he died.

Even now my jaw tightens at the thought of it. At the age of twelve, I honestly believed that my dad had a choice and that he chose to die. And I couldn't understand how a parent could choose to leave their children. If I were a parent lying in a hospital bed with just a mustard seed of faith to make my life better, right my wrongs, and be there for my children, you can bet your sweet ass I'd be begging my god to give me another chance to live, to correct my mistakes before I went off in search of the hereafter.

As a twelve-year-old girl who needed her daddy, I didn't understand why he didn't have enough love and commitment to stay. I've since learned that his decision was driven by his self-destructive nature. My dad couldn't love himself enough to allow life to do anything but leave him empty and alone . . . and ultimately dead.

And my mother? She must have felt real fear, exhaustion, and utter powerlessness, because within six months I'd have a new family. Possibly, jumping right into an instant, "just add water" family made sense to her. Was this all she could do at the time? If she had known what danger a couple of the new family members brought, I have to believe she'd have never done it. I want to believe this, but as I have aged and learned some things that are more than hard to swallow, I know now that she did. She did know and brought it in anyway.

What Ken and Barbie Never Knew

IN MY ROOM I HAD a closet that had a sliding door, and I would sit in there for hours with my dolls. We would have "group sessions" about life, love, and—on this day—death. When I was a child, no one ever explained anything to me; I was left to come up with my own conclusions about how things worked. Ken and Barbie were quite helpful. It seemed they always knew what to say to me, and most of the time what they told me was about getting love in one way or another. At the time, I didn't realize how foolish and self-centered they were—Ken and Barbie, that is. Always looking for the best outfit, driving the perfect Barbie car as if that would determine the amount of love and acceptance they would get.

That year Peter Frampton was my escape music. His lyrics "I'm in you . . ." would set the stage for what I began to believe about love. The song was about being so completely empty that the only answer was finding someone who would fill every part of you, that without love, you were nothing, always empty, always searching.

"It's time to go now, sweetheart," my grandmother said as she came into my room. We loaded the car and drove to the funeral home, where I soon discovered a huge corpse that bore some resemblance to my dad. Except that there wasn't a smile on this corpse's face, not even a fake one.

Before I left my bedroom that morning, I'd grabbed a tiny bear that Dad had given me when I was little. I didn't want my father to forget about me, and I thought Bear—that's what Dad had called him—would be useful to him on his journey to the hereafter. I knew that I had to place Bear into the coffin with Dad before they lowered the lid.

Our family was in a private room away from the other spectators. It was called the viewing room, where we were supposed to view my dead father. Of course, they had seated us in another freaking pew! (I would grow very tired of pews in my life, and I promised myself that I would never belong to another church that had them.) After a fog of people talking, preaching, and reading, our family was directed to walk by the coffin and say goodbye to Dad.

I still don't know exactly how my father died. And, yes, I'm angry about that—still.

You have to be honest. Don't treat your children like they are idiots because they haven't lived as long as you have. Children hurt and bleed, and they have the same feelings as you. You just have to figure out an appropriate way of listening and talking to the children in your family. It can be the difference between life and death.

Waiting in line for my turn to stand at his coffin, I finally saw the opportunity to put Bear in with Dad as I stood with my cousin Melody. She held one of my hands, and I gripped the toy tightly in the other. I thought I would tuck Bear in by Dad's head. But as we got closer to the top of the coffin, my heart started pounding so violently that once again I thought I was about to become Vomit Girl. A horror-movie vision popped into my head: Dad rising up, eyes and lips sewn shut, and grabbing me to make me go with him. I was in big trouble, and I knew I had to make my escape. I ran back to my seat still holding Bear, and that is when I came to the conclusion that death is not only scary as hell but also really gross.

All these years later, Bear still sits on my desk, awaiting *my* trip to Heaven, wherever that is . . . maybe the beaches of Mexico. In any case, I plan to take Bear with me. And when I see Dad again, I might think about giving Bear to him. I never did see Dad actually placed in the ground, and I've had a lifetime of emotions with no closure because of that. Closure was one of the things I always sought without knowing it, because having closure on pain is the only way to move toward happiness and healing. It probably is true that the dead cannot "cross over" because of unfinished business, but it is *our* unfinished business with them that haunts me.

Later in life, when I was living in a treatment facility, I would be asked to write a letter to my dad and drop it in a mailbox. No address. Just drop it in and let it go forever. I have often wondered where that letter ended up. I imagine that someone opened a mailbox and discovered a letter that merely said "Dad" on the envelope. That whoever received it opened it, and when they realized it was seventeen pages long, they read it for entertainment with their morning coffee instead of the local newspaper or a good book. They would have loved the part about my grandmother, who repeated with *her* coffee: "Stephanie, your dad always said that God and coffee were best in the morning."

If, by chance, you are the owner of a letter marked "Dad," maybe you could find me someday and return it.

Even now, as an adult, I still have that childlike feeling that there is a chance that Dad really isn't dead, and that he did get my letter and read it. Kids always have that kind of hope.

1977–1987

High school graduation

Teenage wedding

Trusting Mama

SIX MONTHS AFTER DAD DIED, I was sitting in some stranger's house. Outside the bay windows of what seemed to be a garden room, I could see a huge tree, and I focused on that. I didn't even hear the marriage vows that my mother was reciting. I was unable to take in the fact that the four children this man already had were going to add two extra stepbrothers and two extra stepsisters to my dwindling family of three. One of those new sisters was my little redheaded friend, Nesey, and that was the only silver lining of this very dark cloud. I loved her, and this meant that she'd move her blue bicycle to my house, and we'd be able to play all the time. When I turned around, she was squirming in her seat, looking a little worried. But she was a kid, and she had hope too.

It's absolutely impossible to recall exactly what anyone said that April day. It was something like, "Blah, blah, blah, your dad is gone, and here is a new one. Get used to the idea, Stephanie." I do know that when I was finally allowed to get out of my seat I found a bathroom and did what I had been doing since Dad left me. I puked!

Carl came looking for me and knocked on the bathroom door. "Pudge, you okay in there?"

"Yeah, almost done." I'd been in there for a while, and I imagined all the kids thought I was pooping, which was horribly embarrassing to a twelve-year-old girl. Embarrassing, period, because girls don't do things as yucky as poop, right?

When I emerged, I saw the wedding cake and made a beeline for it.

"Let's go outside," Nesey said.

"Okay, get more cake, and we can take it with us," I commanded. As we walked past two of my new siblings, I finally took a good look at the oldest stepsister, DeDe, who frightened me.

Then I remembered.

I have no idea how long I stood there, allowing my mind to flood with images from a few years before. I couldn't move. Staring at DeDe as she talked to her older brother caused my stomach to turn.

I was remembering a night when mom had let me go for a sleepover at Nesey's house.

I dropped my stuff in Nesey's room, and we raced to the kitchen.

"What are you cooking, Davey?" Nesey asked her oldest brother.

"Tuna casserole with peas," he said blankly, without looking at us. The meal sounded gross, but it was appetizing, and I gobbled it up as I did most of my food. I wasn't concerned with the taste and texture, just the sensation that it filled me up. And the food would only serve its purpose for a while, because in a few minutes it was going to come back up anyway. At age twelve, I'd already learned that food equaled control for me.

The rest of this family wandered in and out of the kitchen, filling their plates and heading to various spots in the house to eat their food at metal TV trays.

"Hey, Steph, want to watch TV while you eat?" said the other son, who'd been quiet up to that moment. Derwin, the younger brother, had the sweetest smile, and he made me laugh with his jokes and taught me how to dance to Michael Jackson. I loved Derwin. But I never was sure why his dad and his older brother Davey insisted on calling him Dodo. Teasing in that meanspirited kind of way is anything but funny and nothing but mean.

"Sure," I said. "Nesey, want to come?" We sat in the tiny living room in front of the small TV. We wolfed down the noodles, creamy tuna sauce, and mushy peas while Derwin made jokes, and Nesey and I laughed.

Then *he* came home. A skinny, unhappy man. And as soon as he walked through the door, the entire dynamic changed. Davey headed straight for his younger brother, calling him Dodo and slapping him on top of the head. DeDe snickered and went to her room and shut the door. Derwin just sat there with a frown, while Nesey ran straight to this man's arms, yelling, "Daddy."

The man was familiar to me because he worked for my dad. Or

was it that he worked with my dad? I wasn't sure, and I never saw any interaction among him, my mom, or my dad. But I'm sure that there was some kind of triangle there; I just couldn't figure it out. Never tried to—until later.

The night during the sleepover I saw something that still didn't fully make sense. After everyone had settled in for the night, and Nesey and I crawled, still giggling, into her beautiful canopy bed, I got up to get some water from the kitchen.

"Stop it," I heard, accompanied by a weird kind of noise. There was movement on the couch, but I was determined to quietly sneak past, get my glass of water, and leave unnoticed. But there was more moving around and more noises. Unfamiliar noises.

It made more sense for me to get to the kitchen than to go back to the bedroom. But I realized I couldn't turn on the faucet without being heard. So I just stood there in the dark.

Finally, there were more noises from whoever was on the other side of that couch, then silence. It was so quiet I thought that if I took a breath I'd give myself away. I kept quiet and huddled in the dark in a corner of the kitchen with my empty cup.

I saw the man who would become my new dad get up and walk off. Okay, everything was fine, I thought to myself. Then I saw her, the older sister get up from the same place and go back to her room. I was reeling with confusion, fear, and disorientation. I didn't understand. I fully understand now that DeDe was the frightened one.

All those images from so long ago came flooding back on the day of my mom's wedding as I saw this girl, this sister who was now part of my family.

Then I heard him . . . the dad. "Don't tell anyone" he almost whispered to her. What seemed like several minutes had past, but it was seconds when I heard her reply. "I never do."

All in the Family

———

ONE DAY NEAR THE END of that month, I was in the backyard, where my dad and I had sat less than a year before. This house had become a place of brutal unhappiness for me. The only good thing was that Davey and DeDe had gone to live with their grandmother in Kansas City, which meant I wouldn't have to be terrified of Davey laughing and grabbing at my nonexistent boobs all the time, and DeDe couldn't glare at me. I now know that her glare wasn't directed at me. It was about what she was enduring herself.

DeDe ran away at the age of fifteen to save herself from the torture her dad, my stepdad, had inflicted on her for years. If only I'd had the courage then to speak up, maybe her truth wouldn't have been ignored and my truth would never have happened. Either way, I am sure she's found her strength. Survivors like DeDe continue to give me strength in my fight for justice.

In the yard, the honeysuckle already looked a bit dry. But I was pinching off the ends to get the honey like Dad had taught me when my memory of him was interrupted by the man walking toward me. When I saw my stepdad, I moved to the middle of the two-seat bench, so he wouldn't sit in my dad's place or next to me. I already hated my stepdad.

By this point I was starting to believe that inappropriate behavior, abuse, and molestation were normal, and that I was not. I never shared what I had seen, heard, and felt that night with anyone else; no one knew. Confronting my stepdad would only mean I'd be shamed for lying, or my mom would, as usual, ignore me or be disappointed in me. I had no words to define it. Trying to stay clear of her disappointment was a lifelong goal for me.

The weird thing was that when DeDe was around—which wasn't very often—she didn't seem to be afraid of her father at all; she was simply defiant. I never told her what I had seen that night. I wanted to, but she scared me just like her dad and her oldest brother did. All I wanted was to ask about the night to make sense of what I'd seen. I sure couldn't ask my stepdad. I was scared he'd beat me to a bloody pulp.

DeDe was several years older than me, had been a cheerleader, and hung out with the rich and popular kids when she was living at home. I always thought she was so pretty, and I used to idolize her in a way that made no sense. But she seemed like a cold person with a calculated look that screamed, "Don't talk to me!" In reality she was screaming, "Help!"

Her sporadic visits opened a new adult world to me, since she found time now and then to tell me some of the things that were done to her or what other men could and would do. But DeDe insisted she was in control and could get whatever she wanted from any man. In my mind, DeDe was a woman. She had answers to questions I never asked. I was just wishing my boobs were going to get as big as hers were.

Davey also came back to visit, and that was a hell all its own. My two new stepbrothers were nothing alike. The one I liked, Derwin, was the same age as my brother, Carl, and I loved having him around. When he was with me, I felt relaxed. Derwin taught me so much. We'd spend hours talking about life and things happening in the world. We'd watch *American Bandstand* on Saturdays and find space on the floor next to the fireplace to practice our dance moves. That actually paid off when I won a ribbon at the community center one Saturday night for a dance contest and also got to take home the newest album from REO Speedwagon.

I hated the way his dad treated him, always ridiculing him. I should have confided my secrets to Derwin, but maybe I didn't want to give him any more to worry about. He tried so hard to please his dad.

Davey was handsome and mean at the same time—one of those guys who always got the girl. I never felt anything but terrified of him. If he were watching TV in the living room, I'd rather pee my pants than walk past him to get to the bathroom. He scared me, scared us all, really, except DeDe and their dad.

When school started that fall, I only thought about a few things: the latest boy I was in love with and the hope that Mom would get me the new school clothes that Nesey and I had circled in the JCPenney catalog.

I had to look perfect for seventh grade. I had a severe sweating problem that year, and I was mortified at the thought of someone noticing the stains in my armpits, so I tried to wear colors that hid them.

Since the brand Polo was hot that year but we couldn't afford it, I thought that ingenuity would be my best option. I bought a pair of Polo socks, carefully removed the tiny riding man from one of them, and placed it exactly, so I thought, on the breast of my Hunt Club shirt so I'd fit in. Thanks to my savvy yet humble friend Martha, who loaned me a real Polo shirt, I was quickly saved from ridicule.

Meanwhile, Carl was as silent as he was invisible after our dad died. With the additions to our family, he just stayed out of the way, making an escape plan. He didn't talk or smile anymore. He seemed to be in his own world. I love my brother, and I know that the pain that he endured caused him to build emotional walls so thick that I couldn't even get through anymore. But he did love me, and I'm sure he was upset by my many bad decisions throughout my junior high years.

To our dismay, our parents told the four of us at home that we'd be moving to a farm outside of town. Our schools wouldn't change, because there was only one junior high and high school, but we'd have to ride the school bus into town. Carl and Derwin were almost old enough to drive, but we had no extra cars.

October turned me another year older, and I was sure thirteen was going to be a magical year. I felt like I was growing into a woman, and the attention boys were giving me was exciting. Nesey and I constantly played with makeup and clothes, and we practiced talking and walking in front of boys. We had to practice everything. It was a crucial moment for a girl when she started to realize her female power over a boy.

But there was another boy—a man, actually—who also saw the changes in me, and wanted to take advantage of those changes for his own evil satisfactions. That summer Davey was in our new house on the farm. He was on leave from the army—or he said he was—and he'd push his tough-guy stories around the kitchen table along with the butter at suppertime. No one seemed to speak much in his presence, and all I wanted to do was stay invisible to him.

But that became impossible.

The Farm

—————

I WOKE TO THE SOUND of cattle being prodded at the barn and groggily went in search of my tooth-decaying cereal and milk. Once again I wondered why Mom was making us drink the disgusting milk with its creamy chunks. I used to watch her try to strain the cream from the fresh cows' milk with a thin cloth diaper, and I always thought it was awful. To get it down, I pinched my nostrils together so I could eat the Frosted Flakes or whatever cereal we had. Then I sat there thinking about my newest boyfriend. I had fallen in love with Jon on the long bus ride to and from school.

But I was worried about hurting Mark. He had been my first kiss. Would he be mad at me when we returned to school at the end of the summer? How could I make him not hate me for moving on? Little did I know that within weeks neither Mark nor Jon would be a thought in my mind; I would soon meet a basketball player six years older than me, and he'd be the one I would give my heart to. But at that moment I wanted to see one more time what Mark had written on the back of his sixth grade school photo.

Having moved so many times, I found it best to keep my favorite things in a trunk; that way, no matter where I lived, my treasures would travel safely with me. To this day, I have four large steamer trunks and many memories to go with them. When we moved to the farm, my trunk was stored inside the barn.

I walked down the stone path, past the green field, past my stepdad, who was finished with the cattle and heading to the house. I pulled back the heavy barn door and made my way through the dusty, dimly lit space to the storage area. I found my trunk, heaved it to the dirt floor, opened the lid, and rummaged through my mementos.

There was Bear, along with letters, pictures, and a collection of penguins. The birds had fascinated me from the time I was nine, when I had seen them at a zoo. My dad started my collection, and after he died, I continued to add to it, probably thinking that might bring him back or at the very least keep my memory of him alive. Turning a little brass penguin over in my hand, I heard a noise and jumped. My stepbrother Davey was there.

"What do you think you're doing, little girl?" His eyes told me that I wouldn't escape with only a taunt. He took another step toward me. "You know, most girls your age have boobs. You don't even have bumps. It's pretty pathetic, huh?"

The penguin fell from my hand as I scrambled to get past him. He grabbed me and threw me down. Dust flew in my face, and I covered my eyes as I wrestled to get away, but his strength kept me prisoner. The rest of the day melted into a dark fog with the green field just beyond my view.

With this episode, I began a new lesson in survival more cruel than any I had ever encountered. I opened my eyes. I was alone. I had been raped.

Dirt, tears, and vomit covered my face, and I was convinced that I must've done something very wrong. God must really be ashamed of me. I felt empty as I sat there in the dirt trying to find the penguin I dropped so I could get it safely back into the trunk. Mom. I had to find my mom.

I retraced my steps from the barn to the house, but this time I didn't notice the cows in the field or the sun bouncing off the grass or the rocks lining the path.

The door slammed behind me, but I didn't call out. I was still shaking when I found my mother in the bathroom, putting on makeup. She didn't look my way as I closed the toilet lid and gingerly sat down. Closing one eye, she applied eyeliner then stopped to scratch her arm.

"I don't know where these hives came from. Wish I could figure out how to get rid of them." She continued studying the mirror.

"Mom, I hurt."

"Me too. They sure do itch. I must be upset about something. I've heard that nerves cause hives." Mom leaned toward the mirror, carefully brushing mascara on her lashes. I had no strength to go on as I tried to get her attention. I fell silent and stayed that way for a very, very long time.

I walked out of her bathroom, unheard. Still alone.

In my bathroom, I locked the door, took off my clothes, and stood in the shower, trying to wash away the humiliation that smothered me. I desperately wanted to get rid of the filth. I stepped out of the shower, toweled off, then stepped back into the shower again and again, convinced that I could cleanse myself from the shame that consumed me.

When I dried off the last time that day, I noticed the bruises on my arms, legs, and bottom. The emotional bruising I suffered was less visible. But when I brushed my teeth, looking into the eyes of the little girl in the mirror proved to be impossible. Unlike my mother, who quickly identified the source of her hives, the little girl in me couldn't diagnose the origin of her own overwhelming pain. All I knew was that I was anything but a little girl anymore.

I learned to survive by shutting down. Blocking memories, forgetting full days. Denying the realities of my past and present became familiar tools in my attempt to cope with the trauma of life.

But He Loves Me

WHEN THE SUMMER WAS OVER, and school started again, I somehow got onto the radar of a boy who was a nineteen-year-old senior in our high school. Oddly, he lived alone in a house but ate his meals at his grandmother's. All I knew was that he was older and a basketball jock, and he liked me.

"Meet me in the parking lot after school," Bob suggested one afternoon. Giddy with the attention, I did as he asked. Finally there was someone older to care for me.

"Is this your car?" I asked with sweat running down my armpits into a pool of embarrassment. Summer's temperatures were following us into fall, and it was way too hot for what I was wearing. I jumped into the passenger seat, kicked away the trash that covered the floorboard, and sat with my books held tightly in my arms.

"Relax, Steph. It's okay. I won't hurt you," Bob said. That he might hurt me didn't really seem to matter. I had been hurt more than anyone knew, and at least, I thought, Bob only had my well-being in mind. He liked me because I was nice and because I was funny. So I thought. So I snuck off to see this boy who was really a man, and, eventually, I got caught by my stepdad. When Bob decided to drive to the farm to see me, my stepdad ran him off. My stepdad's way of running off the gentlemen callers, no matter what age, was an awkward jealous kind of rage—at me, though, as if I was cheating on *him*. I wondered if he had been that way with DeDe.

The thing is, I have no idea why he tried diligently to rid me of this guy, and all the while it was *within* our walls that I was unsafe.

Once he was successful my pain intensified with my isolation; my heart couldn't handle the insult of not being heard about Davey or about my need for the relationship with my nineteen-year-old boyfriend. I found ways to sneak off to see Bob, who told me that he loved me. So it had to be true, right? One night I was able to get away for a sleepover at a friend's house. Now I had an escape route to my boyfriend, and I finally found my way to his place, an ugly brown house. As we walked through the kitchen I noticed an odd contraption sitting on the kitchen table. He mumbled something about a water bong and proceeded to get me stoned out of my gourd, have his way with me, and then he was done. Turns out he really didn't love me after all.

That was the year I was caught hiding the book *Forever* by Judy Blume behind my algebra book so I could learn about sex and love and the rest of the class could learn about putting numbers and letters together to come up with equations. This book was all the rage because it was where my friends and I first discovered that boys actually named their penises. I was trying desperately to learn about life, love, and how things worked.

At thirteen I was still a vulnerable little girl, exposed to every possible predator, a target for any imaginable pain. Abandonment, neglect, and abuse were the original perpetrators of destruction in my life, but I quickly learned how to magnify the devastation by my own self-loathing choices. I was starting to equate sex with love, but I was still confused about why it was always so short lived. The equation seemed to be: I am loved, I have sex, I am not loved. It didn't make any sense. But I was desperate.

Dingy Motels

DURING THE SUMMERTIME, MOM OFTEN sent me back to Grandma's house to stay. For whatever reason, that summer I was once again in Missouri with Grandma, listening to her hum church hymns at the kitchen as she cooked, and I was glad. There the aromas of spaghetti and ketchup mingled with the rose lotion and hair spray that she wore. While she clattered dishes at the sink, I scooted my kitchen chair closer to the table and inhaled the good smells as the steam hit my face.

"This smells good. Thanks, Grandma."

"You are welcome, sweetheart. I always love fattening you up," she said, staring out the tiny kitchen window that looked out toward the clothesline. Grandpa just scuffled into the kitchen, grabbed his strong coffee, and went out the back door without a word. He was off to roll his sweet tobacco in his thin papers to enjoy a smoke. I'd seen those kinds of cigarettes, and I thought they were illegal until I was told that was a different kind of weed than what Grandpa smoked.

Grandma was the essence of safety to me. And her house was a haven. Grandma *was* my home.

My cousin Melody was living with Grandma and Grandpa again, too. She'd gotten tired of her ex-husband using her face as a punching bag, so she gathered up enough self-esteem to go back home and start over again. We shared a common bond that summer, though we never spoke a word about it.

"Hey, Pudge, whatcha doin'?" Melody asked from her seat at the table. Without waiting for an answer, she went on. "Hey, Mom, Pudge and I are gonna go for a walk later, okay?"

"Okay," my grandma said, "but be careful. People drive fast on that dirt road. They stir up the dust, and they can't even see you." She turned and added, "When you head back, go to the grocer on the corner and get a pound of that bologna Stephanie likes."

I don't think I will ever understand how this woman, my grandma, and this girl, Melody, came from the same family as the repulsive great-uncle.

Whispering to me, Melody said, "I'm gonna go see my new boy-friend. Come with me."

I just shrugged, because I had crammed a wound-up forkful of spa-ghetti and ketchup into my mouth. I idolized Melody. I'd do anything she asked.

Abuse victims often learn patterns of living that leave them vulner-able to more endangerment, and my cousin was no exception. For her, "starting over" meant just that—starting from the beginning with more abusive men. The new guys she hung out with proved to be unstable for her and dangerous for me.

We'd walk down the dirt road to get to the dingy, pay-by-the-week motel where her boyfriend was staying, dodging traffic across the high-way. The traffic was easy, though, compared to the company we kept inside. My cousin's boyfriend and his friends were scary for a young girl newly stripped of her innocence. I felt like a magnet for molesters. After a few trips there I had seen a full range of misfits, from the skinny girl with jet-black hair and really long red fingernails to the greasy-haired guy with the whiskers on his wrinkled face.

On our next visit to the motel, I sat on the edge of the bed in a dirty room, waiting for my cousin to surface from another room. Look-ing down at my feet, thinking about what color I wanted to paint my toenails, I turned to see the brother of my cousin's boyfriend. He was grinning, still greasy with the same whiskers on his same wrinkled face. He put his unwelcome hand on my thigh in the hope that my weakness would work in his favor.

Not today! I thought. Somehow I found the strength in my 115-pound frame to muscle his 200-pound body to the floor with a huge shove. As he looked up in anger at me, I scrambled away from him and slammed and locked the bathroom door. I climbed out of the bathroom window and ran across the highway, down the dirt road, and I guess you could say over the hills and through the woods all the way back to

Grandma's house. I was terrified he was following me. Once safely in the house, I went back to my cousin's room, threw myself on the floor, put on her cassette tape, and listened to Bread sing "Lost Without Your Love." Lying on the floor, breathing so heavy as I counted the tiles on the ceiling. Something I did to calm down. I would count frontways and backwards, whatever it took.

Then the phone rang. Jumping, I picked up the black rotary phone and I heard, "Hello?"

The thirty-year-old creep had the nerve to ask me not to tell anyone, and as he put it, to "stop turning me on!" For some reason, I didn't tell and I could have. Then I worried that Melody might be mad at me for leaving, and wondered if she'd remember to pick up the bologna. Now I was hungry.

God, Are You There?

———

SUMMER ENDED WITH MY RETURNING home. I was determined to focus on schoolwork, while Mom was trying to focus on my salvation. Apparently, she thought catapulting me into religion would wash me clean of her mistakes and mine.

"You have to go with the youth group at church, Stephanie," said my mom. Our main way of communicating at that time was through arguing. I had learned that submitting to her was better than getting slapped in the face, or as she called it, "popped in the mouth." Her ability to slap me into silence was uncanny.

I just got out of the car and looked across the parking lot at my classmates. Some I knew, and some I didn't care to know. They were boarding a bus heading to JBU, a small university in Siloam Springs, to see some kind of concert put on by two sisters. I dragged myself across the parking lot and saw our youth minister. He reminded me of my dad, and he was someone I felt safe around. He had two little girls and seemed to be interested in me and my well-being. Seeing him, I thought back a few months ago to the day he had taken me to lunch at a nice country club. I'm sure he asked my mom if he could be of any help with my attitude and wanted to visit with me.

Walking through the doors on my first ever country club visit, I noticed people in plaid shorts and those blasted Polo shirts I couldn't get enough of. This was like the secret Polo shirt-wearing club. I was sporting my Jordache jeans and the Ocean Pacific T-shirt I'd borrowed from Nesey It wasn't a jeans and T-shirt kind of place.

"Have you ever been here before, Steph?" Pastor John asked.

"No, it's nice, though. Thank you. Am I in trouble for something? Did Mom make you take me here?"

"No, not at all. She didn't ask me; I wanted to," he said, reassuring me with a touch of his big hand on mine. One thing I know and have tried to pass on to my children is that there are touches that are safe and there are touches that are unsafe. His was safe.

"I know that you have been experimenting with drinking and drugs," the pastor said, "and I am worried about you."

Wondering who snitched on me, I decided not to lie. "Oh, that . . . Well, I guess I can't lie to you, but I only try it on the weekends." This seemed normal to me.

As we talked through the lunch, I asked if I could have two desserts, and I found myself feeling like any kid of nearly fourteen. Pastor John went on to tell me about the things that would help me: how if I knew that I was special in God's eyes, I would treat myself better. It was then that I started to talk about how some of those in my home were treating me.

The day of this concert was going to be Pastor John's last youth outing before he and his family relocated to another church, and I was sad. Before getting on the bus, I made my way to the basement of the Baptist church to find the bathroom and was stopped by a woman who taught a Sunday school class I'd gone to once or twice. I remember her sitting under a picture of Jesus in the classroom and how I thought their hair looked alike. How she recalled my name was beyond me.

"Stephanie, are you doing okay?" she asked softly.

"Yeah, I guess so. Why?" I was puzzled.

"I know you have been through a lot," she said, "and Pastor John wants me to watch out for you after he leaves."

She said one more thing that stuck with me: "This has happened to others, and we need to have you talk to someone." At first I didn't know exactly what she was referring to; then I wondered if she meant what had happened in the barn. Or what my stepdad had been doing. I had tried my best in my own evasive way to confide in Pastor John, and I guess he found someone to tell. I wonder why he didn't tell the police. Probably because I wasn't specific—something I've always had a difficult time with, especially as a kid. It would be late in life when I would name the act and call out the accused.

When we got to the university, I took a seat and watched the two sisters—Kathie Lee and Michie Epstein—make their way to the stage. At first, I wasn't receptive to the music, let alone the words. Then I looked up and felt like the dark-headed one was looking right at me. Yes, she was, I decided. The songs went on quite a while, and slowly the words made their way into my mind and I took them in, even though heavy-handed religious music usually turned my stomach. After the concert, I bought one of their albums. It had faded pictures of the Epstein sisters, and I listened to it several times in between my recordings of Meatloaf, REO Speedwagon, and Janis Joplin.

There was a small change in me that day, thanks to a quiet voice, a gentle look, and some words of redemption that I felt were aimed directly at me. All these gestures hinted at hope and the possibility that God might actually see me, hear me, and want me to be okay. Thanks, Kathie Lee and Michie.

It was the beginning of a transformation, but it would be a long while before I saw any major changes appear in my life.

The last few months had been full of ups and downs. Carl had been commissioned to the Air Force Academy, and although I was happy for him, I was sad for me. I didn't want him to go. Then mom had suddenly decided to leave my stepdad and move Nesey and me to a different home. That made me happy until, less than a year later, she changed her mind and moved back into the house with him.

I planned my escape from all this with a badly planned suicide attempt.

"Why are you sick?" my mom asked me on the first day of my junior year. "I hate my life," I said, crying, "and I don't want to be here anymore!"

"What did you take?"

"I took an entire box of Dexatrim!" I was so sick! Needless to say I was nowhere near death, but I had to survive a massive headache for days and explain why I could not make it to cheerleading practice that week. I had thought that getting my mother's attention would cause her to really see that I was hurting. But all that happened was that I got in trouble and made her even more angry with me. As mom became more disappointed with me, I was doubtful that she'd listen to any of my complaints even if I tried. My mom had had enough of me for one lifetime.

The Red Truck

IN MY DREAM, I WAS running to cross a street in a neighborhood. Out of nowhere, a red truck came speeding toward me. The driver, hunched over his steering wheel, looked up to see that a person—me—was trying to cross without being hit by his aggressive driving.

I made a split-second decision that it was safer to go forward than to stop and turn back, so I decided to run like hell!

The driver hit me anyway and kept on going. All I could do was put my hand under my knees and pull my limp body to the curb. The scene had played out in mere seconds. Then I woke up.

Climbing out of my bed, I went to find Mom, who was loading the dryer with wet towels. I leaned against the door and told her about my weird dream. "It was awful!" I said, and then shared the more sordid details.

My mother just peered off into the distance, which she usually did when I tried to tell her something. Then she turned to me and said, "I always wanted a red truck."

As years passed and I read quite a lot about narcissistic behaviors, I realized they applied to my mom. They were her own survival techniques, I guess. We all probably have them to a degree, but I have tried to get rid of mine—to fight against being like her. Getting out of my own head and doing what I can for others has helped me. I have learned to listen.

My Heroes

———————

MY TEEN YEARS CONTINUED TO give me so much emotional baggage that I needed my own personal bellboy to carry them around. Really I just needed direction of some sort. Because of the impact that Kathie Lee and Michie had on me the night of the concert, I thought that Christianity was the key, so I tried joining the Fellowship of Christian Athletes. When that didn't float my boat I joined the Future Farmers of America.

For those of us desperate to locate our dream man, this was a perfect opportunity to find either a good Christian boy or one with a knack for driving a tractor. One girl in the Future Farmers was actually there to learn to be a farmer herself. She wasn't chasing boys; no, she was chasing the idea that maybe someday a girlfriend would be acceptable in our society. The friendly farmer girl helped me realize that maybe it wasn't the group for me. She was right. I wished her well on being "who she really was"and moved on into other clubs that fit me more.

Trying on about every personality I could muster to see where I fit in was exhausting. With an angel on one shoulder and the devil on the other, I was divided between the "good" and the "bad"—between the social group we referred to as "soc" and the partying, pot-smoking group called the "hoods." That not only gave me a plethora of interesting friends, but I also passed back and forth what I learned from one group to the other. I felt like a kind of social liaison, always trying to get one kind of person to like the other.

Cheerleading was perfect for a personality that loved to flirt and jump around with nothing to say but "Go Panthers, go!" I also tried hanging out in the parking lot before English class to smoke a joint with people I liked, even though I knew they weren't the best influence on me. I didn't really like pot—or smoking anything, for that matter. I was born with great teeth that I obsessively brushed and wanted as white as possible. But I always migrated toward what society called the underdogs. I referred to them as the unsung heroes of the world who were willing to step out of society's restricted boxes.

One of my favorite unsung heroes was Rusty, a friend who was a year older than I. He was in my algebra class, and we both knew that neither of us would ever pass it. Rusty had been held back, as I was sure I would be the next year. He was an artist, and one of the coolest guys I'd met. Rusty was a bohemian-looking dude with long hair. The art teacher had convinced the principal to give him a big empty space on the lunchroom wall to paint a mural.

Rusty taught me about getting high and was probably the first one to crack open my artistic side by encouraging me to write. He used to tell me that I was different and that my mind worked in such a way that I was sure to go through life misunderstood. His daily talks while I watched him paint opened new ways of seeing things and new ways to approach the world, plus he showed no signs of interest in me the way I was conditioned to think guys always did. "Steph, be colorful, not gray," Rusty told me, and I really took that to heart.

My friend Eric, who loved me unconditionally from elementary school on, was another unsung hero. He always tried to save my ass, my honor, and my soul.

Eric's loving parents took it upon themselves to create a safe environment for the kids of Siloam by opening the Emporium, a great pizza place with games, music, and fun—minus all the things I'd go out to find before showing up at Eric's place. Time and time again, Eric would find me in the Emporium parking lot, mascara-stained tears running down my face as he rescued me from the jerks I always picked. Thanks to him, I realized there were good people—specifically, good guys—in my life who had only kindness, love, and adoration for me just because I was . . . well . . . me.

I even found out that Eric had a fistfight in my honor with the dishwasher from the Emporium. It was the old boyfriend who had dumped me after our romantic bong-induced encounter. He had taken a smoke break in the parking lot where he worked, and when he voiced his twisted false pride over what he had accomplished, Eric handed his ass back to him.

My dear friend Robert saved me on numerous occasions even though he never knew he was doing it. Robert provided safety. When I had to give up cheerleading because of one of many corrective foot surgeries, Robert hung out with me in the afternoon, while his girlfriend, Annette, was cheering. Sometimes we spent the time at a pizza place on the other side of town, and sometimes Robert stayed with me at my house, watching *The Brady Bunch* until everyone else came home so that I wouldn't be alone with my stepdad. I've always wondered if fate put heroes in my life so I'd learn ways to stay safe.

Robert showed me how to boil water for pasta and told me about sauce in a jar. And he'd tell me how much he was in love with Annette. One day we went to pick her up after practice, and I saw her smile at the sight of him. She put her hands on her tiny hips and batted her amazing, long lashes, and love was written all over her face. I always knew he and Annette would marry. They did, and they're still married.

Some people are meant to be together and for always. And others, well, they shouldn't be together ever. Those were the ones I usually picked, but not always, because later I met Bobby. And that was right.

Itty Bitty Titty Committee

MY JUNIOR YEAR OF HIGH school proved to be one of my most experimental years—a lab of boys, booze, and drugs. I seemed to have lost all the moral codes I had been taught by my sweet grandmother. But when you are taught that anything that feels good is wrong, you really don't have much to work with in the way of balance. I tried to spend time with my healthy friends and those who were only a bit less than healthy. But basically I pulled out all the stops and lived a fast life. I loved my friends and would have done anything to be with them. Plus, being with them let me escape my family.

"Stephanie, what'd you make on the algebra test?" The jock next to me reached to grab my paper.

"None of your business." I pushed his hand away as the teacher—we called him Coach—sat back down in his wooden swivel chair.

"Coach, can we do extra credit?" My hand was up before I could censor myself. I was desperate, considering the late-night conversation I'd just had with my mother about my failing grades. I wanted nothing to do with the summer school she'd threatened. I wish now she had taken this kind of stance throughout my education, but for some reason she gave up on the possibility of my academic success somewhere around the fourth grade.

"Henry, you are *not* smart." Coach leaned back in his chair and tapped a rolled-up test against the edge of his desk. He always referred to everyone by last name.

"Henry, why don't you just use your looks to get through life?" He chuckled, and the class broke out in laughter.

I laughed with them but smothered the humiliation I felt. Okay. Maybe I did struggle with schoolwork. But on the bright side, I apparently had *looks*, whatever the hell that meant.

"You're pretty, Steph," was something I heard over and over. Yet all I knew was that "pretty" hurts in some way or another. I would rather have had nondescript looks so that I'd go unnoticed. I had to deal with Mom being ashamed of me because of my looks, and because of my looks men liked me too much.

In any case, I grew up doubting that I was pretty. Thanks to my evil stepbrother, Davey, I spent years convincing myself that I wasn't worthy of admiration or respect, and he launched plenty of verbal grenades my way to make it clear that I was physically inadequate.

At least one gift for my seventeenth birthday was predictable: I was sure to get a T-shirt with the slogan "Itty Bitty Titty Committee" or "Flat Is Beautiful" splashed across a very conspicuous place. A year earlier, as I stood next to my boyfriend during my sixteenth birthday party, this stepbrother whispered in my ear, "Poor girl . . . sweet sixteen and still no boobs." He delighted in pointing out my imperfections. At seventeen, not much about my body had changed.

But now my algebra teacher had declared I possessed "looks," and Coach's suggestion bounced around in my head as I floundered through my junior year. And it stuck with me through my life.

My obsession with physical appearance grew out of my desire to prove that I mattered. Report cards showed that I was stupid and that I didn't count, and Mom's displeasure over my flunking yet another class only solidified that thought in my mind. I was constantly failing anything I had to calculate or read.

Sometimes I wonder if some parents feel it's easier to give up on a kid than to help them fight their limitations. I severely question the educational system in which I was raised, but more importantly I question the lack of guidance at home. That is where it starts. It's because of the commitment of those raising us that we are taught to sink or swim. My hat is off to those who fight to ensure their children have a better education and a better life. In my case, I didn't even tread water with my education, and it would be years before I even learned to properly read and write. Since I couldn't feel validated by my dead father or feel heard by my mother, because I wasn't valued by the abusive stepfather or molesting stepbrother and great-uncle, and I was a dismal failure in academics—I figured I could at least go places by using my so-called looks, specifically, my body. That decision was a choice born out of self-hatred; it was my little-girl coping mechanism for life's horrific injustices. If I were "good," then bad things would stop happening.

I paid attention to my hair, makeup, and boobs (what there were of them). Perfecting my teeth became a high priority. Trips to the mall in the big town of Fayetteville included my watching guys watching girls, and I convinced Mom to let me pierce my ears. I learned what to wear, not necessarily for style but as a tool of seduction—a means of survival.

Most of all, in order to make my body appealing, I learned to starve myself—to binge and purge when I didn't even know what these two words meant. I liked the feeling of control that bulimia offered. I could command my body into submission. At least something in my life could be predictable. The end result was a thinner body that enhanced my looks. Control, fear, and acceptance took on an important meaning for me, and I was becoming an expert at all of them. The illusion that I could control the monstrous eating disorder ran rampant through me.

Utopia

├─────────────┤

THAT SAME YEAR MY ENGLISH teacher had us write a paper about our Utopia. Never really being a good student—not even an average student, for that matter—I was very surprised when I got an A on the paper. Here it is:

My Utopia

Living at Grandma's house I'd get to eat fried chicken, mashed potatoes with as much ketchup as I want. Without my stepdad always making me eat the extra ketchup on my plate with a spoon so I don't waste it. He's so mean and smells gross!

Grandma's house is where I can sit by the TV and don't worry about some gross guy touching me in the places that make me wanna puke! If Utopia is perfect, I guess I'd feel safe then probably. No one making fun of me because I don't have boobs or pulling my hair and laughing cause I'm stupid.

I'd be walking into our living room and my Dad reading a newspaper as he's telling me another story that makes me laugh or sometimes his stories make me cry but that's okay. He liked Dean Martin and Jerry Lewis movies for laughing and the Phantom of the Opera book for crying. But in Utopia Dad wins the hot dog eating contest at his mobile home grand opening, or was it pie eating? Or was it both?

My Utopia is where my brother and I can play office and I'm the secretary who types fast and gets to use the cool pencil sharpener that we plug into the wall.

I wouldn't have to write a thousand times "I will not talk in study hall" because Coach is mad at me again and I get in trouble even if I ain't talking. I would quit getting in trouble. Mom would be home after school and stop leaving me there with my stepdad. Why is he home anyway when it's not after work yet?

The smell of Grandma's house and fried eggs and bacon in the morning, making sure she ain't popped by the bacon grease. Listening to her sing "How Great Thou Art" at the kitchen window while she washes the breakfast dishes.

Even if Grandpa doesn't talk, it's okay because he's safe. He just sits there with his rolled up tobacco that Grandma makes him go outside to smoke and watches a stray cat he named George. Maybe I would have real clothes in Utopia and I wouldn't have to buy the polo socks, take off the polo guy, and sew it to a Hunt club brand shirt from JCPenney's to make it look like a real polo shirt like my friend has. I just want to be like my friend but my hair is really icky and she always looks good. I would live with only Nesey, Carl, and Derwin, because the four of us have fun, we laugh and no one is mean. Davey wouldn't come home and Mom would make my stepdad go away for good. He is so gross in his boxer underwear walking around like no one can see him.

In Utopia Mom would let me sit on her bed like she used to on some Saturdays before she married him. She'd let me go through all her jewelry and see what I liked and got to have when I am old enough. She'd give me that butterfly pen she has. Mom and I would have a special day when she would let me have two squirts of the Shalimar perfume from her bathroom.

If home looked perfect and I got to live here, it would have big trees, a bunch of sunflowers, and dogs. Utopia is where I look like my friend Dana, I have a huge house like my friend Joanne, tons of cool clothes like Martha, I could sing like Tracy, be beautiful like LaDonna, have Brietta's dad, Annette's eyelashes, and Tami's smart brain. Mom would listen to me when I was crying and my Dad would be alive.

Out of Control and Out of Luck

SNEAKING OUT OF THE HOUSE, spending time with my new hippie boyfriend, Chris, and driving my brother's Camero into a ditch while he was trying to better my driving skills were among the many things I was doing in high school—along with flunking every single class I took, including home economics. I couldn't even get a decent grade on how to prepare a meal, change a diaper, or sew a button. Through the years, though, I have learned how to change a diaper—a lot of diapers!

The cooking thing? Well, the truth is I don't like to cook, and when I do, my menu is limited to spaghetti sauce from a jar. As for button sewing, if a button falls off, I toss the garment away and just pick something else to wear. Which is a blessing; I used to go through tons of duct tape trying to keep my TG&Y and Walmart clothing together long enough to get through a long day or night! If you fold tape thin enough you can hem a pair of pants in no time.

When Mom realized that I had flunked yet another math class, she threatened to send me to that summer school for algebra. Completing algebra with a decent, "I'm not an idiot" grade became one of my biggest hurdles in life. Grades were the last thing on my mind, however. What was taking up a lot of my time and energy was trying to sneak off with my boyfriend and hide the black mollies that I had discovered would keep me from eating. I went once to the class and spent the rest of that summer high as a kite.

By the time my junior year ended, and I had spent a bit more time with a group of friends on the infamous wet side of the state line that was referred to as "West Siloam," I was partying and getting busted all the time. My first legal driving night out I was given the huge Lincoln Continental to "go to a movie." Instead, I was talked into making a beer run. I was sure I wouldn't get caught. Passing by the restaurant that my mom and stepdad were sitting in probably wasn't the most thought-out plan. The fact that they saw me was a fluke, but they did. And then they followed me to the store and let me go in, buy beer, and then bust me. See, that's the thing about me. I *always* got caught when I did something wrong.

In any case, I had become a candidate for a different summer program that my mom had planned. Mom, my stepdad, Nesey, and me moved for the summer to Fairview, a tiny town in Oklahoma that barely had a population.

I said good-bye to my edgy friends on our last night out, as we climbed the Siloam Springs water tower after dark and marked it with "Steph was here, now she's gone and left her name to carry on." Poetic, right? My plan was to get through the hell of leaving all the people I loved and deal with my fate for the summer of '82. At least I would get the best tan ever. That would take the two and a half months to do, no problem.

With a bad attitude and tears in my eyes, I sat in the backseat of Mom's cramped Mazda for the five-hour journey to our new summer home, which was anything but a dreamy vacation place. It was, in fact, a small, two-bedroom apartment with a blow-up mattress on the floor for Nesey and me to share.

But change was in this dry, red-dirt air, and little did I know how much change was about to happen to me. After the summer was over, I would carry out my next act of vandalism when I spray painted under the old bridge downtown. This message read "Steph loves Bobby."

Geographical Cures

AS FAR BACK AS I can remember, I was a gypsy in the making. If I'd
been born a century or two earlier, our family would have had a couple
of covered wagons full of our crap and would have moved several times
to start over and try to find a better life. I became familiar with Interstate
35 as a child. In my twenties and thirties I referred to myself as the I-35
nomad. Change can be good, but at some point it was apparent that no
matter where this nomadic gypsy either rode in a car with her parents
or drove her own poor Saab with over 250,000 miles and no brake pads,
she would still end up with one familiar thing—herself! It's like the old
saying: "No matter where you go, there you are," right?

Since 1982 Carl had been in the Air Force Academy and I was
left with only my stepsister Nese—she had grown out of being called
Nesey—my mother, and stepfather. I hated it when my brother left to
go back to school. And I couldn't blame him for not wanting to come
home. Hell, we were all just waiting for our own exit.

It was never his job to raise me, although he tried his best. I will
always feel bad that he thought that some of what happened to me was
his fault, either because he had left or because he didn't notice what happened when I was a little girl. Releasing him from that guilt has been
an important goal in my life. Carl was only twenty months older than
me, and I was not his responsibility. Our family was what it was, and as
with any family, dysfunctional or not, we had lives to live. It had been
time for him to get the hell out of our abusive home in Siloam and on
to better things.

I know that some of the decisions my mom had to make were difficult for her. No doubt when my brother was no longer around, she was
all that more miserable. He was her life, and I can say without resentment

that he was her favorite. He was my favorite, too! My thoughts shifted on the ride that day to Oklahoma. When we got there I'd have to deal with someone I hadn't had to deal with in a very long time: my stepbrother Davey, who had married and moved to Fairview.

Mom had her own issues to deal with. She was always picking the wrong guys for the wrong reasons. That was a mold I, too, would not break for many years. But where had Mom learned this pattern? My grandmother had one of those "til death do us part" marriages, though I did find out years later that happiness was not something she ever felt entitled to. "Sweetheart," Grandma told me, "I decided a long time ago that I would find joy in my children, even if I felt unloved by your grandpa. It was a sacrifice, but I would do it all again."

As for Fairview, I was sure this place held the promise of absolute boredom, solitude, and no friends, let alone boyfriends. What was a girl to do?

As we pulled into the parking lot of our apartment complex, I was sure the next few months were going to be a living hell. I loved Nese, and we would be good for each other. But staying in this cramped place with a stepdad I could barely look at was just not right or fair. Especially when two oil-rig guys across the hall discovered there was "fresh meat," as they called it, in the building. It was a scary game to walk quickly and safely past their door in the hope they wouldn't want conversation or something much worse.

But the absolute worst part was having to visit my stepbrother's home, which we did a lot.

My grandma always told me that God only gives us what we can handle, and I believe that God did, in fact, think I had had enough. Davey's new wife kept him away from me. It was the only way living in the same town with them would ever be safe. Safe enough, I guess. On our first visit to their ugly, brownish-gray, concrete home, she met us at the door. She wasn't an overly friendly lady, but because she kept him from me, I thought she was a queen.

Endless Love

———————————

THE DOWNTOWN AREA OF OUR summer town proved to be nice and quiet, and I met a new friend who introduced me to a couple of really sweet guys. Phil, the older one, was taken with me, and we went out on one date, but it was the younger one, the guy with the big blue eyes and great smile, who would change my life. Bobby finally conjured up the nerve to butt in and ask me out. I am sure some guy code was discussed between the two of them, but eventually the shift was made. I became Bobby's girlfriend, and Phil and I remained good friends.

Bobby had a way of walking that made you want to grab his hand and walk alongside him. He was bubbly and fun, and his laugh melted my heart. He was different from the guys back home, and he had a normal, safe family. I loved riding in his light blue Chevy pickup. We would listen to Alabama's rendition of love songs or just sit and listen to nothing at all.

When you're longing for it, you see the possibility of love everywhere. I saw a future with this boy. He had commitment and real promise. My stomach turned over in agony when I thought of how I would miss him. That summer went fast, and when I left town, I cried the whole five-hour drive back to Arkansas. I had forgotten all about my summer tan.

And when I got home, I felt different. My grades went up, at least to passing, I got a job at a local pharmacy, and I stopped being part of the wild crowd. I imagined a family and a future. Bobby and I talked and wrote letters, and I found myself deeply in love.

We had so many visits, and even my poor, lovesick mother drove me back and forth several times. She was dealing with her own broken heart every time she came home because my stepdad had stayed in Oklahoma.

Eventually he showed up again and lived with us a bit longer, until their marriage finally ended.

Bobby would clock out from his job and drive all night so we could be together, and we soon became engaged. In the face of so much love, my hidden demons finally gave up and left me alone. It was as if they were suffocated by the love I was feeling. I forgot my nightmares, never realizing that secrets, if ignored, will surface later. I just blissfully lived in my new world.

That year I pulled away from most of my friends at school, except for a few girls I was really close to. Traveling to visit Bobby's family was my favorite thing. Being there with the smell of home-cooked meals, card games, and laughter felt as routine and comfortable as if I were putting on a pair of pajamas and my fuzzy socks after a long day. We would sit in a tiny room off the dining area and listen to the men play guitars and sing. I was proud to be a part of his family and never dreamed I would be anywhere else ever again.

I kept trying to impress them. One day I made chocolate chip cookies for Bobby's dad and left the foil-covered plate on the front porch with a note; I wanted to surprise my soon to be father-in-law when he came home from work. He *was* surprised. He walked to the front door and discovered something covered by a mound of ants. Back home in Arkansas, I spent hours with LaDonna and Brietta, looking through wedding magazines, every girl's pastime while she's waiting for matrimony. I thought it would be my once-in-a-lifetime chance to find the perfect wedding dress and begin a perfect life. I had the perfect guy, so I was a step ahead.

As young ladies, we believe that the man we're marrying, whoever he is, is "the one"—the ultimate love of our life. Please heed my warning, however: If you are not completely open with him, it will be a problem later. Love can endure, but it needs to know what it has to endure. If you have that type of honest relationship, with no hidden secrets, consider it a gift. But some of us are unable to voice secrets. Sometimes they are so deep that we also forget they are part of our reality.

Some of my reality was brought to my attention on graduation day when our principal eerily smiled at me. Listening to my name being called as I strode across the stage to accept my diploma—with my family, including Bobby, watching—I felt pride. Until the principal handed me the crimson, leather diploma holder and pulled me close to whisper in my ear, "Please don't open it. It's empty. You haven't passed yet."

Shock does odd things to the senses. Somehow I was capable of walking to my seat, still grinning at all of my friends. The tears would come later. What was wrong with the education system, anyway? Not only would it have been nice to know this bit of information before graduation day, but it was also the school's duty to ensure I hadn't fallen through the cracks. After the ceremony I was told that I'd need to pass more tests before I graduated. Why hadn't my mother told me? Was a notice lost in the mail?

I finally scraped by, passing a test in math as well as a few other things, and I was able to start my new life. I can't honestly say I was pulled out of that educational crack, because when they handed me the results it was clear that I was still uneducated. But apparently even a GPA of 1.9 will get you out the high school door. I just moved on. Moved, period, to Oklahoma.

We had our wedding in the tiny town I was going to live in. It was a pretty ceremony, and I carried a bouquet of peach and white silk flowers. A circle of baby's breath on my head held my veil. I bent my head in prayer as we lit our unity candle, and I gave thanks for the day. I felt safe. I *was* safe.

The only thing wrong was the person who gave me away. During the school year, as Mom was loading laundry into the washer she told me, "Your stepdad and I are divorcing, but he's going to walk you down the aisle anyway. We'll wait until after the wedding." I was so happy to be leaving that I didn't care who walked me, threw me, or kicked me down that aisle.

I damn near ran down the aisle to Bobby, who stood there smiling that smile I loved so much. The wedding was like a prom I had never been to. I knew, no matter what, that we would be okay; my dreams had finally come true. I never imagined that the words of our song, "Endless Love," would be tested.

With our wedding, I felt that life had finally started for me. Even though the normality was unfamiliar, I loved it—the Sunday meals with the family, the card games, the love, and the working together the way a village does to raise a child. I didn't realize it at the time, but I was the one who still needed to be raised.

Bobby and I bought our first home with help from his mom and dad, and life was good. Life was normal. We had a home with maybe a thousand square feet and just enough space to fill with one child and a tiny dog. We were happy.

When we took a trip to Las Vegas for his work, we were two kids in an unfamiliar world that was speeding by. I never imagined that a day would come when I would walk these streets without him as a much older version of myself. The excitement of a place like Vegas can do things to the average person. In this instance, I was an eighteen-year-old girl who thought I had the world at my feet.

I remember the advertisements getting stuck to the filth on the bottom of my shoe. The city seemed to be littered with these cards and flyers offering the services of exotic dancers to the lonely. I was confused as to what they were all about and wondered why these girls would expose their naked bodies to the world. Little did I know that I would later understand exactly why they did it.

Standing there looking up at the massive MGM Hotel was overwhelming. Looking over at my husband, who was looking at me, I just smiled and said, "Hey, let's sneak into the casino and play the slot machines. Maybe we'll get lucky." Bobby grinned at my peer pressure and said, "Yeah, maybe we'll hit a jackpot!"

Porcelain Baby

———————

THIS TIME IN MY LIFE was full and happy. I had finally escaped the hell I had lived in most of my life, and although our home had no white picket fence, I still considered it a dream come true. The dream only got better when I found I was pregnant.

In the evenings, as spring began to show, along with my ever-growing belly, we tried out baby girl names to see what fit. Bobby was so happy that I was pregnant that he wanted to call the baby "Jackpot." One night after a dinner of fried chicken, we went out to the backyard. I was talking about the rotten peaches that kept falling off the lone peach tree next to our clothesline.

"Make jam," Bobby said, and we laughed. I had recently gone to TG&Y to buy canning jars but decided I liked using them for iced tea instead. There are little moments in life that you never forget. This was one for me, because I knew things would never change. Life seemed so simple. As we went back through the old screen door, it hit me, as if our baby had whispered what she wanted her name to be: Miranda Nicole.

It was perfect timing; soon she was on her way to us. Our baby girl was beautiful and very small, and I never thought I could ever love someone more than I already did, until I saw this person come from me out into the world.

Bobby was thrilled at the miracle of her life, and he carried a camcorder around that was larger than our baby, documenting her first days. A friend has said that having a child is like taking your heart and putting it on the outside of your body—it's that type of vulnerability. Sometimes I like to think that even the Big Guy Upstairs becomes speechless at the birth of a child.

As I left my teenage years behind that October before Miranda joined us, I was terrified at the idea that this little thing would depend on me for food, safety, and love. But I had a lot of guidance from my mother-in-law, who taught me the job of being a mommy. Carolyn is the essence of what a real mother is and ought to be. This is a woman who gives all of her being to the welfare and safety of her children and grandchildren.

This is one time in my life when I was happy that I couldn't sleep. I filled the time keeping watch over Miranda. Hour after hour I thought about the definition of beauty and the definition of God's grace. That was Miranda. That *is* Miranda.

I watched Bobby crawl over the floor with the video camera, chasing our growing daughter to get shots of her laughing and cooing. As she pulled the slipcovers off our garage-sale couch and as she raced around it until she was dizzy, we'd soak up the sounds of her baby laughter. *My* only concern was keeping the tiny pink bow I'd pasted on her little blonde head with Karo syrup from falling off. Learning daily what it meant to be a wife and mother, I still tried to get a bit better in the kitchen, spending hours at unsuccessful attempts at making supper, just happy that I had a full set of CorningWare dinner plates. Maybe I still wouldn't be able to pass home economics, but Bobby ate the food I managed to make.

When we first married, we joined the local Baptist church, and I asked to help with the youth, though I was a bit confused as to why I had to be baptized one more time to do so. Apparently the baptisms couldn't get me clean enough. I had already been baptized twice before, once as a baby and again when I was nine years old. I still remember the pond water and my floral dress pinned together between my legs to keep it from flowing up around my waist. Then I was dipped into the water by Pastor Max and cleansed of all the sins I had committed from birth to nine years old. Actually, I now think that my grandmother had me cleansed of all the sins that were done to me, instead of the sins I had done.

For my third cleansing, I was pregnant with Miranda, and I had to make my way to the makeshift area behind the pulpit as the congregation watched. This time I wore a white robe, and I was submerged in a contraption that was basically a bathtub to eliminate the sins that kept me from God. As I was dunked under, I imagined the baby in my tummy being saved by osmosis. She would be free of sin before she arrived.

Butt Paste, Not Toothpaste

POSTPARTUM DEPRESSION FEELS LIKE AN emotional Mack truck ramming its way through your days. The highs and the lows of having children seem like too much to handle at times.

I felt like I was abandoned on an island, and no one could see my signals of distress. The severe shift from extreme high to rock-bottom low simply didn't work with my brain chemistry. If you are a mom, you know the drill. In the middle of a sunshiny, blissful state, you fall asleep, and then the clouds come crowding in and the gray takes over, and you wake up and realize that nothing is the same. We not only feel fat, ugly, and tired, it's as if we are an entirely different person. Not to mention we are suppose to remember to be sexy and ready for our loving husbands when they return from a long day at work.

It sure didn't help that afternoon I was strolling through the grocery and was greeted by a woman from our church. "Hello, Stephanie. Now when are you going to have that baby?" Hoping she was either clueless or cruelly joking, I didn't reply right away. Hiding the bag of chips I looked forward to spending the afternoon with, I just said, "She's eight weeks old already." She stretched a ridiculous grin across her makeup-plastered face and said, "Oh, sorry dear."

All we can remember is what got us into the mess to begin with. For me, if I only had to care for Miranda I would have been fine. All the other duties of being a wife and actually having to shower were bogging me down.

There are too many times when your breast milk decides to set its own delivery schedule—usually at the most inopportune moment, like when you finally find a shirt that fits. Or you've succeeded at dressing yourself and getting the baby ready only to discover you have crap on your face, mascara on one eye, and you have to grab a stick of gum because you have no idea where you left your toothbrush or when you actually used it last. I was so frazzled that one time I mistook diaper rash paste for toothpaste, burned my mouth, and ruined my toothbrush and my dignity.

Before the postpartum crap starts its feeding frenzy on our self-worth, new mothers should be whisked away in a limo and set down at a lovely spa that welcomes both mom and baby, where we can get sleep, nourishment, enjoy playtime, and have a panel of experts nearby for our questions and answers. There should be nurses caring for the infant so we can feel secure enough to melt down or simply sleep. Instead we are ignored and left virtually on our own. No matter the amount of love your family has for you during this time, you'll feel crazy and out of control.

I'm not saying that this condition, which just about every woman in the world has experienced, set the stage for my emotional deterioration, but it sure as hell didn't help. Something was shifting in me, and some old familiar feelings were making their way into my head. My depression was a breeding ground for old ways to surface. My nightmares were just lying in wait for my weakest moment, and when they rose up again, I would not be prepared and neither would my sweet husband.

I decided that I would get a job and take a break from my beautiful daughter, who seemed only to cry when I held her. There was a cool clothing store in Fairview called Jody's Clothing Shop. Jody herself would be on the list of people who tried to save me. I loved it there. The women took me in and sheltered me the best they could, just as Grandma Carolyn sheltered Miranda from a storm she surely felt was in the air.

On the Seventh Day God Said, "Steph, Get Back to Church!"

————

THERE IS A VULNERABLE MOMENT when you want to live your life the way you think God wants you to, while evil is pulling you over to its demonic side. As I sat in church services with my husband at my side and my baby in the nursery, I allowed one of those voices to get louder. I just wasn't sure which.

The thing about church for me is that it has always been about what I have done wrong. Church has been a place to lay down all your wrongs and have another shot at doing things right. But it seemed like my sins multiplied too fast, beginning on Monday morning. By Sunday I had another list to lay down. It was a vicious circle.

Unbeknownst to me, my secrets were surfacing with a vengeance. I'm sure it was due to one specific episode that caused a domino effect. The problems began with disgusting notes left on my car while I was at work. For months, after I'd clock out at Jody's, I'd find seedy, perverted notes on my windshield that suggested that the writer of each note knew everything about me. I was being stalked. I couldn't tell Bobby at first; I thought he'd be angry at me and assume I was doing something wrong. He was the sweetest guy ever, but I actually thought he'd slap me, call me names, leave me, or worse, be disappointed in me. Because certainly I had caused this, right?

Finally, after a few weeks I told Jody, and she helped me tell Bobby. And he, of course, reacted with nothing but sympathy for me and anger at whoever was doing this to his wife. We tried to discover the perpetrator and even met with a handwriting expert. In the end we discovered the note-writer was our next-door neighbor. The police didn't do anything because the notes weren't "threatening in nature." It seemed to be okay with these authorities if someone followed me everywhere, said they were in love with me, and knew what perfume I wore. Call me crazy, but doesn't that send off some serious signs of an unstable person? But I was being treated like the unstable one, and I'd quickly start owning that title.

I was barely twenty years old, and I had no tools to deal with the real world. I had no idea that this event would force my inner child into a catastrophic rebellion fueled by terror and a need to survive.

Predators and Pastors

BOBBY HAD GOTTEN ANOTHER JOB in a different town, Enid. He was committed to moving us from Fairview to make better money, and, I am sure, to appease his young, scared little wife. Staying put in one location wasn't in my genetic makeup, and bless his heart, he tried to do what he could to make me happy. After the stalker left me alone, I was still scared to work, so I quit and stayed home, alone with Miranda and a new puppy. And then out of nowhere a friend of Bobby's older brother decided to pay a few visits and help me learn the right way to groom a dog.

This guy and his wife were friends of ours, and at first I didn't think anything of it. But soon things he said caused me to think, number one, that my young husband didn't really love me, and number two, that someone else's did.

People without the capability to feel their own worth often sabotage everything to punish themselves. If it was my fault that I had been molested and raped, then it made sense to me that I didn't deserve something as real as the love Bobby and his family had for me. It's not a cop-out because it was my choice. I won't even throw a "but" in here because that would negate my accountability. The fact was, once I was victimized by the stalker, my inner child started reeling with terror, and this time I didn't retreat. Something about being followed caused me to sleep with one eye open again and to kick and scratch anyone who touched me. Except this new friend. He'd be my way out as I used the situation to sabotage my marriage. I lost my will to accept love for myself in a healthy way. My old habit of justifying bad behavior was certainly linked to the fear I'd lose it all anyway. I just made it happen quicker. Bottoming out at warp speed, I took Bobby, his family, and the family of this guy down with me.

One weekend I left my baby girl with her daddy and drove to see my mom, whom I hoped could make sense of what I was doing. When I got to her house and saw her there with her newest husband, I froze up and left. I gave in to the pressure of meeting this guy, my dog-grooming buddy. I became a cheater. I'd be lying if I told you it was all planned out, because it wasn't. But as we carried on, I began to feel even more afraid. I masked my fear with anger that simmered until it bubbled to the top and erupted. Those who loved me couldn't get close, because a raging monster might attack them at any second. I couldn't think straight. My eating illness returned and made me spin out of control even more.

Finally, I was unable to stand it anymore; I picked a Sunday after church to tell my wonderful family what I had done. I'm not sure what I was thinking or what I expected. Maybe I was trying to quit before I got fired or simply relieve myself of my own guilt. Having everyone throw me out on my butt would have felt normal. Being beaten would have even felt good. I deserved it.

As it had when I was a teenager, bulimia gave me that familiar feeling of control. When everything else in my life was unpredictable, when everyone else in my life called the shots, when no place felt safe, I could control things by binging and purging. I could determine what food I ate and what food I didn't want to keep in my body.

Bulimia also deflected the anger I felt about others. Instead I turned it toward myself. Stomach pain, hunger, and faintness were my friends in a world gone mad. It felt normal to cause myself pain—and empowering to be the one deciding to inflict it. At times I'd find myself curled up in a ball on the floor of my bathroom, wishing I were dead.

My out-of-control behavior had me bulldozing my way through the lives of others at such a pace that they never really saw what was coming. Other demons surfaced, too, and a mix of alcohol and drugs soon left me in a foggy haze.

My sweet, young Bobby tried to understand, but how could he when I didn't understand it myself? I hurt him deeply, but Bobby loved me anyway. He came to me with open arms, and when his arms became tired, his family took over in an attempt to hold our family together. Still I spiraled into a dark hole.

I couldn't understand my addictive personality or the impact of my buried secrets or my immaturity as a twenty-year-old mother with no coping mechanisms for life's difficulties. I directed my anger at the good people and things in my life rather than focusing on the real issues, the areas of hurt that needed to be recognized.

I didn't see that I was hurting my husband, and I never contemplated the pain I carried into his family as well. Life was all about me and Miranda. I deluded myself into thinking I could do whatever I wanted and not hurt anyone else, certainly not my little girl. I didn't consider the consequences of my behavior, and I never dreamed that I could lose my baby. My most painful life lesson lurked around the corner with each destructive choice, but I was too naïve to understand that the world can be cruel. If you don't follow the rules, you experience many hand slaps until the lesson becomes so painful the only choice left is to numb the pain.

Desperate and hoping that change would help, Bobby moved us to Enid. Finding us a tiny duplex, he tried everything to save us, save me. I took a job at the local Gap store, but I met the wrong people, and any remnants of sound thinking disappeared.

Family members suggested I go to counseling at a church in this new town. Hopeless, I went, although grudgingly. I loved this family so much that I wanted to try it, even if I had no idea how to wash my sins away once again. Another baptism was certainly not going to work. When I stepped forward during the service to meet the pastor and ask for help, he greeted me with a handshake, a picture of Jesus on a religious tract, and an invitation to meet with him privately for marriage counseling.

Well, predators can roam the churches as well as seedy backstreets. During our session he opened his Bible across my lap and recited, "Love is patient, love is kind . . ." I didn't know love was also perverted and as greasy as the preacher's hair. Running his hand up my skirt, the minister used our counseling time to bring pleasure to himself. It was then I learned not to trust anyone.

"I have to go," I told him. It was all I could muster.

"Let's pray first," he slurred out.

"No, thank you." I picked up my purse and walked out, and he stood there, watching me walk off as if he were some guy in a bar checking out a girl.

That was the day I gave up on Bobby, my new family, and myself. I would be asked to give up my baby, too. Now these so-called men of God were no different to me than the evil men in the home I'd left behind years ago. I still loved God very much, but I made up my mind that no man in this world could be trusted. Maybe that's why I never told Bobby about the pastor's approach to counseling. I should've run to my husband and told him, but I couldn't. Shame kept me from it. Certain once again that it was my fault, I didn't have the words to tell my story, so I ran away.

Witchy Woman

WHEN I WENT TO WORK at the Gap store in the local mall, I found another set of friends who understood and fueled my hatred for religion. They started teaching me a different kind of spirituality and new ways to find myself. A scared young girl who had no direction in her life, I was easily deceived, and their beliefs appealed to me.

I met BJ, a witch, at the store. I call her a witch not because she was mean but because she practiced black magic. She was the most dangerous kind of witch—one who appears as a friend. Having traveled to what she called a "craft" store in Oklahoma City during a visit for Gap managers' training, I saw that these crafts were different from those that I was used to. In the 1970s we called these stores—with their potions, spells, and crystal balls—head shops. What I saw there gave a whole new meaning to the word "craft."

"You need to start over," BJ told me, and I believed her. Her counsel made sense. I was miserable, and starting over sounded good. Walking the aisle of this dark, thick-smelling place reminded me of the head shop in Siloam that I'd heard about from some of my pot-smoking friends. I couldn't wait to see what a head shop was or why it was called The Pink Panther. The name probably referred to the pink shag carpet, or maybe after a few whiffs of pot you thought that the posters of the Pink Panther were actually talking to you. While I was reminiscing, BJ convinced me that this store of spells had all I needed to find answers in life.

So when I returned from that trip with what I thought was my New Age outlook, I stood in the kitchen of our rented duplex and told Bobby that I was leaving—and taking my baby with me. I didn't think he would mind. She was *my* baby, after all.

"Stephanie, you can't just take her," Bobby said through his tears. "We will share our time."

I couldn't give him the comfort he needed because I was so wrapped up in the new life I was convinced I had to start. What I wouldn't give to go back in time to that day. I can see him sitting there on the kitchen counter, legs dangling, as he tried to change my mind. Knowing everything, this young man had driven hours to my mom's house to bring me home. He forgave me and loved me. He tried to, anyway.

But in my naïveté, I trusted the wrong people again. I moved in with BJ and her part-time boyfriend, Rick.

"We have a beautiful house, and your part of the rent is only three hundred dollars a month," BJ said, assuring me that she understood that I had no money. This meant my entire check would go to the rent.

I just wanted to find a place where my daughter could play, watch cartoons, and color in her Barbie coloring books. I thought we'd be okay.

On the days that I had Miranda—Bobby also had her part of the time—this new roommate acted like a normal person. We'd watch my daughter drag around her silky blue blanket as we talked about what I needed to do to be happy.

I didn't believe that wolves could wear sheep's clothing or that witches could really cast spells. But they can. During my life I have seen acts of evil beyond description and heard others tell of the torture they endured. Having been lured into the den of evil myself, I know the reality of these acts, these types of people. We all have an internal alarm that I like to think God put there. If you feel it or hear it, listen to it! I should have. Instead, I'd left my safe world to go back to a hellhole existence.

Living in a home where someone practices witchcraft is terrifying. BJ did her best to tell me that religion was a waste of time. At night in her house, I started locking my bedroom door, afraid I would relive my childhood experiences. I could hear the roar of drug-induced laughter as BJ and Rick watched *A Clockwork Orange*. Most of the time, after I returned home from work, I'd eat a little food, lock myself in my room, and fall across my bed and cry. I begged for someone to save me, though I was the one who had put myself in that situation. I had found safety with Bobby, only to discard it and come full circle back to a horribly familiar feeling.

"Steph, get out here and join us. You're such a party pooper!" her boyfriend said through my closed bedroom door. The guy creeped me out! Having to fight him off after he kept coming into my bedroom, I began to realize that I had found myself in yet another dangerous situation.

I made the decision to drive to Mom's house every other weekend in Norman, a few hours away, to create a better place for Miranda's visits. One sure thing was that, contrary to *unpopular* belief, when it came to the safety of my daughter, there wasn't anything I wouldn't do to keep her safe and us together when I was allowed. Though I had a less-than-trustworthy car, I started my nomadic practices again. At least my mom's home was man-free at the time and safe.

The chaos in my life grew worse. As my buried secrets surfaced, I needed more alcohol to mask the pain of childhood sexual abuse by my great-uncle and stepbrother. I needed more drugs to numb my heart to my stepfather's leering eyes and inappropriate touches. I needed noise and a frenzy of activity to drown my inner cries that arose from my feelings of abandonment by my father and neglect by my mother. I needed a man to validate my worth. I never recognized that Bobby was trying to be that man.

But I believed that no one cared. My desperate cry for help and my overwhelming need to be worth *something* to *someone* all went unnoticed. I wanted to be rescued. Instead predators fed on the remains of my soul.

Someone Say Something

|————|

ONCE I STUMBLED ONTO THE worst possible attorney in Enid, the divorce was filed and the process started. The first session of court seemed like a bad appetizer to a very bad meal. Sitting in a kind of large boardroom with all of Bobby's family and my one family member—my mother—everyone listened as I shared my plans.

"I was reading in a magazine at work that I can go to California and learn about art and stuff." I planned to become an art curator. Miranda would be happy there, and she could see her Daddy whenever he wanted.

The judge looked at me in confusion. "This is your plan? To move Miranda with you?"

Yes, it was my well-thought-out plan, you see. I actually thought I could go to California while Miranda was with Bobby and his family, so I could make a place for us there and be close to my big brother. With Carl stationed in California, I thought he'd have time to continue raising his little sister as well as her daughter. I assumed Bobby would be okay with this plan, too.

I had gone over this not only with Mom but also with the attorney who was supposed to guide me, and no one had said I was freaking crazy to think that the world worked like this! The attorney's level of commitment pretty much equaled the low funds I could supply. It wasn't just that I was up a creek without a paddle; I didn't even have a boat.

I'm sure the judge rolled his eyes, although it went unnoticed by me, and he said, "I wish you well in California, Stephanie." Then the judge said, "Okay, you have joint custody," and read the rules to us all.

My mother said nothing throughout the session. Of all the times I needed her to speak up and even tell me I was an idiot—because I was—she just sat there. I had just destroyed a family, broken a young man's heart, and wrecked my daughter's future. I don't justify myself by saying someone should have questioned my dysfunctional thinking, but I do think neither the court system nor the educational system prepared this student to understand anything about the world. Because if I had been capable of reading the actual documents in the first place, I'd have seen that I stood to lose Miranda if I did *anything*—and anything included my moving to another state.

If you don't understand the workings of the legal system—even if you think it's wrong at times—find someone who does. But it's not the best idea to ask for help from those who have no clue what's going on. Or who know but don't care what happens to you.

The Dark Hole

———

AT LEAST I STILL HAD a job. I locked the sliding gates that shut the Gap store off from the rest of the mall and was walking the cash drawer back to the safe when I heard, "Steph! Hey, Steph!" I looked out into the mall. It was Rick, and he was waving at me from behind the closed gate.

"Be there in a sec." I locked the store and reluctantly met him outside, behind the building. "Where's BJ?"

"Don't know, and who cares? You can ride with me." Rick was already strung out on something. An unsettled feeling swept over me, but I climbed into his car anyway.

"I think I'll just head home tonight."

"Come on, Steph. Jeff is having a great party. Go with me."

Jeff was a bartender I'd dated off and on. I went with Rick not because I wanted to, but because I feared the consequences if I didn't. Rick scared me.

The party was in full swing when we arrived; everyone was drunk or stoned—or both.

"Hey, Jeff, look who I found." Rick took my arm and guided me through the maze of partygoers.

"Cool. Hey, Steph, have a beer."

I switched gears in my head from working Stephanie to party chick Steph and joined in, shaking off the feeling that I was in danger.

"Hey," a strange girl said to me.

"Hey," I said back, wondering if this conversation would have more than one-syllable sentences. She reached over, pushed the bleached hair out of my eye, opened my palm, and placed a tiny pill in my hand. After that, there was nothing but fog.

Until there was pain—excruciating pain.

I was lying on a mattress on the floor, and Rick was on top of me. I focused on *not* screaming. I clenched my teeth and shut my eyes. *So much pain.* When I opened my eyes again, a different guy was on top of me. I was crying, but that didn't stop either of them. Frozen, I lay there waiting for my escape. When I finally got back to BJ's house, I called a friend to help me get to the hospital ER. Then she called the one person who despised me most—my mother.

That night, I lay on an operating-room gurney with my mom at my side. She was silent, but she didn't have to say anything. The look on her face said it all. Disgust.

The IUD that served as my birth control device had lodged inside me so deeply that it caused internal bleeding. The nurse who administered my IV sedation for the DNC I had to have was crying. My mother was not.

Handing me a clipboard, the nurse quietly said so my mom couldn't hear, "Honey, you need to sign here. The doctor has written this down as date rape, and we've called the police. Will you give a statement?" With tears streaming down my cheeks, I just looked at her and said, "I don't remember who it was."

This little girl inside me was screaming, but no words found their way out of my mouth. I wanted desperately to tell my mom I had been hurt again. But I couldn't. My mother stood in that hospital room holding my stuff in a plastic bag. I had no idea what she was thinking or feeling. She shook her head, and then I lost consciousness.

Trust Me

————————

WEEKS PASSED, AND I WAS doing everything possible to forget what had happened. I had also forgotten that I was supposed to make plans to move to California. I rolled out of bed and did what I knew would be the best thing to start the day. I took a shower and headed for work.

"Hello, can I help you?" I had somehow landed the job of assistant manager at the Gap store. I finished folding a pair of boot-cut jeans and looked up, trying to figure out what jean style fit the personality of this tall man with a waxed mustache. I played a mind game to get through my hours at work, like my childhood church games: What jean style matched the customer? Boot-cut, slim jeans were a sure fit for the skinny, true country boy, the one who rode a combine for fifteen hours a day during harvest time. The curvy, loose-in-the-hips jeans were for the woman who had just given birth to her third child—the one who knew she would never again see her younger figure in the mirror. But she needed to remind herself that her looks could still steer her husband's eyes away from the TV long enough to make her feel pretty again.

"Would you go on a date with me?" The man asked in a German accent as he scanned my body with a calculated look. I looked up at him, bringing myself back to the moment, and replayed what this stranger had just said to me.

I paused, but only for a few seconds. "Yeah, sure, but I'm not divorced yet." My desperation for love trumped reality. Reason eluded me. "We just had our hearing, and I have joint custody of my little girl, but my divorce isn't final."

"That's okay. I will pick you up after your shift tomorrow night."

"Will there be anything else?" I stared down at my feet. Alarms would've sounded for most stable people, but I wasn't stable. I craved what no human could provide. Dignity. A sense of self-worth. Value.

As he paid and exited the shop, I realized that I hadn't figured out his jean personality. I should have known it would be the too-tight-in-the-crotch style. I also realized that I hadn't heard him ask my name. I only remembered that he had said his: Thomas.

Once I had a few dates with Thomas and I believed I had fallen in love with him too, I fixated on the future, hiding the past deeply in that place in my mind that was trained to lock it away. Thomas seemed to be everything I ever dreamed of. And I was convinced he really loved me because I slept with him. Didn't that seal the relationship? Didn't sex equate to love? Wasn't a person supposed to protect you once you gave yourself away to him? He bought a toy and a book for Miranda, so obviously he loved me enough to embrace her. He introduced me to his life, his friends, and his relocated German family, who were the reason he was in Oklahoma in the first place. His aunt was kind to both Miranda and me. Yes, I was sure we were in love.

Thomas owned a restaurant in a small town outside of Enid, and I became his waitress as well as live-in lover. I didn't need my assistant manager job anymore, so I quit and left everything behind, sure that Miranda and I would be fine.

The attorney in my first custody suit was encouraging me to make changes in my life. He decided to counsel me. After one particular attorney-client meeting, I was upset and went in search of Thomas at work. I found him in his office. He was leaning against a file cabinet, laughing with a new waitress while he acquainted her with the restaurant and himself. I barged into the room, ignored the blossoming boss-employee relationship, and unloaded my custody concerns.

"My attorney says I have to create a healthy home environment or go back to court." Bobby and his family were worried I was making the wrong choices for Miranda, and they wanted to amend the joint-custody arrangement.

The new waitress looked down at her nails. Thomas turned toward me, crossed his arms, and rolled his eyes. "Okay. We will get married, and I'll rent that house on the corner and get a dog." Funny how he thought a new marriage, a rented house, and a dog could make my life appear stable.

"I think we have to wait before I can get married again."

"Not if we go to a different state and find a judge who will do it."

"I can't lose my daughter, Thomas!"

"I will take care of it." Thomas waved in my direction, exasperation punctuating the jabs of his arms in the air. "Now get back out there and clean off those tables. The doors open soon."

I hurried out but leaned against the closed office door. The new waitress and my husband-to-be were laughing again.

After clearing the tables, I finished my makeup in the bathroom. As I drew a thick line of black eyeliner over each lid, then under each eye, and finished the look off with dark red lipstick, I replayed our conversation. I resolved to do what Thomas said. After all, he was older, and he seemed sure this was the right decision. He would help me. He would take care of me. Thomas would fix my problems. I was driven by only one thought: *I will die if I lose my baby.*

Justice of Anything But the Peace

A FEW DAYS LATER, I finished my restaurant shift and walked into Thomas's office. It was late, but the next day, after a long night of partying, Thomas and I and our two witnesses were ready to drag our hungover bodies to Wellington, Kansas, for our blissful ceremony before a judge. Thanks to the pot we smoked on the way, what little judgment remained was clouded. It seemed to make sense to drive to Kansas in search of a judge who would marry us. I had also picked BJ of all people to be a witness. For some reason, she was in favor of this union between Thomas and me. Sadly, she was all I had.

It also seemed that, although Bobby and I had only been divorced six weeks, marrying Thomas was my best option. Why didn't I know then that I had the power to make a real choice in my life? That one option was to not let this happen?

"You're the one for me," Thomas had assured me. "I've waited for you my whole life." There were three others he'd waited for his whole life, too, but I didn't find out about them until later. I was the one who supplied his green card and a face and body to abuse, as I also found out later. But at that moment, I believed Thomas was the way out of my witch's dungeon, so I agreed to marry him.

"Honey, are you sure about this?" The judge performing the ceremony looked at me with sad eyes. He seemed to understand my predicament.

No, I'm not. I'm so afraid . . . more afraid with each passing day. Can you help me? I wanted to cry out, but I couldn't. I didn't. Instead, I said, "I am," followed by a very weak, "I do."

It was done. I left bad place number one and went to bad place number two.

"Are you crazy!?" my attorney yelled over the phone the next day. "Get into my office as soon as you can. This is not good, not good at all!"

When I had tried to contact my attorney before the courthouse wedding, he didn't have time to advise me. Despite the fees I paid, he rarely paid attention to my calls.

Sitting in the huge leather chair in his office, I twisted the leather button on the chair's arm until the button broke off. I hid it in my pocket and stared at the floor.

"Stephanie, you've messed things up," the attorney said. "You will lose joint custody. We'll try to make a case for you. We'll hire an expert witness, but it may be impossible to show you are stable." Regardless of his heartless behavior, the attorney was right. There is no way to make something out of nothing, and I had nothing that proved I was stable. "Also, your *new* husband will have to be interviewed by the court's expert witness," he added.

I walked out of the law office, past the reception area, and felt the eyes of every staff member watching me. I imagined they were shaking their heads in disappointment. I made a habit of doing stupid things and losing the respect of those around me. These people had fresh evidence of my foolish choices.

When I got home, I found Thomas in our bedroom and told him he would have to be evaluated by the expert witness—a psychologist. He resisted. "This is stupid, Stephanie. This is your problem, not mine."

My eyes rested on something red sticking out from under the bed—a bra, much larger than what I wore and my least favorite color.

"You will go with me!" I said. "You will make me look good, and you will stop having sex with that new waitress." I grabbed the bra and threw it across the bed. "If you can't do that, I'll leave." I thought the threat would scare him, because he needed me in order to remain in this country. But it pissed him off instead.

His open palm landed across my face. "Don't ever talk to me like that again," he said as blood oozed from my bottom lip.

I sucked in a deep breath and didn't exhale for many years to come.

I Just Want My Baby

ONCE I WAS OUT OF BJ's house and not supplying her rent money, she turned from what I thought was a friend into an enemy. Confused by the way she supported me one day and hated me the next, I still tried to be kind and to see her when my beat-up car could make it from Pond Creek to Enid. But it was difficult to get there very often. Thomas wanted my full attention, BJ wanted to sell my soul to the devil, and I wanted to keep Miranda.

When news of this marriage mistake hit Bobby and his family, things changed overnight—literally.

"Steph, get those breakfast plates out to the table by the window," Thomas demanded while he stood on the opposite side of the serving window at the restaurant.

I heard the phone ring and then Thomas say, "German House, can I help you?" Standing there with two plates of cooling eggs and toast, I froze at the look on his face, wondering who he was talking to. In his broken English, he got nasty, said things in anger, and slammed the receiver down. I shook my head, hoping it was only a vendor who had sent the wrong food shipment. But somehow I knew it was Bobby calling about Miranda.

I soon found out that the judge had changed my visitation, altering it in a way I couldn't handle. "Just go see your attorney, Steph," Thomas said nonchalantly.

So I did. Sitting in the office that automatically turned my stomach, I listened as the attorney read the new custody rules. Why is it that attorneys have to have some huge, ornate desk between themselves and the client? Is it a barrier so they don't get too close and too personal? So they don't have to have real human contact?

He sat on his side of the barrier and recited the hard reality: "Stephanie, you no longer have joint custody of Miranda. The custody will be given to Bobby, and we have to go back to court. Until then, you will have no overnight visitation with her. You can see her two nights a week—Tuesdays and Thursdays—and that is it until we get back to court and fix this mess."

I wanted to melt into a puddle under that dark mahogany desk of his and die. All I could come up with to say was, "When do we go back to court? How long will I be restricted to seeing her only six hours a week?"

The lawyer pivoted his leather throne in my direction and glared at me. "Nine weeks."

During this hellish waiting period, some days were too much; the pain seemed too hard to deal with. I would stand outside Miranda's preschool and talk with the owner, who was a friend of mine. She convinced me that taking Miranda and running would only cause more pain and trauma. This woman was tough, and I enjoyed riding around in her Corvette on our party days together, but I also knew that under her fake tan and rough demeanor she was wise. I'll be grateful forever that I listened to her. I really only wanted to grab my baby and leave town.

I watched my daughter go up and down the metal slide in the pink shorts and Minnie Mouse T-shirt I'd bought her at Kmart, and I felt close to death. How could I stay away from her? She wasn't even two years old. I wasn't allowed to even take her in my arms when I wanted. And she couldn't sleep next to me after we read our bedtime stories.

Soon, though, the judge would fix it. He was nice, and after all he knew me. I had seen him at one of the strip clubs I frequented to talk to my friends who worked there. I'd soon work there myself, when one of these friends showed me how to make a quick buck. The next morning I returned to BJ's house to get the rest of my things. Our stressed friendship was on its last legs after I'd found out that I had been paying the entire rent—not half of it—since I moved in there.

A day earlier I had taken Miranda back to her dad's. This ritual included my stomach knotting up, head aching, and tears burning in my throat because I did not want her to see me cry every time. Also, the ritual included a visit to a local bar in Enid called The Flamingo. I'd enter through the back door since I was a regular, and then I'd shuffle sadly in and find my seat at the bar. The owner's wife would bring my usual order of fried hamburgers with grilled onions and a tap beer. "Honey, you okay this time?" she'd ask. "I know it's hard to have to drop her off, but just stay busy and possibly a little drunk and the time will pass quicker." It was good advice. Except for the drunk part, I guess. Closing the bar meant I'd have to sleep it off at a friend's place while trying to avoid Thomas. On waking, I would be hung over, tired, and angry at life. An alcoholic fog filled my head as I drove, and I swore I'd never drink again. I felt terrible!

When I got to BJ's, I tried my key in the front door, but it wouldn't turn. Then she opened the door, and with a tone of a snot-nosed teen-ager said, "It won't work, Steph. I changed the locks."

Stunned, I asked, "What? Why?"

"You don't need to come in here anymore," she said. "All of your stuff is right over there."

"There" meant the lawn, where I could see the few belongings I had. I didn't mind so much until I saw the one thing I cherished most lying on the ground in a broken glass frame. Miranda's picture. Then I came unglued.

"You stupid bitch! I'll kill you!" I shouted, as if all of my life's angry moments were rising to the surface at once. For what seemed like hours, I picked up my stuff and crammed it into my beat-up car, screaming that BJ owed me money. Holding Miranda's picture close, tears all over my crumpled AC/DC T-shirt, I walked over to her with a piece of the broken glass in my hand. For a moment I would have sworn I was looking at the devil. And I wanted it dead!

Then I heard Grandma's voice loud in my head: "Stephanie Ann, put it down and walk away!" Before I did, I had to listen to BJ mock me about how I'd lost my daughter.

As I turned my back, she yelled, "Go to hell, Stephanie. You're a loser!"

"I can't," I taunted her back. "You'll take up all the space there."

The Pink Tent

WITH ONLY A FEW MORE weeks left until the judge's hearing, I waited with nothing but hope. It was my day to see Miranda, and we played. Usually we went to the local McDonald's, where we could eat chicken nuggets and fries and I could watch her climb those kid-sticky colored tubes.

"Panda Bear, let's go buy that tent we saw for your birthday!" I said as I scooped her up in my arms when she got to the bottom of the slide. Her second birthday was going to take place two weeks after our court date, and my celebratory attitude was surfacing.

"The pink one?" she said with excitement.

"Yes, the pink one." Hoping that Kmart would actually still have it and that we'd find it before my visiting time was over, I ran into the store and went up and down aisles with Miranda bouncing in my arms until we stopped right in front of the most beautiful pink Barbie tent. I promised her I would get it ready because soon the judge—"the mean man," as I referred to him—would give her back to me. Then our time was up, and although she was only two years old, she also knew that the visit had to end. But she didn't understand why. Neither did I.

My spirits plummeted, and I reacted with yet more destructive choices.

I set up the pink tent in the empty playroom of the house I lived in with Thomas. But it wouldn't be empty for long. I had plans—dreams that drove me, tormented me, and mocked me. Dreams of welcoming my baby girl back home.

"Hurry up, Stephanie. We have to be in Enid in an hour." My husband of eight weeks paced the floor as I applied finishing touches to my makeup. "You are so slow!"

"Thomas, do you think the hearing will take long?" I hesitated, then scrutinized the not-quite-grown-up little girl in the mirror, certain I would need the waterproof mascara.

"I don't care. You won't get her back anyway." Thomas's Red Roper boots continued to pace.

"Do you remember what the expert witness said to do?"

"I will say the truth but not the whole truth." Thomas's jaw clinched.

"You have to—"

"I don't have to do anything!"

We drove to the Enid courthouse in silence. My future and the future of my daughter rested in the hands of this man, this fake, who offered me only a counterfeit love. Thomas parked the car and left me at the bottom of what seemed like a million stairs leading from the sidewalk to the front door of the courthouse. As I gazed up, I recalled the song "Stairway to Heaven" but quickly changed the words in my mind. This was my stairway to hell.

"Excuse me, where is the restroom, please?" I stopped the first lady who looked at home in the building. After she directed me, I hurried into the nearest open stall. The door slammed behind me as I dropped to my knees and spewed into the toilet.

"Are you okay?" A woman's voice sounded from the other side of the stall door.

"I'm sick. Could you hand me a wet paper towel, please?"

"Of course . . . are you throwing up?"

"Yes, but I'm used to it."

I gathered what little strength remained, and, looking in the mirror, I realized I would enter the courtroom with the stain of regurgitated breakfast cereal decorating my dark blouse.

So there I was—twenty-two years old, with bleached hair and dark black eyeliner—and the stench of vomit.

I proposed to fix my mess by telling the judge I was sorry. *I made a mistake, and I would fix it.* Surely he would listen. Surely he would believe me. Surely . . .

I walked through the courtroom doors to my attorney's side. When I looked up at the robed figure, I saw the familiar face.

I smiled at him, but he responded as if he'd never seen me before in his life. Not only did he shun my sunny demeanor, he acted as if the very sight of me made him ill.

"You're late. Where's Thomas?" My attorney didn't appear happy either.

Scanning the room, I didn't see my husband anywhere. As a matter of fact, I saw no one on the side behind me; the seats designated for my supporters were empty. Like the pink tent in my baby's playroom.

Finally, after the session started, Thomas walked in with watery red-colored eyes. He was stoned.

Mom didn't show. I was alone. Again.

The witnesses who found their way to that stand on the worst day of my life were my ex-husband, his family, my old witchcraft-practicing roommate, and a stoned German with a turned-up mustache. My team was made up of the lying, drug-using dregs of society, and it had the weakest link. Me.

As BJ spouted off pure lies, I just sat there. She had no regard for two things: truth or the Bible her hand was on.

I left the courthouse with shattered dreams. I returned home to an empty pink tent.

Go Ahead, Hit Me!

DURING THE NINE-HOUR COURT SESSION, it had been brought to my attention that Thomas had a few wives in Oklahoma, one in Germany, and a couple of kids. After that, Thomas pretty much dragged me to his car to leave, and then he drove to his restaurant to get the profits from the night before. Then it was back to the house. Thomas had embezzled his money from places he had worked since entering our "land of opportunity." He took every opportunity to use the people around him. Soon the authorities would come collect his ass and send him back where he belonged. I wanted to help that happen.

For now, I opened the rusty gate, walked through the yard, past a new puppy that I had thought my daughter would play with, and made my way to the back door. Despite all my hopes, my baby had been here only twice before on daytime visits and was yet to have a sleepover with mommy.

I went upstairs to the bathroom, where I dropped my purse and knelt at the porcelain vessel that I had been comfortable with since I was twelve. With the self-hatred I felt that day, contempt ran through me rapidly, and all I needed was to gag myself into oblivion and vomit up anything I had left in my stomach. Bulimia is a less-than-ladylike thing to practice, but it was the quickest route for me to rid myself of any poisons in my heart and soul.

There were no conversations until Thomas banged on that bathroom door sometime later.

"What the hell are you doing?"

No reply.

"Stephanie, come out of there now!"

Still no reply from me.

He hit the door with his fist and stormed off. When I finally came out, I had no idea of the time. I went to the kitchen and found a bottle of liquor under the kitchen sink. Thomas was nowhere to be found, and the car was gone, too. I assumed he'd gone to the restaurant to see his girlfriend.

I sat on the bench along the kitchen wall and imagined "someday." Someday, I thought, I would have a kitchen that had a long table with bench-type seating on either side. Someday I would make bacon and pancakes with chocolate chips in them for my baby girl and the brothers and sisters I was sure she would have. Someday I would fill a home with laughter and cartoons would play in the background as I washed dishes and did laundry.

But at that moment I had no someday, and the only chance I ever had of that happening was gone at the slam of the gavel, when I was pronounced "unfit to be a mother."

It was getting dark, and I had already thrown back several swallows of the brown liquor that I had never acquired a taste for. There's no telling how long I sat there before Thomas's car pulled into the driveway and the back door screeched.

"I'm glad you came out of bathroom, finally," Thomas said. "What do you do in there?"

"Nothing," I managed to get out.

"Are you drunk? Hey, you're drinking my bourbon."

"Not yet, but I will be soon," I said.

He just twisted that ridiculous mustache and said, "You'll have to get over what happened. Stop crying. We'll go have fun."

"I can't. I don't want to live anymore."

As I sat there, Thomas went to get his cordless phone, and I realized that it was true that I had nothing to live for, but that I could also take him out with me and save the world from his presence.

I had so many thoughts in my head that day. So many voices drowning out the voice in my soul that I am sure was God trying to get me to listen. All to no avail.

After Thomas walked off, I looked down at my lap and realized that I had the phone he was searching for, and I remembered why.

"I will get this asshole out of this country," I thought out loud. "Yeah, that's what I should do!"

I snuck off to the upstairs deck and called 4-1-1.

"Information, can I help you?" the voice on the end of the line asked.

All I could think of was, "Please, can you tell me a number to call to report someone who needs to go back to Germany?"

I'm sure the person on the other end of the call was rolling with laughter, but she actually said, "Do you mean the number for immigration . . . to report an illegal immigrant?"

"Yes, that's what I need. Thank you!" I couldn't believe I was doing this.

Thomas slammed the door open and grabbed the phone.

"Who the hell are you calling, you stupid bitch?"

For some reason I calmly turned to him, no longer afraid, and said, "I just reported you." He walked away. I wasn't afraid of abuse or even death. That, too, was on my list for that night.

Before I did anything, though, I wanted to call my brother, Carl, to ask him why Mom hadn't been at the courthouse earlier that day.

I made my way to the phone by the kitchen, dialed, and waited for Carl to pick up, as I heard Thomas coming back down the stairs. "Who are you calling?"

Carl answered just as Thomas grabbed the phone and hit me across the face. He had done that before, so I was familiar with the feeling.

"Hello, who is it?" my brother said.

"Carl! He's hitting me!" I called out, while I tried to fend off Thomas's blows. I heard my brother say that he would have his Air Force buddies from Vance Air Force Base in Enid come out to beat the hell out of him. They might have shown up at some point, but by then I was probably in the ER again.

Pulling myself away from Thomas, I went to find Miranda's tiny white snow boots, where I kept some money hidden. I grabbed them and hid in the bathroom.

I sat on the side of the claw-foot tub and watched the water fill it. Something about the sound of water soothes me, no matter what. It was amazing to think that in such a short time I had lost custody of my daughter, gotten drunk and beaten up, and that now I would end my life.

The pink tent was waiting.

Please Let Me Die

THE BATHROOM WAS JUST ACROSS from the makeshift play-room, and when I opened the door, I could see my destination. With pills already popped and more alcohol than my malnourished frame could possibly deal with, I knelt, a picture of my daughter in my hand, and crawled into the tent. Drifting into oblivion, into death, I hoped.

But I was shaken to my feet like a rag doll, and as my eyes opened and closed to the sight of Thomas, all I could do was throw up at the smell of his disgusting cologne. His daily ritual of mustache sculpting left each end of it stiff and flipped up, as if he were Snidely Whiplash from the Dudley Do-Right cartoons. He seemed to wear the same jeans every day—and those awful red cowboy boots.

I had no idea what I was doing when I met him. At that point of my life, my alcohol and drug intake clearly made someone look better than they were—inside or out.

"Damn it!" Thomas yelled. "What am I supposed to do with you now?"

He called the sheriff, who loaded me into his truck and hauled me to the ER, where my stomach was pumped. When I woke, my throat was on fire, and I was told to take the hotline number for suicide attempts. I had to check in with them and give them my whereabouts. But I had no idea where I was going to go. The first person to pop into my head was Bobby's sister, Cheryl. She was a friend who always was ready to rescue me with open arms.

The sheriff drove me back to Enid. Looking over at me, he said, "You know, honey, everyone has a reason to live." As I stared out the window at the night, he went on, "You do too." Without looking at him, I said, "I know. Her name is Miranda."

Miranda and Bobby had left town after the trial and were tucked away in Fairview, where his parents still lived. I called Cheryl from a pay phone, and we decided that, at least for that night, I would go to the duplex where I'd last lived with Bobby and Miranda. I could get some sleep after we took pictures that we could use to file an assault charge against Thomas.

Cheryl got me into the bed that Bobby and I had shared as husband and wife, and then she went to sleep on the sofa. Later, a couple of hours before morning, I found my way into my daughter's empty room and climbed into the tiny bed that smelled like her. That's when I turned over yet another leaf. This one would not prove to be any better. Honestly, it was worse in most ways, but it was yet another plan to survive. I needed only to make more money, find a better lawyer, and win my daughter back.

Once everything came out in court that awful day, Thomas was eventually extradited back to Mannheim, Germany, where he was thrown in jail for more reasons than those I had found out about in court. He hadn't paid any of the child support he owed, and he was found guilty of robbery in another Oklahoma town. He'd been a busy guy. I was surprised he had time to ruin my life. But he did!

1988-1993

What's really going on behind this smile?

Visitation with my baby girl, Miranda

Street Smarts and Bullshit with a Smile

LOSING CUSTODY OF MIRANDA BROUGHT my problems, mistakes, and life-threatening decisions to a whole new level. I still had to rid myself of childhood memories, but now I had to deal with the terrifying realization that I would not be able to create any childhood memories for my baby girl.

To legally rid myself of Thomas, I had to circulate a newspaper notice asking his whereabouts and requesting a divorce. Because he was in Germany, I couldn't just annul the mistake. I added it to my growing list of failed marriages, but I wasn't done yet. Was I a hopeless romantic? Yes, something I inherited from my mother. Well, hopeless for sure about love. But I was also a survivor when it came to adversity, especially when I realized that Miranda was worth living for, even if I couldn't share a house with her—yet. That would be my new reason for living, my new life's goal. I couldn't do it if I were dead, so I decided to live.

As my moves stacked up, my belongings dwindled. With Cheryl's help and love, I found a tiny apartment in Enid that I called the "rathole" because mice and rats had also taken up residence in the building. If you can't beat 'em, well, join 'em, right? Occasionally I had to stand on my cheap wobbly kitchen chairs in the middle of the night because I heard the squeaking sounds they made, and I vowed to one day live in a beautiful home and have enough money for pest control.

"Stephanie!" my neighbor said, banging on my apartment door one night. "Are you okay in there?"

"Yes" I yelled back from my perch. "I screamed because I saw another mouse. Sorry!"

Now that I had to support myself in the real world, I had to learn my way around. I found out that my ability to bullshit with a smile would take me places. Maybe that eighth-grade algebra teacher, Coach, was right after all, because having "the look," I realized, gave me tools for survival. I was still unaware of what the look was exactly, but apparently it worked. It made me appear to be someone who needed to be taken care of. Still vulnerable. "Empowerment" was a word I had not heard of at that time. Some of the people who stepped in to help would be bad for me, but I also learned street smarts. And as for the smile, most of the time it was bullshit. Inside I was crying.

And I needed a job. Walking into a local restaurant that I heard was a popular place, I met a woman who would soon be my waitstaff trainer and a trainer of life experiences as well. She was a strong woman with long, dark hair and the toughness of someone who has seen more than she probably wanted to talk about. But she also still had a softness around her eyes that said she would take care of me and show me the ropes. Thanks to her, I was able to learn a trade that would carry me through life—waiting on people.

I worked hard, and Sneakers became my home for years to come. I lived a restaurant-nightclub life, a life that is fast and furious and gives you little time to ponder the realities of your world. My nightlife in a bar is best described as illusion. The amount of alcohol consumed there would allow anyone to become anything they wanted to be, temporarily, anyway. And there's such an energy that you feel as if you are flying. The sounds that reverberate off the walls—of music, voices, and clinging glasses—is a high. For people like me, who have to keep moving, it was the perfect place. I think Tom Petty put it perfectly when he sang, "If you never slow down, you never get old."

Learning the names of the regulars and allowing them to pour out their stories as I made a living pouring booze into them was my job. This was a business like any other, and although we made sure that our customers were safely tucked into cabs when they had too much of the happy elixir, they still had to face their own realities when they walked through the front doors of their homes. We gave unsolicited advice on how life should be, and it must have been good advice, because the customers always came back for more. Some of them were the most interesting people I would ever meet. They became my adopted, dysfunctional family.

It was the beginning of a lucrative lifestyle. Daily lunch groups, like the women who came in after Bible study, needed my almost-girlish attitude, which they thought begged for forgiveness, when actually I was just begging for tips. The group of men at night wanted only to look me up and down for their own pleasure. They never heard a word I said, but they left the biggest tips—and a few phone numbers. Day in and day out, for fifteen-hour shifts with a few breaks that were also spent there, I was riding high on little food and a lot of stress, and I loved every minute of it.

The Man in the Round Specs

ONE OF THE REGULARS, A man who came in nightly, was actually the owner of this establishment, I later found out. He had a darkness about him, and I found his aura of mystery intriguing. It wasn't an issue that he was twenty years older than I was, though it should have been. Paul wore a dark suit and round John Lennon specs. He was distinguished and quiet, and when he looked at me, I thought I'd never be the same.

And I wasn't.

Like clockwork every evening at six o'clock, there he was: Paul would walk through the front door and up to the bar where my Greek buddy, Tony, the bartender-turned-lover, would pour Paul's usual Myers's rum and Coke. Paul would take his drink to a spot at the "commuter" bar that stood right in the middle of the action, in between the serving bar and the wait station, and he'd watch me like a hawk until closing. First he just stared, never saying a word, and finally he approached me about having a drink with him. For a month or so I refused until he wore me down, and I finally agreed. From that point until the bitter end of our relationship, I belonged to him, and he told everyone that was the case and that I was not to be bothered by anyone else again.

Working long hours and seeing Paul only after dark never struck me as odd. I was out of touch with reality. To this day, I'm amazed at the level of insanity in my life at that time. I viewed it all as normal behavior. Well, it *was* normal then.

One evening Paul walked in as usual and sat at a large table, my table, with about twelve other people. I went to him and started to hug him, but he pushed me so hard away that I nearly fell to the ground. The look in his eyes actually frightened me. I had no idea what was happening.

I went to a girlfriend of mine who worked the same shift and asked, "What did I do?" She took me into the office, sat me down, and explained that Paul was there with the "real people" in his life. Real people? What exactly did that mean? Well, one of them was his fiancée. It turned out that I had thought I was special, when really I had merely become his late-night booty call.

"Steph, he's been engaged to that woman next to him for months," she told me. I was so ripped apart that I stormed out the office door, jamming my leg into a piece of kitchen equipment on the floor.

Hurt and confused, I resorted to survival mode. I got up, walked into the ladies' room, added more makeup, put several Band-Aids on my gaping wound, and went right back out to that table. I did such an amazing job that it was one of the most productive tipping nights I ever had. I guess Paul was impressed that I could shut off my emotions when I needed to. He got rid of his guests as well as his fiancée and returned to the bar before closing to find me.

It was one of many nights when the staff locked up, drank some of the inventory, and then hit some of the other town bars for more. I was so angry at Paul, but he decided to join us anyway after he left his "real" girlfriend. This night would be unforgettable: not because I woke up facedown on top of a grave in the local cemetery, necessarily, but because I woke up there alone! It was one of the most disturbing memories I have. Even worse, I had no idea how I got there.

As the sun rose, I began moving my head from side to side, only to see tombstones all around me. Surely, I thought, I had finally died. My next feeling was one of relief. Yes, I was tired and dirty, but if I were dead I wouldn't feel my throbbing head or the wound in my leg.

Hearing my name called brought me back to the earthly plane, and I looked up to see the sheriff coming to my rescue. This sheriff somehow had a way of showing up to save me when I got in trouble.

Apparently I had been dumped in the cemetery because things had gotten violent the night before, and I had said that I wanted to be dead. Probably Paul and I had argued about his "real life" versus the one I thought I was a part of. Leaving me in the cemetery to honor my "wishes" was undoubtedly meant as a cruel joke. Someone in our little group—I never knew who—dumped me in the graveyard and left me there. I never spoke of it again, and the sweet, chunky sheriff who graced our restaurant weekly never did either.

I kept busy with my shifts and dealing with the interesting characters who sometimes came crawling in already wasted. One night a group of pretty messed-up people came into the restaurant. Whatever they were strung out on had them slurring every word as they tried to order. I told them I couldn't serve them any more alcohol, and they called me a few choice names. I then calmed them down by acting as if I'd get their drinks. I told Tony to act like he was pouring but not to really do it. After they left the restaurant, they decided to return to our nightclub, which was in the back of the building. I'd spread my shift between both places that night, and I was watching the register so one girl could have a smoke break when one of these guys saw me. He took out a small gun and put it to my head, demanding that I give him the money out of the cash drawer.

At this point I must have been just as insane as he was, because I started laughing, that kind of nervous laugh that made me look crazy. Surprised, he asked, "What is your fucking problem?" Ignoring the tiny gun at my right temple, wondering if it was really loaded, I said, "I've had a very bad day, and this is a perfect ending. Just take the money and enjoy the whole five hundred dollars of it. I don't care."

Well, my sheriff buddy told me later that the stoned-out-of-his-mind dude was so shocked that I wasn't scared that he was caught off guard long enough for security to jump him from behind. Once again, I was saved. My guardian angels were working overtime for sure. Either I was under the illusion that I was invincible, or in spite of my will to live for Miranda, my will to live for myself was still challenged.

Business picked up after that night, as everyone in this small town waited for more action. Clearing half-emptied highball glasses and ashtrays full to their rims with cigarette butts and sticky gum, I wondered if this was going to be my life forever. One of my friends, a giant of a man, grabbed me from behind and lifted me high in the air.

"Come on, Blondie, let's go party!"

I loved Gary. He knew when I needed a lift, literally.

Diamond Raindrops
and Disco Biscuits

YEARS LATER, AS MY DRUG-INDUCED fog lifted, I could actually recall some details of those alcohol- and drug-filled days, or the party-like-a-rock-star nights that took days to recover from before I'd actually remember what I had done. It was like watching a movie for the second time, when you catch things you missed the first time. The people that I ran with were some of the kindest souls I have ever known—and the most lost. But I wasn't looking for safety. I was looking for acceptance. A day of hard work and pranks was something I got used to. Numbing the days that were vacant of my daughter was the only coping skill I had.

After closing one night, as I sat at the bar with my usual dish of pasta in front of me, I realized it had a funny odor, but I shrugged it off. Really wish I hadn't. I dug into the steaming plate of pasta, swirling the noodles around my fork to make the perfect amount to fill my mouth. Everyone was watching for my reaction. I looked over at my boyfriend the bartender and noticed that his Greek features were very intense and his black hair was getting darker before my eyes. The liquor bottles on the shelf were moving, too. Thinking I needed some air, I got up to go outside, into the rain. Now color me crazy, but some of you will know what I am talking about: Suddenly the raindrops were like diamonds and looked like they might shatter into a million pieces when they hit the ground. I am not kidding. I was so fascinated at what I was seeing, and I still didn't know that I was tripping! This drug recollection may sound intriguing, I know, yet it's anything but that. If you live on the edge, it's only a matter of time before you fall over it.

I guess that after a few minutes I went back inside. When the cook came out of the kitchen things got very scary. His voice sounded like a slow-motion film clip, and when I looked at him, I swear his face was melting. I felt like I had stepped into another dimension and was overwhelmed by fear that I would never get back to Earth again. At first I believed that psychedelic mushrooms had been cooked into my pasta sauce, but later I was told that apparently the new dishwasher had dropped acid into the sauce. I gasp now at the thought of how I survived things like that—things like standing in the road in my go-go boots, trying to dodge cars.

From my teen days with the quaaludes we called "Disco Biscuits" to this point, the only thing that had changed was my age. I was still making dangerous choices, and the stakes only got higher the higher I got! The last thing I remember of that night was seeing ghostly images of Dad. Looking into the huge, ornate mirror behind the bar, I saw him. I was sure I saw him staring back at me and shaking his head.

I woke to a few friends sitting in the floor at the rathole apartment, and they jumped when I said, "Good morning." I hadn't been the only one who had dropped acid that night. I'm pretty sure the term "dropping acid" doesn't count if it was dropped on you without your knowledge. It's another experience I will never fully understand or forget.

The pranks weren't always drug related. Once, in the dead of winter, I found that my only jacket had been submerged in water and placed in the walk-in freezer. This kind of prank wasn't as deadly.

That I survived nights such as these is miraculous. At my own hands, the day I lost custody of Miranda, I mixed Xanax with Dexatrim diet pills, and here I am still. At the hands of others, I continued to dodge everything from drugs, pistols, and a lot of bad decisions, and by the grace of God I am still here.

Strong coffee and a dose of B12 from an EMT friend that I was fortunate enough to have and I was ready to start another day. Getting a ride to work, I was noticing—as I often still do when in Oklahoma—the beautiful skyline when the sun hits the red dirt. It can create such a stunning image that no drug could ever manufacture. I was alive, I was okay, and I was late for work.

I swept the front porch, and while I was wiping down the large chalkboard that we took turns writing the days' specials on with colored chalk, I saw Paul. He showed up, hung over again and looking for me. He tried to tell me that he was unhappy and didn't want to marry the woman he was engaged to. He was also losing the high-powered job that provided him the lifestyle he was living. He had moved into a smaller home, he explained, and he wanted me to marry him and live with him and his kids. It was me he was in love with, he repeated. He would fix everything, and I would be happy because he believed it was his job to take care of me and my job to hang out with him. When I didn't answer, he added, "The boys really love you, Steph. Will you do it for them?" I said no, and he left and drove all the way to Arizona.

But eventually he returned. It would be months before I finally convinced myself to marry Paul, but I did move in with him. I was juggling other jobs besides the restaurant at the time, and they kept me busy. I had been introduced a few months earlier to a girl who took me under her wing and taught me one more way to earn money. Along with the rent and my partying habit, I had to make monthly child support payments so I could have my every-other-weekend visitation with my baby girl.

Do Guardian Angels Get Tired?

"YOU LOOK LIKE SO MUCH fun," said the girl who was at one of my tables during one winter night shift at the restaurant. She was a bit drunk and laughed when I told a joke, even if I messed up the punch line, which I always did.

"Come party with us, Steph!" she said. "We'll come by and get you if you don't have a car."

I was thinking how great it would be to go to a fun party, because I had busted the window on my old car that morning when I thought that throwing a pan full of steaming hot water on my frozen windshield was a good idea. I did need a ride.

"That would be great, but I don't get off work until midnight."

"No problem. We'll be there until, like, morning, so who cares, right?"

"Right," I said, knowing that this would be a bender and glad I didn't have to clock in the next day until 5 p.m.

When Jan picked me up, I was finishing a touch-up of my eyeliner and lipstick in the restaurant bathroom and trying to wash some food stains out of my jeans.

"It's freezing outside, so grab a jacket!" Jan said, climbing onto the vanity countertop and kicking her boots on the cabinet while I talked about the idiot guy who had spilled his creamy lobster sauce on my jeans. Now everyone would think that smell was me. Damn!

"I live close. Let's go grab a pair of my jeans. Those smell like hell!" she said wrinkling her nose.

"Great! Cool, thanks, Jan!"

Running out of the restaurant, I caught a glimpse of Tony looking worried. Even given my drug use of the past few months, he thought I was at least a little safer with people I knew. This new crowd was a whole other ball game, and one I'd strike out of quickly! But my sporadic relationship with Tony due to his situation at home didn't really give him much authority to tell me what to do. I figured out he was not going to leave his struggling marriage and be with me, and I was, once again, just a fill-in. To be honest, I would have been able to live with myself in spite of his being married, until his wife came to the restaurant for a visit. In my defense—not that I am saying I deserved defense—I just didn't know. His wife was truly in the dark about our fling. Blind—no, really—she was blind.

At Jan's house, watching her kiss her girls goodnight and leave them with her mom made me sad. I wanted to hide inside my tiny apartment and wait for the weekend, when I would see Miranda. But the loss of her and the need to numb just about every thought in my pounding head made me do things I should have stayed clear of.

We pulled into an empty space on the side of the road and walked to the house. It looked like rich people lived there, and I thought the party would be fun. My mood could adjust as quickly as a chameleon changes colors. "Adapt to survive" was my motto.

Inside, the house was packed with people of all ages, but I didn't see a single person I knew, which was odd because Enid wasn't that big.

"Here, drink this," Jan said. "We have to catch up." I took a sip and she said, "No, silly. Slam it!"

I chugged down the gold-colored liquor from my Dixie cup.

A moment here with my personal disclaimer. Coming clean about my life before I got "clean" is tough, because I have so many kids in my world today who will be shocked, I hope, at these stories. But I have to find my truth and share it. I realize I cannot keep everyone off the streets, but I can attempt to keep someone else from wasting time trying to be cool—or at least keep them from wasting their lives trying to fit in or numbing the pain they need to deal with. This is one of my missions in life.

Whether you are eating qat in Yemen or chewing coca in Bolivia, getting hooked on a substance that removes your sense of clarity is not good, no matter what "they" say. The thing is, I don't judge the user as much as I judge *myself* as a user. My authority derives from my experience, so all I can do is tell you about my experiences, to the best of my hooked recollections, and demand safety where I can provide it for my children, others' children, and anyone I might help along the way. But first I have to finish telling you what I did and why.

After I set the empty Dixie cup down and found a little food in the kitchen, I looked over at a glass-topped table big enough to seat ten and saw people crammed around it. My curiosity pushed me into the crowd. There were piles of white powder all over the table and flat razor blades sitting in a small box, except for one that some guy was using to shape the powder into skinny lines. Everyone was laughing their heads off as a guy pressed one side of his nostril and tried to snort up the powder in the other nostril, but scattered the substance all over the place.

"Here, asshole, let me show you how it's done!" another guy said. "You're wasting it!" He took a twenty-dollar bill and rolled it so tight it barely had a hole. Then, with great precision, he snorted the stuff right through the tiny opening and into his nose without wasting a spec.

I was mesmerized by the newness of this world—or perhaps by the three shots of whatever it was Jan kept handing me to slam. Finally, a girl turned to me and said, "Come on, cutie, try it."

"Okay, whatever, sure." The man handed me his rolled-up bill, and I tried to be cool and act like I knew what I was doing. With my knees on a chair, I bent over and quickly sucked this white dust up my nose, thinking that if I did it quickly, I would look like an expert or something. But as I sat up and put my feet to the floor, I felt nothing, just a very, very cold sensation in my nose and throat.

"Hmmm," I said, and walked off to find Jan in the backyard, where I saw a pool. A hammock hanging next to the house caught my eye before I found her. It looked very inviting because all of a sudden I was very tired. I curled up in it and talked with a guy sitting in a folding lawn chair, and then it hit. I had a jolt to my system like none I had ever felt before. I was ten feet tall, and nothing would ever hurt me again. I was so wrapped up in this feeling that I never noticed people suddenly running past the pool and jumping the wooden fence.

"Whoa, what's going on?" I wondered, but before I could roll myself out of the hammock, the guy next to me had bolted, too. When I stood up, I saw police officers, but none of them saw me—yet.

"Well, what are *you* doing here, young lady?" a familiar voice said. "It's too cold for a pool party, don't ya think?" The infamous sheriff stood there as I watched the other cops handcuff a few people and take them around through the side gate. "I am out of handcuffs, but you gotta ride in the patrol car," he said, like a disappointed parent who just found out his child had lied or flunked an algebra test.

From the back of the car as we drove away, I could see a woman still inside the house, as if nothing had happened and she just needed to clean up after the party before she could go to bed. All I could think was how dirty that house had to have been, and that I should have helped pick up before I left. I had no idea until I got to the station that nearly six hours had passed since I'd arrived at the party.

Different people have their own versions of "a night in jail." Once I got past the sight of the toilet that did actually sit in the corner of this cell, I found a spot on the floor and awaited my punishment. I fell asleep against the wall, and in a few hours it was morning. Reading my name from a clipboard, a really cute policeman let me out and motioned for me to follow him to his car. Silently, he took me to my apartment, and when I asked him who paid for me to get out, he just shrugged as if he didn't know or care.

Pushing the door open to my humble apartment number 108, I flopped onto my waterbed, and hit my head on the edge where the padding was supposed to be. Adding once again to my growing list, I promised myself that when I got enough money, I'd buy a real bed instead of this one I got in the divorce from Bobby. It was like floating in a pool on a cheap mat.

Later that day I went back to work, and though I told myself I definitely would not discuss what had happened, after a few days I finally told a friend who worked in the kitchen. She just laughed and said, "Honey, you got some pretty tough angels watching over you, but you are wearing them out!"

I would like to tell you that I changed, that I never again used, never drank too much liquor or put myself in danger. But, honestly, this was just the beginning of a long and dusty trail. I was thirsty, hungry, and desperate to fill the void in my soul. I spent weekends at parties, took road trips to concerts, and did anything I could to make every hour between leaving Miranda and seeing her again go as fast as possible. When I finally had her, we'd just hide from the rest of the world.

You Got the Look

———

THIS ADDED OCCUPATION WOULD PERFECT my ability to shut my emotions down and perform for those who wanted to exploit me for their pleasure. I didn't care, as long as they paid accordingly. There's a whole underground world of bars that open when regular bars are closing, and that's the world I entered. Thanks to my new friends, I had a large selection of costumes and stilettos I could borrow, and I did things I never imagined I would do. It was as if there were an entirely different person living inside my body, one who didn't care if the outside of her body was touched by strangers.

One of my new friends explained what an exotic dancer was and said, "You've got the look." It was the second time someone had told me that. This is when I realized the body could actually be a commodity. Driven to be independent and without any need for someone to take care of me, I used this new realization for my financial gain.

To keep the "look," I had to starve myself thin so I could pull my body to the top of a brass pole, grab tight, flip upside down, do the splits, and gently turn myself over without injuring myself or the clients. I wore five-inch stilettos that could puncture an eye if I wasn't careful.

Music was the part of the job I enjoyed. So it was easy to let it move me and allow my mind to escape long enough to make a few more bucks before sunrise.

I had to find ways to escalate my energy to make it through each morning, so I was glad when Paul introduced me to coffee—something I'd never be without again. I'd scuffle into his kitchen, trying to ignore the looks of disgust he made when he was sure I'd been out all night partying. I ignored him, found the dark chicory coffee grounds, and proceeded to start a lifelong ritual of drinking coffee so strong you could almost stand a spoon up in it.

There was a weird type of corporate climbing in a stripper's world in those days. You could actually just show up and meet the entertainment boss or connect with the pit mom, and if he or she liked the way you looked, you would get floor time. If you were lucky, you would get to hit the center stage. I knew how to flash a smile, and after Paul demanded that I add some enhancement to the two small bumps on my chest, I was noticed even more. When the girls and I had the funds, we'd drive from Enid to Oklahoma City or buy cheap tickets from Oklahoma City to Dallas, where the men paid a hell of a lot more for us to swing around that pole and keep them company.

Dallas was a different world. But while I flew in and out of a few of the gentleman's clubs—where the men were anything but gentlemen—I always seemed to migrate back to Oklahoma and Miranda. I wore out the road from Enid to Oklahoma City to Dallas when I couldn't afford to fly, but my little convertible Rabbit would get me where I needed to go. Between my regular job and hiding this other occupation—because I was sure to lose Miranda if anyone found out about it—I rarely had time for sleep. I hardly slept anyway.

One time I'll never forget is the night I ended up with a chipped tooth. "Hey, gorgeous, sit with me," a customer ordered. I could tell he wasn't a nice guy, but he'd bought the usual bottle of bubbly just so I could be his hourly companion. After a while, I could see why this creep had to buy company. He was such an ass! When I finished putting my time in with Mr. Wonderful, I got up to leave, but that wasn't what he had planned. He grabbed me and jerked me back into his huge lap. As I said a few choice words, I watched his face contort in about fifty different ways. Add booze to a character like that, and you've got an instant fight.

I pulled myself away and called him a . . . well, I'll leave that to your imagination. Well, never mind, I called him an asshole. Then the guy actually took the cheap champagne bottle out of the bucket and swung it at my face. I thought he'd miss for sure, because he stumbled back as the bouncer caught him, but I was wrong. He swiped that bottle right across my teeth, and bam! I had a snaggletooth until my friend Dr. Jim, a dentist, could fix it. Hazards of the occupation, I guess.

Crazy parties at big, fancy houses made me feel alive. They where places where I felt I could put my personality on autopilot. I watched groups of people standing over a table playing cards, or so I thought. Then I saw a familiar sight.

I've never had a problem throwing myself into a group of strangers. I squeezed between two large men who were huddled over the table and saw the familiar powder on a mirror. One girl took a razor blade and started sectioning off the white lines, and for a minute I thought I might back up and walk away, but I didn't.

She looked up at me. "Want some?" she asked.

Leaning over the mirror, I inhaled the cocaine. My bottoming-out was around the corner. My pattern of partying would cause pain not only to my constantly bleeding nose but also to my soul.

Living with an alcoholic made it easier to live my hidden life. The spans of time I was MIA I could explain away to Paul because he was just as foggy as I was and twenty years older. I had an unfair advantage, I think. I was making it through the days and the nights with muddled thinking and no sleep. The less I hung out with Paul, the more frequent my cocaine use became. Finally, Paul claimed it was time to get married. So we began plans for me to become his eighth wife. I cleaned up my hidden life, stopped dancing, and spent days trying to be a mom to two of his boys; his third boy was my age and didn't need my mothering. I created a space where my daughter could come safely. A change was starting in me that I was unaware of, one that was guiding me toward more stability. I had only one-word prayers in those days: "Help!" Someone was listening, but sometimes it takes a very long time to realize it.

Bottomless Pit

THE SHOPPING CART WAS ALMOST overflowing. Clothes, perfume, jewelry, makeup, and all the foods I craved filled my KMart cart, and I still wasn't finished with my shopping. I hadn't hit the baby clothes and toy aisle yet, but I would before the night was over.

When I felt bad about myself, I often strolled the local KMart and stuffed my cart with all the things I wanted, pretending I could afford everything in the store. My fantasy tour included items for the babies I would one day have and pretty dresses for Miranda. After spending hours in the store, I parked the loaded cart in an aisle and walked out.

Strange, but it filled a need in me to know that someday I would be able to take care of myself and my family. I'm glad I chose a fantasy game, though, instead of actually shoplifting. For me, what mattered was the idea that if I acted as if this was my reality, then maybe one day it would be. My dreams have always been about having a home and a family. Of course, if home and family had been packaged and put on the shelf, and if I didn't have the means to get them, I certainly would have swiped those!

Some of my other habits in life weren't as harmless. In fact, most of my actions during my later teen years and early adult life were destructive—outward evidence of my inner self-loathing. The abandonment and neglect of my parents laid the groundwork for my not believing I mattered. The sexual abuse by my stepbrother, great-uncle, stepfather, and any other predator, including a preacher, solidified my self-hatred. No one paid attention to my cries for help. No one listened. No one cared.

So why should I?

The numbing continued, and so did the booze, drugs, and sex. And I sheltered a secret. Many.

Once the lunch shift at Paul's restaurant ended, I had a few hours before the night shift began. I'd then go from the night shift to the late shift in the nightclub connected to the restaurant. Still wearing my small black apron with three pockets—one for pad and pen, one for change, and one for the makeup I continuously applied—I started clearing uneaten food from each table, putting the plates into the black bus tub. For a moment I stared at the cheese-covered fries and half-eaten potato skins with oily cheese dripping from them, and then I hurried to the back, grabbed a napkin, and scooped up the scraps. I sneaked into the bathroom and gorged myself on someone else's leftovers.

As I crammed the greasy remains into my mouth, I felt a sense of temporary relief from the empty feeling I carried with me. I didn't stop at binging. Clubbing one night, I heaved over the cold toilet of a bar I was in and saw a pair of puppy dog eyes staring back at me. I'm certain that if this furry creature could've spoken, he would've said, "You are so stupid, lady. You are blessed to have food at all, and here you are, throwing it up. What an idiot."

I picked up the tiny creature, cleaned it in the sink, slapped a handful of water on my face, popped a mint into my mouth, and headed back out to show off my discovery.

We were living in an old, wooden house that used to be rented to one of Paul's many secret girlfriends. Paul had told me that we needed to move there because he had lost his big house and all his money, but he didn't tell me how.

"Go over there, Steph, and clean it up. We've got to move in for a while."

When I asked why, he simply told me to trust him. *Right.*

"Just trust me, and get it ready for us. The kitchen is a mess." That was an understatement.

Taking my new furry friend with me, I walked into the kitchen, opened the refrigerator, and found it full of moldy, maggot-infested food. A normal person would've thrown up at the sight and smell, but I saved the vomiting for my controlled episodes; I didn't waste such responses on things like fuzzy, green food. I slipped on yellow rubber gloves and went to work. Somehow the work ethic that grandma taught me filtered through and carried me through life. If I had a job to do, no matter what, I did it with passion. Even if my grandma might have been disappointed at the work I was actually doing.

After one of my visits with Miranda, a girl I worked with informed me that Paul had yet another girlfriend—another of the girls at the restaurant. You would think I wouldn't have been shocked, but I've never lost the ability to offer the benefit of doubt to everyone, even if they don't deserve it. After each disappointment, I continue to grasp at some unrealistic hope that the person will change. It's the definition of illusion, I suppose.

Leaving the restaurant, I headed home to rid myself of the food I'd eaten. Crying all the way there, I rushed into the bathroom and threw myself to the floor—right into a pile of crap that my sweet little puppy left for me.

I hated that musty dump of a house, Paul, my job, my body, and my life. I felt a familiar rage work its way up from my belly, and I began violently punching myself in the stomach. I pulled my hair, screamed, cried, and basically kicked my own ass. I ended the tantrum by smashing my hand into the mirror that covered the medicine cabinet.

I called a girlfriend, and by the time she arrived, I was feeling almost catatonic. The doctor checked me out. I didn't need stitches, but he gave me the number of a good psychiatrist, one of many numbers I would receive in those years for counseling.

Nightclub Wedding

IT WAS THREE YEARS FROM the time I became Paul's girlfriend until I became his wife. He took me to get my first passport, and I was sure that our upcoming honeymoon to Spain would be the one and only time I ever left the country. I never could have imagined that someday I would fill the pages of two passports with stamps from the countries I visited.

Finding something to wear to the wedding—my nightclub wedding—was next. My friend and I searched for the perfect dress, which, I told her, laughing, could be anything but white. We settled on a cream-colored lace dress that tightly fit my 118-pound body.

"That is a perfect weight for you," Paul would always tell me. Believe me, he meant it, too. Every morning he would wake me very early, and before I was really awake, we were a mile into our daily runs. There were, of course, benefits to running. It gave me more endurance and allowed me to push myself even harder. So there I was: perfect weight, perfect dress, and after a few hits on a perfect joint before the ceremony, I had a perfect calm.

We had transformed our nightclub into a chapel, sectioning it off with chairs for about twenty guests. After convincing my brother, Carl, to walk me down this short aisle, I was married for the third time. I am serious when I say I cannot remember anything about that wedding. The only thing I have from that day is a picture of my brother and me. He's gripping me tight, as if to say, "No, Pudge, don't do this!" But I did.

Standing there, released from Carl's grasp, I looked at the preacher we'd hired to perform the ceremony. He asked, "Do you take this man?" For a minute I had to remind myself which man it was, and then I said, "Okay."

Paul glared at me, as did the preacher, and I quickly said, "I mean, I do. Sorry." Was I ever sorry!

Our Spanish honeymoon is just as cloudy; Paul and I pretty much drank our way through Spain. We hopped a plane to Madrid and checked into our hotel. But when I opened the window of our beautiful room, expecting an amazing panorama, I found myself looking at the wall of the hotel next door. So much for the view. I turned instead to the tiny television and messed with the wire antenna until I got some reception and watched a cartoon in Spanish. Paul was passed out, and I wanted to go home. Wherever that was.

Leaving the hotel the next day, we rented a car and drove south toward the Mediterranean. All I remember of that journey is seeing workers harvesting olives. Finally Paul stopped the car, and I got out, walked to the edge of the sea, and took the deepest breath I had taken since the doctor first slapped my baby butt. It was as if I were standing at the edge of my life. I thought back to a painting by Maxfield Parrish and laughed, thinking of Tony. He and I would search out prints by Parrish, and my favorite was of a girl standing at the edge of a cliff. I was reminded of a conversation we'd had. "Tony, I don't know whether I should jump," I said. Wrapping me in a hug, Tony said, "Into what?"

Before dinner that night we walked into a shop, and I stared into a case of beautiful porcelain art pieces. Paul came up behind me and asked, "What's caught your eye?" I pointed to a baby doll so delicately made that even the lace on its dress was porcelain. "I guess this will have to do," I said, "because I know I won't have any more of my own. I don't deserve to." I stood there, hugging myself as tears fell. Surprisingly, Paul bought the doll, and I got her safely all the way home to Oklahoma.

Who's the Girl in Spain?

ON OUR WAY BACK TO Madrid, we stopped in a tiny village so I could look for an adapter for the hair dryer I had packed and naïvely thought I could plug in without an electrical converter. I was walking up a narrow sidewalk when I caught a glimpse of my reflection in a shop window.

In the reflection, I saw a young woman with long, crimped, bleached hair and an even, tanning-booth tan. She was tall, too thin—a size two—but somewhat slumped, with the weight of her world on her narrow shoulders. Outwardly she looked perfect and in control—hair, skin color, body size, and boob size all altered at her command . . . at *her husband's* command.

My reflection scared me enough to stop me in my tracks. After being told repeatedly that my look was all I had going for me, I decided that I had better make it work for me. But why then had I changed so much about myself? Why had I changed my baby-fine, straight, dark-blonde hair into an unnatural color? Why didn't I like my pale skin? What was wrong with a five-foot-eight-inch frame that was probably a true size six or size eight and should weigh around 135 pounds?

Paul broke my trance when he shrieked, "Hurry up, Blondie, there is a bullfight up here. Let's go!"

Shaking myself back into the present, I noticed a group of Spanish men staring at me as they approached. As they got closer, they paused, eyed me up and down, and smiled, saying something in Spanish and motioning with sweeping arm movements that the sidewalk was all mine, and they'd take to the street in my honor. I smiled back and said, "*Gracias*," which was all I knew aside from "*Donde está baño*," and then

I yelled at Paul at the top of my lungs, which caused these men to turn and look at me with worry on their faces, "I'm not Blondie!"

I never was able to allow the real me to surface. All those years it was as if I were standing in a lineup at a game show, when the announcer says, "Will the real Stephanie please stand up?" There were about ten different versions of me staring at one another, confused as to who the actual Stephanie was.

The authentic me? It's more like the bohemian-looking girl with dark-blonde hair, a sun-damaged complexion, a bit round in the hips, who's standing somewhere in the middle of the lineup of Stephanies, looking tired and hungry. She's the one who wants to move to the front. But she is still too scared to, for now. My life felt like the life of that poor bull I saw in the bullfight arena. Coaxed into following something enticing or colorful, lured by the illusion that it's a good thing, and quickly realizing I have to fight to the death for survival. So far I have been luckier than that bull. The arena I was still in presented a bit more danger yet.

When Someone Else Chooses

WHEN WE LANDED BACK IN Oklahoma and made our drive back to the dump where we lived in Enid, all I could think of was seeing Miranda and giving her the gifts I had brought back from Spain. It didn't take long for reality to set in, however. Although Miranda was thrilled and ran right into my arms, her dad was not so happy, and neither was his new wife. That never mattered to me, because I only wanted Miranda, and our time together was so precious and rare that I relished every moment of it. I'd learned to block Bobby's disappointment, and I honestly didn't care what his wife thought of me. I think Bobby thought I'd eventually give up the fight for our daughter. I never did.

Waking one particular morning, with gray clouds that matched my mood, I looked for Paul, expecting to find him in his usual spot in the tiny backyard, sitting at the wrought-iron table he'd moved from the big house with his coffee and newspaper. He wasn't there. I could smell his Crabtree and Evelyn aftershave, so I followed it and found him in the living room with his nose in *The Power of Positive Thinking*. I thought Paul reading the book was a good start to a conversation we needed to have. With the excitement of a child, I waited until he looked up and signaled it was okay for me to talk. I stood there until I couldn't take it any longer, and I blurted out, "I'm pregnant!"

Why the hell I thought this would be good news to an aging man I will never know. I guess I thought that since he said he wanted me to be happy, he would, in fact, want me to be happy. I couldn't have been more wrong. The next several minutes seemed to go on forever.

"This isn't a good idea," Paul told me pointedly. He already had three children, I had one, and he was too set in his ways to even entertain the thought of more. Plus I was only twenty-three years old and had my whole life ahead of me. But it was my life we were talking about! Apparently at forty-two he didn't think he had that much more life ahead of him.

Why is it that the selfish-minded think that having a child takes away from the life we have ahead of us? In fact, the only thing subtracted is sleep, and we can catch up on that when we are old, or in my case, when I am six feet under for the nap of my afterlife.

In the end, Paul made the decision. He said, "No, Steph." I would have to search for the place to have what felt like an evil thing done, and we would have the matter under control within a week. I grabbed the Yellow Pages and locked myself in my haven, the bathroom. I let my shaking fingers do the walking, thinking how stupid that little Yellow Pages ad was, and found the As. Alcoholics Anonymous? Not yet. Abortion? Yes.

Your Life Flashing Before My Eyes

I WAS SITTING IN THE passenger's seat of the old Saab, looking out the window as Paul drove south on I-35. I thought I could hear the question "Where are you going now, Steph?" over and over in the noise the car made as it sped down the interstate. I was sure that once the deed was completed, I would emerge to find that the gray clouds had overtaken the blue sky.

I thought back to the last few hours, how Paul had asked from the other side of the locked bathroom door if I had the bottle of anxiety pills. The pills were prescribed by a psychiatrist Paul thought I needed to see. After finding the medicine, I climbed into the small shower stall of the awful house. I wanted to wash my hair, but instead I just slid to the floor of the shower and held my tummy and cried. I wanted my mom, though she was never an option for a soothing conversation. I wanted my grandmother, who I'd call soon. I wanted everything or nothing. I had no idea what I wanted except that I didn't want an abortion. But it didn't matter what I wanted.

Whether it was the medication I swallowed or the multiple rum-and-Cokes the night before, I wasn't fully in my right mind as I was dragged to the clinic. We weren't turning back until we had taken care of the problem. Defiance was usually my constant companion during this time of my life, but rather than fighting off the victim mentality, I allowed myself to be a victim once again.

We pulled into an empty parking lot, an indication that either the business was not thriving or that the people carrying picket signs had in fact scared off other girls who needed to get their problem under control.

The building was an ugly brown that reminded me of mud. The sidewalk was cracked, and it didn't look like a dime had been spent on landscaping. This was not a place where people came to hang out or stopped to smell the roses. I walked inside with Paul behind me to ensure I wouldn't try to escape, and he practically pushed me to the front desk.

The young woman slid open the small, glass window and gave me a weak smile. I'm sure I looked so pathetic that she felt sorry for me. She gave Paul the paperwork, and he paid right then and there, because, she said, we would want to leave as quickly as possible when I woke up. "It is better that way," she said, adding that on waking I'd be able to resume my life without as much as a blink of the eye. She was wrong.

I sat there looking at another patient, a girl about my age with tears streaming down her face. She was alone, and I wondered why she didn't get up and run out. No one was there to stop her. For a split second I thought we could run off together and keep going until we arrived somewhere safe, where we could keep our babies. I knew Miranda would love this new child and welcome it with open arms. Isn't that how it's supposed to be? Why was Paul rejecting this miracle rather than embracing it?

The nurse came out to collect me before I could put the plan to run away into action. Guess I drew the short straw that morning. My luck had run out.

I walked into a room with only a cot and a trash can, sat on the edge of the bed, and asked, "Why is there a trash can?"

"That's there for when you wake up, because you will be very sick," the nurse informed me. I was already very sick, though, and used it before the procedure even started. The nurse gave me a pill, and without asking what it was, I popped it and did not wake until I was sitting in the car driving toward home. I don't remember any more about those few short hours, except that Paul had also decided that I needed food, so we pulled into a Waffle House. To this day I can never set foot in one of those places. I'm sure they are decent establishments, but for me the sight and smell will forever turn my stomach and rekindle memories of an unforgiving heart.

"She'll have coffee," Paul said to the lady behind the counter. We were sitting on short revolving stools, and I held my face in my sweaty hands.

Ignoring him, the waitress with gray hair and blue eye shadow asked, "Honey, what do you want?" She looked worried. "You look pale as a ghost."

"Nothing, thank you." Her question rang in my ears the rest of that day. *What do I want?* I wondered. *To be dead.*

As time went on, I remained a coward in my relationship with Paul. Sure that I would never have to go through this hell again, I decided to brush the experience under the rug, which already covered so many ignored issues that one day I was sure to trip over it. Never speaking of it again with Paul, I let that story go untold.

Lemon Soup

——|——

DECIDING THAT SINCE I WAS imprisoned, I might as well find some kind of silver—or at least gray—lining, I took advantage of experiences that taught me about cultural differences in the world. Meeting Paul's family and spending holidays with them was tolerable, even educational at times. For Christmas 1988, his very proper, elderly mother gave me the Vogue book on etiquette, explaining that I needed to learn about manners.

"Stephanie, this will help you to improve on those things in which you need help," she very pointedly said to me, with an eerie smile stretched across her wrinkled face. She thought this was the perfect gift for me after I'd taken a trip to New York City with them, where she noted my less-than-proper manners.

We had gone to an upscale restaurant, where I had my first meal of lobster. I will never forget how intimidated I was by all the silverware in front of me. I was sure I would embarrass myself. Two forks here and a tiny spoon placed, for some odd reason, at the top of my plate. All I needed was one clunky fork to mix all this mess together and devour it. Or, hell, no utensils at all. Give me mashed potatoes, and I'd scoop them up with my fingers right into my mouth!

Once the meal was over, the waiter brought out a fancy bowl of clear liquid. I looked around and waited to see what I was supposed to do with it. I hadn't ordered soup, but I assumed this was something rich people ate after they finished their fancy meals.

So I straightened up in my plush chair, subtly picked up the soup-spoon, and proceeded to eat the soup. After a few minutes, everyone at the table was looking in my direction, including Paul. I was sure he was proud that I had become a cultured young lady. To my astonishment, he said, "How is the soup, dear?" I looked at him and answered, "It is actually very plain, but the lemon floating in it helps a little."

The entire table burst into laughter, and his mother told me that what I had mistaken for soup was the finger bowl that I was to clean my fingers in after having had lobster. Paul made some very snotty remark, and I stood up and said, "Well, now, I'll find a straw—if they have things such as straws in a place like this—and go drink the toilet water. So if you will excuse me."

That didn't go over too well with Paul because I embarrassed him, and I was scolded for days for my remark. He was probably scolded by his mom. Poor guy was always trying to earn mommy's approval.

After overhearing me try to read through *Peter Rabbit* with Miranda one evening, Paul had discovered that my reading level was elementary, and he suggested I take reading classes. At first I just cried with humiliation, but I quickly decided he was right, even if I never admitted it to him. "Steph, you spell the word 'have' h-a-f-t. And I don't know where you learned to pronounce words, but you always say them wrong," he said as we drove our usual route from work to home.

I started thinking about how my grandma spelled "have" that way in her many letters to me. With my misspelled words, incorrect pronunciations, and my notorious dangling prepositions, I'm sure it was maddening for an educated man such as Paul even to have a conversation with me. Remembering graduation day and my empty diploma, I had to agree. I was completely uneducated. Paul kept after me about it, probably thinking I wouldn't listen, but I had already signed up at the vo-tech school in Enid. I just didn't want him to know. It was my idea to better myself, and I didn't want him to have the satisfaction of feeling as if he'd molded me into someone better suited for society. Childish defiance versus gratitude, I suppose.

Within a year I was devouring books like candy. *Animal Farm* was my first. From that point on, I had a new escape. I became obsessed with Ernest Hemingway, whose *A Moveable Feast* became my favorite. Of course, right? Since moving and eating were two things I knew very well. Anytime and anywhere I could find time to flip another page of another book, I did. I even read at stoplights driving to and from work when I'd come to a cliffhanger in a story and needed to find out what happened. It's safe to say that I became preoccupied with reading and with bookstores. I'd found my niche.

Even at the local grocery store, I'd find the aisle that was lined with paperback books, and I'd sit on the floor and read them right there. When Paul took me on trips, I would go off on my own to find the oldest possible bookshops, ones where the moment you walked through the door, you were hit with the scent of history and the written word.

Once in Taos, New Mexico, I found the most amazing bookshop with tattered books everywhere. "Where have you been?" Paul asked, when I finally made my way back to the bar he was sitting in.

"I found a used bookshop," I said, crawling onto the bar stool between him and some guy wearing a full Indian headdress. Paul grabbed the paper sack that held some of the books I bought and dumped it out onto the bar for inspection.

"Well, let's see what you are reading, little girl. What's this?" he said in a condescending tone, loud enough that the wasted Indian chief next to me looked up from his highball full of whiskey.

Grabbing the book, I said, "It's a book about self-love, something I need to learn."

"Steph, it's not a self-help book," he said. "It's about masturbation!"

I melted into the stool, humiliated, while he laughed so hard he had to remove the round specs to wipe his eyes. The guy next to me gave me a look as if to say, "Indian chief says your man's name ought to be Donkey With Mean Mouth." In other words, Paul was a complete ass!

From that day forward, I would learn all I could about the world. I not only acquired manners and read grammar books, but I would rise far above those who thought themselves better than me. In short, I'd prove to Paul, his mother, and my mother that I was worth being educated and that I wasn't stupid.

A time would come when I would find myself back in that exact New York City restaurant as a much older version of myself. This time, though, I had my own guest, and I paid the bill. But not before I took the finger bowl and thought, "Should I do this right, now that I know the difference?" Nah. I scooped up a spoonful, and I smiled.

Finding Answers

———————

AS I WAS LEARNING THINGS at warp speed, I was also learning about myself. It was starting to occur to me that I had a lot of problems—especially because the signs were getting harder to ignore. I'd gone back to working at night, living in a very self-destructive way, hiding my identity under different stage names, and covering my face with a ton of makeup to ensure I'd go unnoticed in the places I worked in. I still had to look at myself in the mirror, and, most of all, I had to hide this part of my life from my grandmother, as well as from everyone else. If she asked me how work was going, at least I didn't have to lie that the restaurant jobs were keeping me busy, adding, "Yes, Grandma, I am trying to get rest and have regular bowel movements." That was always very important to her, because she knew I was never very healthy or regular. You gotta love grandmas and nanas.

Out of the blue one weekend while I had Miranda, my grandma called. She said she wanted to make sure I knew she loved me no matter what. It was then that I confided to her about my drug use and drinking. She started praying overtime, and her praying eventually paid off. Between Grandma's voice on the other end of the receiver that Saturday morning and Miranda's need to read and reread Dr. Seuss's *ABC* book and her *Peter Rabbit* pop-up book, I had a few moments that, in spite of myself, were building a firmer foundation for my life. I just didn't know how to follow through. Or how to orchestrate a plan.

But a visit to a friend helped boldly push me in the right direction. After a lunch shift at the restaurant, I drove from Enid to Edmond, a town I hadn't heard of, to visit someone at a hospital that had a treatment facility for drug and alcohol abuse. I was happy to offer her some support, advice, and direction. My goal was to help her. Little did I know that my introduction to this place would be the first step toward my own recovery. I have heard many times that it doesn't matter what got you to the point of healing as long as you got there. I do know that once you have been guided (or thrown unwillingly) into change, there is no turning back. Being introduced to the life of recovery really messes up a girl's drinking and drug use! When I got to the hospital, I saw a directory on a wall plaque in the elevator, and I was struck by one title—Recovery Counselor. *What was that?* I wondered.

I got off the elevator and asked the man at the desk for my friend. While he searched his paper for her name I looked around at the setting of this place. Some patients were talking and crying while music—a soothing piano tune with a windy, Celtic sound—played. Others were sitting and just relaxing. It made me want to lie down in a field of flowers and just spend hours looking up at the clouds and making shapes out of them. Sitting there, I felt something very unfamiliar, and as I waited for my friend to emerge, I asked myself, *What is this feeling?* Quietly a voice, maybe my own, said, *Peace.*

It had been weeks since I'd last seen my friend, and the person who entered the room was not the same girl I had said good-bye to at the nightclub. This person looked almost angelic—a big difference from the strung-out girl with black circles under her eyes and the smell of cigarettes on her breath. We hugged hello and talked about people we knew and the things that had gotten her to this place. She said that her recovery counselor was a sweet lady, and if I felt like I needed someone to talk to, I should call her. After a while, I hugged her good-bye, took the business card of her counselor, stuck it in the hip pocket of my frayed jeans, and forgot about it.

There is nothing in me that thinks for one minute that my willpower alone can help me; only divine power can do that. I have made many choices in my life, and since you've gotten this far in my story, I'm sure it's easy to see that on my own I had made a pretty big mess of things. My drive back to Enid was full of conversations with a God who I felt was sitting in my passenger's seat. Or maybe I was finally going crazy and hearing voices.

But the conversation went something like this: "Steph, you have choices," God seemed to say. "What are they going to be?" At that moment, it was the choice not to be late for my shift.

After several weeks of being back in my insane life, everything seemed totally out of control. I was enraged most of the time, usually at myself but occasionally at others. I had gotten into a fistfight—or more like a slap fest—with a customer, a large man who was less than a gentleman in a gentleman's club in OKC. He'd picked me up off the ground and basically thrown me across the room. I missed the brass pole, but I hit my head so hard on the edge of the stage that I passed out. For weeks I toggled between partial clarity and partial insanity. As I began to regain consciousness, it became obvious to me that this was a bad place, that my relationship was a bad place, and basically my entire life was a bad place.

When the bouncer called me an idiot for hitting this giant of a man because he'd cheated me out of a couple hundred dollars, I gathered my things from the back, said good-bye to the pit mom, and gave her a hug. Then I walked out of the club, sat on the grimy steps covered in old cigarette butts and trash, and felt like one of the discarded cigarette boxes on the ground. The sun was rising, and one of the bartenders came out and asked if I needed a ride.

"Hey, Blondie," he added, "you should have worn that outfit on stage last night," chuckling as he assumed I wanted him to sit down next to me. "Really," he said, "the cheap wife-beater T-shirt, cutoffs, and stilettos . . . you look sad and pathetic. Men like that."

Why did everyone call me "Blondie," and why was pathetic a good look?

Well, I was done with that, done with bad men, and most importantly, done with looking sad and pathetic! I got up, said good-bye, reached down to unstrap the five-inch heels, and I set off barefoot in a new direction.

Glazed and Confused

———————

"TWO DOZEN GLAZED DONUTS, PLEASE," I said, never looking at the lady on the other side of the see-through donut case. Without
going into the long, detailed description as to why one of my major food
groups consisted of dripping glaze, I thought the donuts in the case at
that moment were the most beautiful, intoxicating things I'd ever seen.
She boxed the donuts and then added extras to make two baker's dozens.

Handing over the money as if I were making a drop to get my fix, I
smiled and walked out with one thing in mind—finding a secret place
where I could devour all twenty-six donuts. I didn't mind that they were
the discounted, stale ones. I was already feeling fat from the two beers I'd
had that morning, and it was about to get a lot worse. As soon as I shoved
the last donut in my mouth, I did what I do best. I puked.

The vicious cycle of taking an upper to wake up and a downer with a
couple of beers to calm down can create havoc and induce some deadly
side effects. Between the time I woke up and the two o'clock shift at
the restaurant, I'd popped amphetamines, gone for a run, cleaned the
tiny crap hole we lived in, drunk two of Paul's Michelob dark beers, and
taken a shower. The time between driving to the donut shop on my way
to run errands and getting to work was a fog. From passing out in my
car in the back alley with vomit on my shirt to waking up with a nurse
standing over me was an absolute blackout. The nurse said, "You're okay,
now. We moved you upstairs to the psych ward. You just rest." Panic set
in immediately, then fear, and then my third survival instinct: to bullshit
my way out of anything!

"Thank you, but I won't be staying. Can I please call my husband?"
I asked.

As if it would make me feel better, the same nurse said, "You're okay here. We didn't have to tie you down." I was really confused.

A tall and lanky man in a white lab coat walked in and talked to me about eating illness, drug use, and, of course, drinking. The blood work showed all the substances in my body. He thought it vital that I find help and go into a treatment facility.

Until that moment I'd completely forgotten about the card the counselor at the treatment facility had given me. I began explaining how I'd already thought about getting help and that if I could have my clothes back, I would call the number on the card and speak with the counselor.

After several hours, I was discharged, and my friend took me home because Paul was nowhere to be found. It's still pretty foggy as to who found me in the first place. I won't even venture a guess as to how that played out.

When I got home, I dug through the dirty laundry for the jeans with the counselor's business card in the pocket. Then I sat on the bathroom floor and left a message. When she returned my call we talked for an hour or more, and the next thing I knew I was packed and had told Paul that I needed him to give me a ride to a treatment facility in Texas.

On I-35 Again

———

THE NEXT MORNING WE WERE traveling down I-35 heading south into Texas. I uncrossed my legs to stretch them out, feeling numb from the three Bloody Marys I'd consumed an hour back. We'd hit a bar in a kind of hole-in-the-wall establishment that had no problem serving alcohol with breakfast. Raising my glass in a toast, I said, "I dedicate my last drink to sobriety!"

"You drunk?" my husband asked me. For some reason, I just stared at his face, wondering why I felt like a child on her way to boarding school. It was possibly because I could have been his kid, since his oldest son and I were the same age, and because Paul was dropping me off for what we both thought would be a month—twenty-eight days, to be exact.

"Maybe, but who cares," I said. "I won't get a drink for twenty-eight days, so I might as well be, right?" Rubbing my eyes, I felt the tears welling up but vowed not to allow them to surface.

"Steph, this isn't for your drinking. I agreed to this because you keep throwing up your food, and you need to stop!" We both knew what he meant. And I wished I could have kept the donut experience from him. I sat there while he peered disapprovingly at me, as he often did. I was just glad that after he'd joined me and thrown back a few Myers's rum-and-Cokes that he was even able to drive me to the treatment facility.

Feeling assured that everyone probably showed up at a place like this smelling of booze, I wasn't too worried about being tipsy. We pulled into the parking lot of Parkside Lodge–Westgate, which had to be the ugliest building I'd seen since the abortion clinic. There was no park, no gate, west, east, or otherwise. The freestanding brown building looked like a nursing home that had been converted to house lost souls like me.

The old Saab made a hissing noise when Paul turned off the ignition.

He looked at me and said that he knew it needed to be fixed, but he hadn't taken the time to do it. "I'll be back to visit you next weekend, Steph. And I'll have someone help me bring your car here for you so you have it when you get out."

I was suddenly having doubts about this recovery gig. I started to cry and couldn't control it. "Please don't make me stay," I said. "I don't have a problem. We just drink too much, and you get mad at me!"

Deep down, though, I knew I had to go through with the plan. I walked up the sidewalk to a side door and hit the buzzer. A scratchy voice said, "Hi, welcome. We've been expecting you, Stephanie," as if I were coming for a spa weekend. Rolling my eyes, I pulled up the end of my favorite AC/DC T-shirt and wiped my runny nose.

"Here goes nothing," I said. The door clicked open, and the smell of canned vegetables filled my nose. I was certain then that this place had been a nursing home; it smelled like the green beans and boxed potatoes used to feed toothless people with colons so weak they couldn't digest water.

Around the corner I met the intake nurse, who took my drawstring duffle and purse so quickly it was like she thought there was a bomb inside.

"Okay, well, here you go," I said in a sarcastic tone that I thought would forever make Nurse Ratched dislike me. I probably could have won her over with a winning smile that said I was not as bad as she had sized me up to be. But when she looked past my shoulder to see a man bringing a steamer trunk to my room, it confirmed to her that I was high maintenance and was used to having people wait on me. She probably thought that I had someone else puke for me, too. She couldn't have known that my life was in that trunk, and I was anything but anyone's princess.

I dragged myself to the nurses' station. As soon as I sat down, she commanded, "Go pee in this cup," and then added, "I *will* be going through that trunk, honey, to make sure you don't have any mood-altering items in there." I dropped the plastic cup on the floor and apologized, and, apparently annoyed, she handed me a clean one.

"When you get done, come back and tell me from the beginning why you are here." Her expression reminded me of the look I always got from my mother, and I wondered why women hated me. Then I remembered my grandmother. She loved me and would welcome me with open arms when I was better. The thought of my grandmother made me wish I were eating her plate of noodles covered in ketchup instead of peeing into a cup in this bathroom. My stomach growled fiercely. "I am so hungry," I said out loud to the stranger in the bathroom mirror. "But for what, Steph?"

Nurse Ratched was waiting, tapping on the bathroom door impatiently. She motioned for me to sit at the chair with the armrest for blood work and said, "Tell me when you last ate and what."

"Twenty-four glazed donuts from Dunkin' Donuts two days ago, but I threw them all up in the alley behind the donut shop right after."

For a second, she looked at me with sympathy, and I noticed how blue her eyes were. I could tell she knew exactly what I was talking about.

"Oh, and I did have three Bloody Marys this morning," I added. "I guess that's food, right, since it has tomato juice?" I was trying to be funny when I was really terrified.

Not answering my question, she wrote on her clipboard and drew my blood. She could see I felt like I was going to pass out and handed me the tiniest cup of orange juice. It was one of those plastic juice cups from an old country diner that serves breakfast to people who wake up as soon as the rooster crows and whose lives seem simple and enjoyable.

I'm So Hungry

RUBBING THE BARBIE BAND-AID ON my arm, I thought of the pink Barbie tent, and I shook my head at how far I'd come since the night I tried to kill myself. Or maybe I was wondering if I was still bottoming out. In any case, I followed the nurse down the hallway to what would be my room for the next twenty-eight days. Or so I thought—because it would take this staff a lot longer than twenty-eight days to crack through my doubts and fears. Hell, I spent the first twenty-eight days just trying to figure out how to get food secretly to the room I shared with my roommate, Susan. With our tight schedule and a strict menu that limited even my ketchup intake, I was about to jones myself into a coma from the withdrawal of sugar, carbs, and other comfort foods that were easier to throw up. Not to mention all the booze and cocaine I was accustomed to having. All the healthy crap I was forced to eat was not filling my hole, and it was harder to upchuck!

After the kitchen closed, Susan, who had been admitted a week after me, and I would sneak through the swinging doors to the fridge and swipe sandwiches stored in little Ziploc bags. Some kind of ham, cheese, and mayo concoction that the normal patients got to eat. Laughing like we had just hit a bank, we'd hide them under our shirts and walk the quiet halls back to our room, eat them with the speed of a starving animal, and hide the plastic behind the picture frames on the wall. Then we'd throw ourselves down on the twin beds, laughing as if we were drunk.

You may not understand the high of food. But think how difficult it is to have an addiction to something that you *have* to consume every day. I will never, ever minimize other addictions—like drugs or alcohol—having had time with both of them myself. But having to learn to eat something normally that you are addicted to is horrible. I am still learning. There are days now when it still kicks my ass. Especially when I think my ass is too big!

Susan was a fellow tortured soul with a huge scar over her eyebrow that went up her forehead. It was weeks before she felt comfortable enough to talk about it. In a car wreck with her mom, she had been slammed through the windshield, and this memory was now embedded in her face. This beautiful girl had such a sweet spirit. Our bond of children, as well as our illness, kept us close during the first few years of recovery. Her son was the same age as Miranda, and we spent hours talking about how I would get my baby girl back after I was clean and sober. Susan's faith in me convinced me this would happen. Later the reality would be revealed: Miranda wasn't going to get to live with me yet. But I'd fight whoever I needed to until that happened. Including myself.

Poor Me, Poor Me,
Pour Me Another Drink

AT THE BEGINNING OF MY stay, the intake nurse led me to another office and handed the paperwork to my assigned counselor. The nurses tagged patients with their addiction of choice, whatever was controlling the patients the most. The counselor looked up from her desk and said, "Well, you have been categorized as a 'bulimarexic,' a new compound word for 'bulimia' and 'anorexia.'" Then she added, "Let's say, bulimic/anorexic/drug addict/alcoholic, etc."

With each title I felt like I was sinking deeper. The combination meant that I'd not only have sessions in the eating-illness program, but I would also have to work on substance abuse, too, in what they referred to as a concurrent program. Well, of course I would have to do double duty. Making things easy for myself is something I have never been good at.

The counselor asked me to sit and tell her about my life. The sagas of my past and present and where I wanted to be in the future came pouring out. I told her why I drank, why I used drugs, and why I allowed myself to be victimized and abused, adding that the self-destructive things like exploiting myself seemed to make sense. With only twenty-five years to cover, I mentioned everything that everyone had done to me, things that tagged me "abused," and my confusion and loss. I used up the entire box of Kleenex on her desk, and when I was done, I realized that I had been staring off into space and had not once looked at the person I was speaking to. I was in a daze, a victimized, sad daze.

She straightened up, and for what seemed like an eternity, we looked at one another, at the walls, the floor, then back at each other. She was cataloging my stories and my reactions, and coming up with a plan for dealing with me. In short, she was processing me. Finally, it seemed that she was ready; she had made her decision on how best to start me on my path to recovery.

This was her answer: "Okay, Steph, get the hell out of my office, girl."

I was so confused by her tone of voice that I responded, "Excuse me, did I offend you?"

She then said something that I will never forget. "You need to fully understand something about recovery, Steph. It's only your responsibility now."

I must have had such a blank look on my face that she decided I needed a bit more direction. "I have heard what you said, and it was horrific, the things that happened to you. But now I have it all, and you are free to walk out that door, choose to live your life free of your demons, and become strong. In here, you will learn how."

Sometimes you hear things that mark your soul. For me, this was one of those times. One problem we have as human beings is an inability to be accountable for ourselves. There is no way we can go back and make the monsters of our past accountable for what they do to us. They'll face their own judgment day. And make no mistake, they will have that day. But we have to understand that the abuse put upon us was not about the real person we are, the person God intended us to be. We weren't created for the abuses of this world, but if we have endured them and we use that experience to help others, then we have survived.

Hearing slogans like "You gotta give it away to keep it" confused me, until I learned that talking, sharing, and finding common ground with others was what healing was all about. If I kept my story inside and I was quiet about the circumstances that brought me here, then what good was I? Silence for me has never been an option. Breaking silence has been my survival.

I won't say that all of this had to happen to make me who I am, because I don't believe that. But it did happen, and now, standing there in that hallway, I realized that I could either use the time to save my life, or just be pissed off that everyone in this place could not fix me.

It *was* my responsibility.

Stripped Away

WHEN YOU FILL A BUILDING with a bunch of people who are used to loud, late-night parties and a plethora of illusions bouncing around in their heads or flowing through their veins, you think you'd get mass hysteria and chaos. But this building—which I still drive past on I-35— was the opposite of that. The place was quiet, peaceful, and structured, all things that none of us knew existed in the world "out there." Mostly the facility was safe. Safe from the people who enabled us, and safe from the biggest enemy of all: ourselves.

"Wake up, it's time for fooooooood," Clint hollered from the other side of our bedroom door. He had been admitted a few weeks after Susan and me and was the one and only guy in our eating-illness program, which had historically been filled with girls.

"Come on, I'm starving!" Clint shouted. He wouldn't go to the dining room without Susan or me.

Stretching myself awake, I was glad I had learned about the power of coffee in my life. One thing about recovery . . . the programs allow for a huge addiction to coffee, thank the lord. I was happy that coffee drinking didn't count as a "switched addiction," like shopping or sex. If there was ever a time I would have become a smoker, this would have been it, but I somehow escaped that one. I slid into my jeans and put on my flip-flops.

"Okay, we're coming. Hang on, mister!" I got Susan moving, and when she was ready, I opened the door and found myself face-to-face with one of the most gorgeous smiles I'd ever see. The young man it belonged to was tall, dark, and beautiful. His vulnerability when he checked into the treatment facility had struck us immediately. Walking down the hallway, which was sectioned off from the drug and alcohol addicts' floor, we walked arm in arm, like the Three Musketeers, to our morning eggs from a carton, toast, and coffee.

"Hey, who is that?" Susan asked, pointing at the new guy.

"I wish I knew," I said.

Clint let go of us and ran to the food line, leaving Susan and me fixated on the handsome new face. His name was Todd, and when he turned and winked at us, we hurried to catch up with Clint. One of the first lessons in recovery is never to get involved with someone else in the program; it is said to mess up your personal recovery success. I'm sure there are exceptions to that rule. But for me it was very important not to try to find my own identity through some guy again, especially in this place. Sober or drunk, my looking for love before Bobby and after had always turned out very badly.

As the weeks passed, though, I couldn't help dreaming of a love affair with Todd. I wondered if he was the one for me because he was sober, or was it because he was so hot? We exchanged looks and flirted, and the time we spent sitting together outside, while he lit up with all the smokers and I coughed my way into oblivion, drew us closer.

So there I was again. Forming an illusion in my head. Migrating toward the perfect love and the perfect man. But, see, the amazing thing was that I really didn't even need this guy to exist. The illusion that I could create his love for me was stronger than the reality of it. I could have a love affair all on my own, in my own little head. Todd was my friend, and although he did give me a kiss or two when the nurse wasn't looking, we weren't in love. And after another new patient made her way into our little safe world, he migrated toward her. My make-believe love affair ended.

I focused on becoming the valedictorian of my addiction classes. They'd start so early, and it would take our colorful classmates the first half of the class to stop laughing when the doctor teaching claimed he was an "addict-tologist."

I'm Healed!

"STEPH, YOU HAVE A VISITOR," said the nurse, as I got up from a Sunday nap.

Sundays were the only days when they didn't wake us at 6 a.m. to follow a routine that resembled that of a military camp. Still groggy, I asked, "Who?"

"I think it's your mom."

She was sitting on a couch in the huge visiting area, wearing perfectly pressed white jeans, a tucked-in, buttoned-up red shirt, and the sleeveless sweater vest that was her usual fashion choice. She carried a black leather purse in which she kept everything extremely organized. Mom always looked very well put together, while I have always been a messy, tattooed, bohemian gypsy. We had the usual surface conversation, though I tried to add more depth. "Mom," I asked her, "can you tell me about Dad's addictions?"

"Well, dear, he was just someone who could never be honest," was all she said.

Then we talked about the food or how my hair looked thin and my face looked tired. Before leaving that day, she handed me a book that belonged to my father. "Maybe this will help," she said, hugging me good-bye. As she walked away, I could smell her Shalimar perfume.

I looked at the faded cover of my dad's very own *Twelve Steps and Twelve Traditions* book, which he used to carry around while trying to twelve-step himself into recovery. When it came to serious issues, my mom was always good at finding words from her Bible, addiction-fighting pamphlets, or even a line from a movie. All I wanted, though, was a mom who would hold me as I cried over the abuse I had suffered, someone who would say she was sorry I was molested by those awful people. Or simply to believe me. But she never could talk directly about that. I had to make do with a birthday or Christmas gift, like a picture or a piece of jewelry, or words etched on ceramic angel figurines. Words such as "I am proud you are my daughter" or "With God everything is possible." Could it ever be possible that Mom would be proud of me? Proud of what, though? She really didn't know me.

When eight weeks had finally passed and I was ready for the outside world, Paul drove to Parkside to bring me home. He had made a few visits during my stay there, once dropping off my white convertible VW and then later picking it up.

"Why did you bring someone to drive my car back to Oklahoma City? I thought you were leaving it?" I asked on one of his visits, which usually lasted about an hour, tops. Looking out the window, I had seen an unfamiliar woman standing next to my VW and wondered if I'd been replaced. I would finally find out on the ride home that he had sold my car to her.

I packed my things, said good-bye to my friends, the counselors, and even Nurse Ratched, who had warmed to me. Then I walked the long hallway that led to the locked door that separated me from the scary world where people still drank, used drugs, and even ate.

There, standing at the office, arguing about the bill for my treatment, was my husband. This man had always seemed so perfectly in charge of things. Twenty years older, he was stern, made all my decisions, and never once allowed me to be anything but perfect. But today, he looked different. He seemed not only very old but also mean. Less heroic and more like a gross, aging guy living with a young girl he could control. It struck me that I was leaving one locked facility to be a prisoner in another. The problem for Paul, though, was that I had gotten stronger and smarter. Now, at twenty-five, a bit more educated and sober, I was going to be a problem for him.

Nevertheless, for a short while I would find myself giving Paul the benefit of the doubt. Perhaps he had changed while I was gone. I would be happy to see his two younger sons; I had missed them. But even more, I'd missed Miranda, who I would see the next day. That made me ready to bolt from that wonderful, life-saving place. I was going to see my baby girl! Miranda was undergoing play therapy to deal with the separation from me and adjust to Bobby's new family after he remarried. I was willing to do anything to ensure that, number one, our daughter knew she was loved beyond belief, and, number two, that no matter what, I wasn't going anywhere, even if she was afraid that I had because I lived in the facility for eight weeks. Someday I knew she would thank me for it, because eight weeks would seem like nothing compared to forever.

While I played this over in my now-clear mind, I ignored the fact that when Paul finally walked over, he didn't even hug me. Not that he ever did. He just twirled me around for inspection and said, "You look very sexy. At least you didn't lose the look."

As we drove the three hours back into my old life, I felt less and less sure of myself, about Paul, and about life in the world outside. The farther I headed north on I-35 to Oklahoma and away from Texas, the more scared I felt.

Mom had said I could come to see her whenever I wanted. As I began to realize that Paul hadn't changed but I had, I wondered if I might live with her. I decided to try. I put an overnight bag into the old Saab. Thank goodness I'd made Paul put this beat-up car in my name because it would become my home.

Don't Get Too Attached

AS INSTRUCTED BY MY TREATMENT counselor, I changed my playmates and places. This meant that I needed to avoid falling back into restaurant and nightclub work. So I went to retail. Still avoiding the need to ask mom if I could live with her, I sought out other avenues. As luck would have it, a very kind woman I was working with at a boutique said she and her husband had an extra room, and I was welcome to stay there until I figured things out. Bob and Jackie were the coolest old couple I'd ever met. With some friends' help, I moved what little I had into their home.

"Hey, Steph. What's this?" one of my friends asked.

"Uncover it and look," I said.

"Whoa! It's a hamster, cool!" My trio of pals gathered to inspect my new pet. I told them that my counselor told me to get either a plant or a pet to take care of. And if I could keep it alive and healthy, I would be ready for a relationship with another human.

Laughing, one guy looked at me and said, "Good luck with that!" Once all my boxes were unloaded, I took my friends for a cheap lunch at Taco Bell to thank them for their help.

I was happy there for the few months I stayed. I had fun watching Jackie and Bob make Caesar salad nearly every night from scratch while they drank large quantities of white wine. We'd laugh watching their old dog run around with a diaper on because it had trouble controlling its bowel movements. As they turned in early from too much wine, I would just go to my little room, read some of the paperbacks I found at a garage sale, and talk to my hamster that was simply called "Hamster."

Maybe I wasn't getting as attached to my pet as I was supposed to. A few weeks later I came home after work to find poor Hamster on his side. He wasn't just asleep. He was dead! Feeling horrible, the only thing I could think to do was to take him to a vet. Putting him in my car still in his tiny cage, I went to the nearest place and walked in, never expecting that they'd look at me like I'd lost my mind. Apparently a vet's office isn't for the rodent community.

"Excuse me," I said when I realized I was being ignored.

"Can I help you?" the girl at the front desk said.

"My hamster is dead, and I just wanted to see if someone could tell me what I did wrong. Maybe I fed it too much."

She got up, went to the back, and surfaced with a really sweet-looking man who took a look at Hamster, poked his rock-hard belly, and said something in vet language that was suppose to explain to me that the poor thing's insides had exploded. I still looked confused, so he broke it down for me. "Basically he needed to fart and couldn't, so he blew up inside."

With a pouty drop of my head I said to this nice vet, "Can I leave him with you?"

"Sure, we can take care of him." I pushed open the door to leave, and he said, "Are you going to get another one? I can tell you what to do to prevent this happening again."

After the little bell hanging from the door stopped ringing, I said, "Oh, no. But thanks. I am anything but ready to try to care for anything or anyone else but myself right now." On my way back to Bob and Jackie's I felt bad, but I wasn't too depressed. I thought to myself, *Note to self, hamsters blow up if they need to fart and can't!* Plan B was that next time I would try a parakeet. Poor bird!

Franklin Street

MOM HAD MOVED TO OKLAHOMA with a third husband, but after discovering that she had again chosen badly, she divorced him. The weeks and months after that were the first and only time I really saw my mom happy. She worked at a university, attended school full time, and found her way not only into a bachelor's degree but into a master's as well. I had never before seen my mom being the mother I had always wanted as a child, and I wondered how long it would last.

She bought a home on Franklin Street, and surprisingly, she and I started to bond. I loved that place. It was tiny and safe, and I didn't mind having to pay some rent and part of the bills. That made me feel like the home was really mine, too, at least until another male playmate found his way into her life. Then she'd be out of mine. That was inevitable. But until then we'd bake cookies and play in the backyard when I had Miranda.

Miranda and I always had our every-other-weekend visits at her grandma's house on Franklin Street. Life felt good, and I felt clean. We hung up a tire swing, and I found Miranda her first bike at a garage sale. She'd play all day and into the night, catching lightning bugs, and she and her best friend, Kate, would sit on the doorstep of my mom's house talking and sharing confidences, as five-year-old girls do. Safety was never a question.

Meanwhile, the clear thinking I had gained from treatment kept me from letting Paul bother me too much. He wasn't too happy that I'd put myself in treatment after we'd only been married two months to start with, and now that I was living with my mom, he'd surface from time to time and try to talk me into getting my own place, since I didn't want to live with him. I'm sure he thought that if I did, he could regain his power over me. Eventually, he was successful. But for a while I stayed strong.

I was pulling a few shifts at a restaurant in Norman as well as a restaurant in Oklahoma City. I typically worked three different jobs, and I was trying to only have ones that didn't require me to be scantily clad. During this time, I went to my meetings and practiced a sober life.

When I heard about a new place in downtown Oklahoma City that was looking for someone to work lunch shifts only, I went to fill out an application. I thought it would be perfect. I could do day shifts there and save the night shifts for the other two places. But first I had to get hired.

I met Jerry, the manager of the restaurant, Interurban City Express. When Roland, the head bartender, walked through, he said to Jerry as he smiled at me, "Hire her!" Jerry hired me, and the restaurant became my home. My coworkers became my new family. I loved that life. I always have. And I knew that, given time, I would be even happier and healthier. As long as my weekend visits with Miranda never were threatened, I could do anything.

Keeping Paul from bringing me down was the most difficult challenge I had. Since I'd returned from Parkside, I'd prayed that he'd get sober, and then he actually put himself into the same treatment center. Before he left, he showed up at my doorstep and literally fell to his knees and begged me not to leave him if he followed through. He came out sober and very unfamiliar to me. What I couldn't overcome was my inability to speak up and empower myself. At least I still could find the wherewithal not to move back in with him. I was still fighting to overcome the nightmares from my childhood. I had tools, even though I wasn't as healed as I thought. I would become stronger and find my way to the good people in the world. And back to school to finish my degree.

He's So Quiet

MY RESTAURANT DAYS WENT ON, and I discovered that I loved bartending. It was the next best thing to therapy sessions—both for me and for those I listened to. The idea that a drunk man's words are a sober man's thoughts is so true. I have always enjoyed learning about people, and many have chosen to tell me their stories, holding nothing back. Customers told me many intimate details of their lives and wondered what I thought. They trusted me. This was a gift, and I have kept their confidence. People just need to talk, need to be heard. But there are some people who never say anything.

Over time, while I worked at Interurban, I would often see a man—Mark—quietly walk in. This was a man who changed a lot about the definition of life for me. He'd sit down with a lively group of customers whom I waited on every day of the workweek. This group seemed tight. He never missed a chance to sit with his friends after work, drinking his gin and tonic, playing liar's poker and listening to what everyone else had to say. He seemed to have a cloud over his head, but I had no idea why. For the longest time I didn't get to know him; he would sneak away from the crowd as quietly as he entered.

As time passed, I found out he worked on the third floor of the building that the restaurant was in. He always dressed the same—in work slacks and a logo golf shirt. It drove me nuts that he would always button all three buttons on his shirt, and I vowed one day to just walk over to him, undo the top one so he wouldn't look so constricted, and say, "Mark, just take a breath." He was probably the most unapproachable person I had ever met. I had no idea that the wheels were in motion for us to come together. I didn't even think he knew I was capable of anything but making sure his gin and tonic always had lime in it. But he did notice me and when that happened, I was shocked.

One happy hour shift I filled the restaurant's aged popcorn maker with kernels and, as usual, forgot about it. The smell of burned popcorn soon notified everyone that Steph was working. Roland, the head bartender and my friend, always announced on the afternoons I'd clock into the happy hour shift: "Steph's here, the popcorn is gonna get burned!" He, Mel, and Kelly were three of my favorite people at the restaurant. We made work fun.

"Hey, girl, you take the Globe table tonight," Kelly said, as she leaned over to put the lime in a Tanqueray and tonic for Mark. That's what we called this particular group because of their company name.

"Okay, but why?" I asked. "I had them last night. You should have them. Mark is here, and he's the best tipper." The waitstaff knew we all were supposed to share the best-tipping tables. But Kelly was up to something. Plus she knew I was short on my child-support payment to Bobby that month, and I never missed a payment, ever.

Pushing two tables together to make the group more comfortable and setting the white paper napkins in front of them, I took drink orders without their asking, because I already had them memorized. I was getting slammed with customers, which made the shift zoom by, and that was my favorite feeling in the world.

Old Habits

"HEY, STEPH, IF YOU'RE GOING to the Virgin Islands, does that mean you'll be a virgin again?" Corey, the busboy, asked. He was referring to my upcoming trip to the Virgin Islands that I had agreed to go on with a guy I was dating. Rolling my eyes at him, I went to clock in.

I had a few unsuccessful blind dates that friends set me up on, and I started dating a man named Jim. Always smiling, Jim enjoyed life, and he won my heart. We'd spend a lot of time together, and when he talked me into a trip to the Virgin Islands, I dug my passport out of my trunk and then went to Walmart to find a new bikini.

Grabbing a few extra friends to join us, we headed to St. John, the smallest of the US Virgins. Jim had a place there. After landing in St. Thomas to catch the ferry to St. John, I found myself being dragged to a tiny airport bar, the kind that looked like a tiki hut, and offered local beers. When Kris, one of the people with us, suggested I have a beer, I didn't think twice. Days—and a few too many drinks—later, I realized that I'd been only two weeks away from my two-year sobriety birthday. I'd blown it! I'd relapsed.

After a week on St. John, I was offered a job at a local bar. With some fruity drink decorated with an umbrella in front of me, I looked past the bartender, who was handing me paper to write my contact information on, which he claimed would suffice as an application: "We do things simple here on the island." I was staring at the most beautiful scenery. There I was with the opportunity to live on the island, have an easy job, and never have to deal with my jacked-up life at home ever again. But something was missing: Miranda. Without her, no place on Earth, however tropical, would feel good. I boarded my relapsed butt onto a plane and went home.

And soon I was migrating back to my old life. I ditched the restaurant job in Norman and began working a few shifts at a strip club.

After my shift ended at Interurban, I'd sneak off to my other place of work. I convinced myself that I didn't have to drink all the time, even if I needed to get a few more bucks to stuff in my dresser drawer. I didn't really feel that I was regressing since I wasn't drugging anymore. I didn't know if my need to stay unrealistically busy was because I felt pressured to pay off my treatment bill or what. Regardless, I was dancing again, and I wasn't proud of it.

Not too many people knew about my other occupation, but one customer, Gene, did, and he was always very kind to me regardless. He had seen me dance, though I didn't know it. Gene took it upon himself to be the one I talked to while I bartended at my day job. He understood why I needed the extra money and didn't seem to think that what I did was seedy. Once he brought me a yellow rose from his rose garden and sat at the bar while I poured him a white wine. "Yellow is for friendship," he said.

"You know," Gene added in a matter-of-fact tone, "I'm really not the president of the company upstairs." Laughing, he told me how he loved telling everyone he was the president of this insurance company in the building.

"Huh?" I said, putting the cork back into the wine bottle without looking up at him.

"Mark is the president of Globe," he added.

"Oh, Mark, the quiet guy?"

"Yep, the quiet guy who watches every move you make," he said, grinning.

"Yeah, sure he does. I am *so* his kind of gal." We laughed and turned the conversation to the guy on the other side of the bar, the one who wore a full leather suit in the heat of summer and who ordered Dr. Pepper and cognac. Ugh!

Gene had a way of planting seeds that had nothing to do with a rose garden.

Just Say No

ALLOWING PAUL BACK IN WAS a huge mistake. One day at the restaurant, I realized that the idea of having to serve him and his friend nauseated me. Even though he had proven his sobriety to me, I still couldn't stomach the fact that he had such control over me. Subconsciously I believed he owned me.

"You know, Steph, I am tenacious," Paul told me, "and I won't give up until you come home." All the while he was peering at me with those stupid specs. The manipulation was more than I could fight. "The boys miss you," he added. That was always a clincher for me. Bring kids into it, and I'll do anything just so they can feel secure and be happy. I took the bait.

"See, I told you," Paul said, looking over at his friend. "She belongs to me."

I just stood there, frozen. Would I ever not be a piece of property that was either neglected or coveted for the wrong reasons? Would I ever learn that the human body is not a commodity and cannot be owned?

Kelly was behind me, and she put a hand on my shoulder to get me moving. I had a full section, and a table of catty women was complaining that I was ignoring them.

"Steph, you okay?" Kelly asked. She knew me well and was always able to quietly give me the strength to do what I needed to do for myself. I can still see her standing there, with a face worn out from her own very tumultuous life. Kelly—God rest her soul—was always there for me as I went from one side of the proverbial tracks to the other, though I didn't realize it. Sickness took Kelly from us years later; I miss her.

"I have to work, guys. I'll get your check in a minute," I told Paul and his buddy. Heading to the catty table, I dug into the pocket of my apron and took out my pen and pad.

"Can I take your order?" I asked, feeling nearly invisible.

"Finally," said one of the snotty women. Scratching their oh-so-important meal choices on the order pad, I smirked and walked off to call out "Order in!" After the crowd diminished, Paul left, and the women, too, were eventually ready to leave. I was untying my apron at the front of the restaurant by the hostess stand, as the women walked out. One of them paused, turned to me, and said, "Sorry those women I'm with were so rude. I thought I'd speak up and tell you I was sorry." Wow, someone was actually apologizing for treating me like crap for no reason. Interesting.

I smiled at her and said, "Finally."

Sometimes Timing Isn't Everything

⊢————————⊣

ROSE GARDEN GENE. HE WAS walking in for happy hour and I was suddenly recalling our conversation about Mark. It had been stuck in the back of my mind until now. We were getting very busy, and Kelly decided to play matchmaker regardless of the fact that I was now spending time with Paul again. She knew how miserable I was. Punching the necessary information into the credit card machine to run the Globe table's bill, I noticed the quiet man approaching me. He had never said two words to me. Or maybe just two words—"Thank you"—when I gave him their check. But this time he had started to walk out the front door and suddenly turned around and made a beeline toward me. I assumed I had made a mistake on the bill.

"Hi, did I ring the bill up wrong?" I asked him.

"No," he said.

"That's good."

"Um, I was wondering," he said, "if you'd like to have dinner with me sometime?"

He stood there with his hands in his pockets, and suddenly I felt I was looking at a little boy. After watching him force this question out, which looked painfully difficult for him to do, I had to let him down gently, because I wasn't going to be able to accept. I decided to go with the truth.

"Thank you so much, Mark, for asking me, but I am getting remarried to my ex-husband this month." I felt a huge prickly knot in my stomach that traveled to my throat and almost cut off my circulation. It was like God himself had sent Mark to stop me. I wanted to scream that, no, I really wasn't remarrying, but I had no idea what to do or what to say.

"That's fine," he said, and walked off. As he was leaving, all I could get out was, "Mark, have a good night."

I untied my apron and set it by my purse. Kelly came hopping back to the workstation as I was feeding my timecard through the time clock.

"Well?" she said, lighting her cigarette.

"Oh, that . . . well, he asked me out, but I told him I was getting back with Paul, so I couldn't go out with him."

"Steph, are you crazy? That asshole treats you like shit, and Mark is really sweet," she said, shaking her black curls back and forth in disgust.

"He is, isn't he?" I said

"What . . . an asshole?" Kelly said.

"No, Mark, silly. He is sweet, isn't he?"

Before I left, I set the ketchup bottles I had filled on the table for the morning shift to put out and then walked out into the dark to find my old Saab.

As I inched homeward on the congested freeway, I had plenty of time to think. I knew I had to pick up where I'd left off in my self-preserving attempt to find out who I was. But for now, home seemed to be mostly in my car on I-35.

I always had good intentions for myself but no strength to follow through with them. I didn't want to be anywhere near Paul. But I did want to be near Mark.

By May, Paul was claiming it was time for me to become his ninth wife. I didn't comment. Nor did I buy a wedding dress. I just listened to the plans he'd already made. But May passed with no wedding, only an increasingly frustrated Paul. I wonder if marriage, for some, is really about ownership. Sitting with my coffee and thoughts one morning, I asked myself why I chose to marry so many times. Bobby was for love. Thomas was for fear. And Paul? Well, because he pretty much told me to, and then he tried to tell me to again.

I let Paul convince me to quit my job at Interurban City Express. I kept the restaurant job in Oklahoma City that was close to Paul's house and the stripper job he didn't know about. Months later I was ready to start saying no to this man: "No, I won't be your wife again." "No, I hate the scent of Chanel No. 5 and the look of white denim miniskirts." And

"No, I won't have sex with you anymore!" I was gaining my voice in this new personal independence movement. I had also gained a bit of extra weight that I was not happy about. It didn't take long for me to realize that I was pregnant again. My last no had come too late.

I needed my friend, so I drove downtown for a visit. Kelly helped me figure out a plan, and after a lot of talk and practiced speeches with her, I felt ready. I went back to the house, allowed myself some sleep, then come morning I marched into the kitchen, prepared to make a stand. He had convinced me that leaving my job at the restaurant made sense for his family's needs. He'd convinced me in 1988 that "Steph, you need tits." This man had convinced me that without him I would be flat, stupid, and homeless. But I wasn't about to be convinced that I couldn't keep this baby. He'd already made me give one up. I would leave, find my own place, and raise the child and Miranda. The baby and I would be fine. We'd be a team. I didn't need him. Hell, I didn't even want him!

I started the strong chicory coffee that was Paul's favorite, placed his cup in front of the newspaper to interrupt his reading and sat across from him. He looked up and said, "Let's go for a run. How's the weight?"

I was stunned, because for a moment I thought he already knew I was pregnant, but he was only referring to my not being able to get into the ridiculous white denim miniskirt he liked me to wear.

"Uh, fine, I guess. Why?"

I was right; he wanted me to wear the damn skirt when we went out later that day.

"Well, you see, umm, that isn't going to fit," I said, hoping he'd catch on, and I would not have to explain how in some mysterious way I had gotten pregnant even after being so very careful with contraception. But I had to say it: "I'm pregnant again."

Paul got up, took his coffee cup to the sink, and washed it out as if he were scrubbing tar off of it. Then he sat it on the kitchen towel and leaned against the sink.

"Well, we know how to fix that."

Without saying a word, I got up and walked away. My prepared speech had vanished like a puff of smoke and so did my power to make a stand. I was six weeks pregnant, and after a full night and day of not talking about it, I found myself helplessly in his car as if paralyzed. We were on the same road to the same doctor's office, and I let the same thing happen.

There are times when completely giving up seems like the only choice, and for me, it wasn't about pro this or anti that, it was that I was physically unable to speak up, speak out, and say no. If you are raised with the feeling that you don't deserve to exist, then the last thing you have is a voice. Spending my entire life fighting for my own existence didn't give me the strength or know-how to fight. In my head I could play out every possible scenario that made me feel big and powerful, but in the real world I was as weak as my feelings for this man. Choice made. Life ended.

And my life? I felt as if I were the one who had died—again.

Freedom

MANIC DEPRESSION SET IN, AND aside from the time I spent with Miranda, I stayed in bed, ignoring my work schedule. One morning I was awakened by some type of spiritual intervention, and I turned over in the guest room bed, where I'd been sleeping since visiting the clinic, and looked out the window. I lay there thinking back to a conversation that I'd had earlier that week with Jerry, my boss. "Steph," he told me, "you can come back whenever you want. We miss you." Only minutes after I woke up, Paul came into the guest room and demanded that I help him with the plants he'd bought earlier that morning at a nursery. "Get up, you've pouted long enough. I want you to plant the front beds before we go get groceries. I'll do the back."

Moving at his command, I swung my legs over the daybed that I had gotten for Miranda and me to share. I took my mug of coffee and went out to the front yard, where a tiny hand shovel and flats of zinnias were waiting for me. I knelt to start digging. With each jab into the dirt I picked up my angry pace. Forcefully, I jabbed the trowel into the ground over and over until I was murdering the flowerbeds as if they were Paul. I could see the neighbors in their yards enjoying the morning breeze. People were cycling by. Birds were chirping. For a small community on a weekend morning, it was a dream setting, but I was caught in a nightmare. I wasn't sad; I wasn't even angry anymore. I was simply determined.

I went back into the house and ran water over my hands as Paul announced it was time to shop for groceries. Maybe in some settings this sounds normal, but that wasn't what this relationship was. It was about who had the bigger stick, who could bully the other. And just because I was losing most of the battles didn't mean that I had to lose the war.

At the local gourmet market, Paul repeated his usual grocery-store mantra: "You go find the milk and the things on your list. I'll meet you at checkout. Don't forget to pick the cashier with the biggest boobs." I just rolled my eyes and went off in search of the items I needed. When I joined him a few minutes later, he asked if I'd gotten the bag of dry beans he specifically wanted.

"Where's it at?" I asked him.

Looking at me as if I were a toddler, he said in his condescending voice, "Steph, don't dangle your prepositions."

Oh, that's right—with all the reading and vocabulary classes, I knew how to rephrase that. I looked at him and with a steady voice said, "Okay, where is it at, asshole?" I felt as if I had made up for all of the meek moments I had experienced with this man in this single moment. He was pissed, but I was happy!

Later that day, after planting the rest of the flowers, I got up, went into the kitchen where he was standing, and said quietly, "I'm leaving."

"Okay," he said, "while you are out, can you pick up some coffee?"

"Sure," I answered. That was that. It was finally over, and I never wanted to look back. With my few belongings packed, I went to the bathroom, sat on the closed toilet lid, and wrote to my two aborted babies. It was as if I had to have closure with him and the two children I would never know before I could leave.

I didn't know how to start the letter, but "Please forgive me" seemed to work. Here's what I wrote:

Dear Unknown,

I will write to you together, because you were from the same blood.

The state of my world when I conceived you both was unsettled, but when I discovered I was pregnant, both times, I felt that I had hope and the possibility of once again being a mom—your mom. The difference was that the man I was with didn't want to bring another child into the world either time, and I allowed the decision to be made by him. I would like to say, "Don't pass judgment on this man for convincing me that the best thing was not to bring either of you into the world," but I can't.

I judge him, I judge myself. I had no voice either time to speak up and save you. For this I am truly sorry.

I know our society has two very different convictions about what I did, but I also know that because I was forced, I can feel victimized for you and with you. I was a victim, too.

I'm sorry I was weak and unaware that I could tell that doctor I wanted to keep you. This will always have to be between God and me. Did I make the best choice for you?

I will never know.

By asking forgiveness and letting go of my guilt, remorse, and sadness, I can feel you are in a better place. I won't say I made the right choice. With no forward-thinking ability at the time, I just allowed that choice to be made. As for the guilt, remorse, and sadness? I still feel them each and every time I allow myself to.

I can't claim to have the same sense of loss as a parent who lost a child, but my loss is my own, and sometimes I embrace it. I have shed many tears for you both and have numbed my mind numerous times through the years when I'd start to ask myself why I did what I did. I am sorry, too, for the moms-in-waiting who go through so much to conceive and bear children. It breaks my heart to see their struggle, and I beg for forgiveness, mostly from myself.

This is a clear-cut case of not being able to go back and change things. I have to live not only with the consequences but also the reality of my history. I believe I will have to answer for this. But I also know that the love that surrounds me will give me comfort, as I am told I am forgiven and that you are being taken very good care of.

"Until we meet again," was the only thing I knew to end it with.

I cleaned some smeared mascara off my cheeks, walked out of the bathroom, grabbing the squeaky duck Miranda played with in the tub, and left.

For good.

Writing on the Wall—Literally

DURING MY RECOVERY IN TREATMENT I had been told to find home groups—Alcoholics Anonymous and Narcotics Anonymous meetings, as well as an Overeaters Anonymous meeting. There wasn't a big calling for bulimic or anorexic meetings. I found a great place that brought someone else into my life, who would never leave, no matter the time or the distance—Marie. This woman had a philosophical way of looking at life that would give me the courage to keep fighting.

She supplied a place for me to live after leaving Paul once and for all and when I didn't want to stay at my mom's. I had given up that tiny apartment in Norman when I gave up my job at Interurban City Express.

Still trying to stay sober in a kind of hit-or-miss way since I had been back from my trip to the Virgin Islands, I just kept going to the meetings and spending time with Marie. She would help me remember that even in so-called recovery, there is pain. Over massive amounts of coffee, she and I would discuss those philosophical questions in deep conversations that sounded a bit like a Beat poetry reading. We talked about what we thought pieces of art meant and how we hoped and dreamed about what life could really be like. She was always reminding me, "Steph, out of chaos comes opportunity."

Pulling into Marie's driveway one afternoon, I said, "It's like the new me will be able to start here, spending time in this little house."

"Then let's call this house The Beginning," she proclaimed, and so we did. "The beginning of our futures, our new attitudes, and our boundaries." She added, "Now let's go talk to your manager at Hooters. Seriously, Steph. You aren't working there anymore!" My plethora of occupations, from waitress to stripper to hula girl advertising the grand opening of Hooters on Northwest Highway was soon to be no more—well, pretty soon, anyway. Marie and I would sit for hours writing on the walls of her house. Literally. I'd say something, and Marie would say, "Write that on the wall!" Grabbing a pencil, I began noting things that we didn't want to forget. Something I heard from Marie really stuck. She'd seen a great saying one day and shared it with me in writing. "Don't mistake my kindness for weakness."

To this day I have a similar wall in my home. As odd as it might sound, when I am hit with something I want to remember—a saying, thought, or quote, for instance—I write it on the wall. If I didn't, my entire body would be covered in tattoos reminding me of things like "Keep it simple," "First things first," or "Don't be silenced!"

Sitting on the stool in Marie's kitchen, I'd watch her take loaves of French bread from the pantry to make her famous French toast, and we'd discuss how to live honestly in the world. As we learned to be authentic with ourselves and others, she was always encouraging me to be a writer. "You have to tell your story, Steph," she'd say. "It will save someone from making the same mistakes!" I have learned that the writing process also helps me make sense of my life.

We have to have people like Marie in our lives, friends who are forthright and honest not only with us but with themselves, who won't let us be manipulated by our own bullshit.

I have to say that during this time in my life, I had a great deal of clarity even when I made a mistake. Even if I regressed and relapsed, I didn't try to justify what happened by blaming reasons beyond my control. I understood that I had choices and that there were consequences for each of my choices. If I could see the choice and the consequence, I could at least make a conscious decision to do something or not.

I did go back to my job at the restaurant, and I felt happy about it. Fortunately, I was also sober—for a while, anyway.

Seeing Jim for a while helped me to find joy again. Although he was dealing with a cranky, bedridden father and a whacked-out ex-girlfriend who flooded his basement when she found out about me, our time as friends was special.

I sometimes spent weekends with Jim at his lake house, and for a time I did something I hadn't done since I was in rehab: I slept. The drinking didn't seem to consume me, though others in recovery might argue about that. If I wanted red wine with the steak dinner Jim made for me every Sunday night before we watched *Star Trek*, then I'd be a Trekkie, drink wine, eat dessert, and enjoy life. The man had a calming way about him, and he taught me many things, including one very important lesson about mechanical empowerment.

"Hey, Steph, come out here a second," Jim said from the carport at his lake house.

"Okay. Are you alright?" I saw Jim on the ground, looking at the tire of my old Saab.

"Yeah, I'm good," he said, "but it's time I taught you to change a tire, girl. This old thing will give you trouble, and you need to be prepared."

"Oh, okay. What's the first step?"

Jim looked at me with that great smile of his and said, "The first thing you should know is it doesn't take a penis to change a tire!"

We burst out laughing. And I learned how to change a tire. Sweet Jim and his golden retriever, Ginger, spent many days showing me and Miranda a joyful part of life. Then he moved on. And so did I.

In the middle of all these changes, I felt that there was another thing I needed to do: amend what I had done wrong to my brother. He was stationed at an Air Force base in Moreno Valley in California. So without an invitation, I drove west to see him. I'd saved enough gas money, asked for time off work, and prayed that the old Saab with its 250,000 miles would hold up. Without hotel money, I could stop at roadside areas to sleep for free. I also quickly learned that the showers at truck stops weren't that bad either.

When I got to Amarillo, Texas, I detoured to get a closer look at what someone had told me was a landmark piece of art—The Cadillac Ranch. Sitting in a field, looking at all the Cadillac cars face down in a ditch, I was overcome with ambivalence. I suddenly felt afraid to keep going. Carl probably wouldn't want to see me, I decided. I always felt I was such a disappointment to him. After all, it was on one of his birthdays that I'd announced on the phone that I had fallen in love with the German and was getting married. Then, after that eight-week marriage was over, I called him again. This time I convinced him to walk me down the aisle for my marriage to Paul. My brother was always my hero, someone who would gather me up and try to put the pieces of his broken, wounded little sister back together.

But on that day, in the field, I couldn't follow through. I got back in my car and drove through the night, eating peanut M&Ms until my teeth hurt. I headed back to Oklahoma, went to Marie's house, and worked on plan B, C, or possibly Z.

Eventually, Carl and I found our way back to one another, as we always did. I begged for his forgiveness and let him know how wrong I was for allowing Paul to keep me from being with him during a very special time, his marriage. It was easier for me to let Paul overpower me than to fight for my need to buy a plane ticket to the wedding of my only brother. So, I missed it.

Working backwards to amend my wrong doing, I felt blessed when Tony showed up during a lunch shift with a promise that he'd remembered and I'd forgotten. It was our birthday month, and one of my favorite bands would be in Dallas. After the concert, Tony and I found a tattoo parlor with red-carpeted walls and a cool, old barber chair. Biting on the tough piece of beef jerky Tony thought would help, I proceeded to get my first of several tattoos.

"Here, baby, pick this tat. It's a Pegasus. It's a symbol of freedom." After the ink had burned its way into my skin, we went to look for posters by Maxfield Parrish, the artist we both liked.

"I found it, baby." Tony said in the low, sultry voice that always melted me. He loved calling me "baby." "It's your favorite picture."

"She's standing on the cliff," I said of the girl on the poster. "Is she going to jump or not?" I asked Tony.

"Baby, that's up to her."

La Rouge

———————

WAKING UP FROM AN EVENING nap at my mom's house, tired and strung out on coffee, I made my way to the shower to wake up from what little sleep I had between my happy hour shift at the restaurant and my late-night shift dancing. I made a lather out of my favorite Caress soap, rubbed up one leg and down the other, and used my pretty pink disposable razor to finish my three-star spa treatment.

Sobriety doesn't promise self-preservation. It's acquired. I was thinking back to a conversation Kelly and I had after a lunch shift, and I laughed to myself.

"Steph, it's not prostitution!" Kelly told me.

"Sleeping with a guy so I can get new car tires sure felt like it," I said.

Kelly snuffed out her cigarette and patted my hand. "Oh, Steph. It's not selling yourself. It's survival." When she got up and headed toward the kitchen, I said loudly over the noise, "Hey, Kelly!"

"Yeah?" she yelled back.

"They were really good tires!" We just laughed.

I toweled off, took another swig of my life-jolting elixir, and bit into some toast. I have always been a breakfast-anytime girl. It's the one meal that comforts me like no other. I'd tell my friends, "No matter what time of day, if it turns bad, you can always start it over with breakfast."

Wiping the mirror, I noticed that my nail polish was chipping, so I decided to get to work early so I could touch it up in the dressing room.

Mom was out a lot after work with her friends. Even if she made it home before I left, she'd assume I was working a late shift at one of the restaurants or perhaps going out to party with my friends. She never actually asked me what I was doing.

I was grateful for this time when she kept her door open to keep up with my moves. My relationship with her never afforded me the luxury of truth, and, judging from my childhood experience, even if I had cashed in some time for a shallow talk with her, it wouldn't have mattered. My talks with her would make you think she was listening, but it always seemed she was just waiting for her turn to talk. We kept things on the surface. That way she and I could coexist when we needed to.

She would have been disgusted if she knew where some of the money I gave her for expenses came from. I used to think she could tell that there was some evil connected to the twenty-dollar bills. I'd chuckle to myself, knowing that the cash she took came from some lonely old guy willing to pay me to act as if I loved only him for an hour. Money *can* buy you love; it's just not real.

I loaded my bag with items that clearly marked me as a stripper: T-backs first. In the '70s we called them "thongs," not to be confused with the flip-flop thongs for your feet. Five-inch stilettos or, my favorite, the five-inch, white patent-leather boots with the zippers. (Those boots always took me back to a time when Mom got me the coolest go-go boots when I was about eleven, and Dad said, "Steph, you look too old in those. Please don't wear them.")

Since strippers are a kind of contract labor, you have many locations you can drive or fly to in order to work for a night or weekend. You have to sell yourself and be your own agent. Appearance is the only thing that matters, so you'd better work it and work it hard!

Okay, makeup, perfume, and hair spray, check! If I didn't have what I needed, I could find it at the club. That was a perk of this job. Our pit mom always kept one of those dainty drugstore mirrors with the cheap gold trim on the counter. On it were drugstore perfumes and makeup, as well as packs of gum that we'd chew not only to erase the taste of cigarette smoke but also to curb our hunger, so we could get through a shift without eating.

Finding myself again on I-35, with my music blaring, I morphed into character. I left Stephanie behind and became the exotic dancer who could shut the entire world out until about 4 a.m. Sober or not, this desperate attempt to make more cash also provided an escape from reality. And I really needed the money.

Working the restaurant job during the day was fine, but it didn't quite pay enough. The numbers were ticking higher on my car's odometer and there were more and more needed repairs. Plus, I still had a treatment bill that had no refund policy on it, even if I had slipped out of sobriety.

Turning toward my exit, I couldn't shake the thought of quiet Mark from my mind. *Why had he asked me to dinner?* I still saw him at the restaurant. Maybe after I slammed back a glass of wine and hit the stage I would feel better. I was a master at numbing my feelings—or so I thought. I'd let my alter ego—the one without self-assurance—start to work.

"I just can't let go of this insanity, not yet," I told myself. "You are only making money, and it's fine." Even though my share of mom's rent and bills was generously small, I still had to buy gas, and, most importantly, make the child support payment that I was determined to never send late.

I also had to buy books and pay tuition for college courses that I had signed up for, because I really wanted to pull together some type of degree. I enrolled in a French class, and my professor, a sweet woman, let me bring Miranda to my Saturday make-up classes. Miranda would sit with her coloring books while I tried my way around a language I probably was never going to use—not even at a place called La Rouge.

I pulled into the gravel lot and parked in the back. La Rouge's neon sign was flickering and probably would do so until 4 a.m. The owner's entrepreneurial experience undoubtedly taught him how lucrative the combination of lonely men and desperate girls could be. If you had enough money to buy red carpet and black paint, you could get a few mirrors, fix a place up, and call it anything you wanted, as long is it was either red this or red that. Or even, as one place called itself, The Red Dog.

Behind this red façade—another French word I had learned—was the dressing room. Where the real talks happened.

Jesus Was a Hippie

"HEY, STEPH, HOW'S IT GOING?" the large guy at the back door asked.

"Good, Jimmy. How are you?"

"Better, now that you girls are here. The day shift girls are always so rude."

"I bet they are, Jimmy, but they probably hate getting up early to be here."

"Well, good luck, and have a good night. Don't forget to tip those who send the clients your way," he said, as he winked at our secret contract.

Pushing the door open for me, Jimmy rubbed the top of my head like a protective big brother. "Steph, you should have worn more than those cutoff shorts and T-shirt. It might be cold after your shift."

"Maybe I'll be a hell of a lot richer when I leave, and I'll get that rabbit fur coat from Sears I saw the other day. It sheds, but it looks so cool!" I said.

Jimmy just laughed.

The other girls were pouring into the back pit room, and one dark-haired girl sat next to me on a wobbly stool as I carefully began my black eyeliner ritual. With a match in my hand, I melted the eyeliner and ran its gooey substance across each lid in a thick line that was sure to stay put as it dried.

"Hey, you got an extra T-back tonight?" the other girl asked.

"Sure, in my bag there." I pointed to the ground, which was sticky with hair spray and leftover vanilla body spray that we'd all used to cover ourselves. It was like a protective coating applied each night, as if we thought it would keep the hands of clients off of us.

"Can I use this pink one?" she asked. "It's really pretty."

"Sure." I didn't feel like talking too much that night, which was unusual for me, but I had so many things on my mind, and I was always worried that someone who knew me might come in. I tried hard to keep my worlds separate. I had a daytime job, a nighttime job, and a mommy job, along with a part-time, try-to-go-to-college-and-finish-my-education job. I did an amazing job of hiding each one from every-one, it seemed. Mostly, this night I couldn't keep my mind off that quiet man who had wanted to take me to dinner. He'd never want to if he knew what I really did.

"Steph," the dark-haired girl said, as she slid my pink slingshot of a panty up her long legs.

"Yeah, what's up?"

"Do you think we'll go to hell for this?"

Right away I noticed the pit mom looking up at us. She was prob-ably younger than she actually appeared and always had her head in some tabloid magazine while an unfiltered Salem cigarette hung from the corner of her mouth. The only time I saw it come out of her mouth was when she flicked the lipstick-ringed thing into a full ashtray. Until this night, when she set it on the edge of the tray, looked at the girl and me, and proceeded to talk in her raspy voice of reason.

"Girls," she said to us, "Jesus was a hippie and one of the most ridi-culed people in history! Listen to me for a minute." I held the Baby Soft perfume I'd picked up from the mirrored tray and paid attention.

"A week before Jesus was crucified, with all the judgment and mock-ery and so on, he still held his head high, knowing exactly what was about to happen. But he held onto his beliefs anyway. Knowing that he'd be redeemed and all."

All of us sitting within earshot stopped moving, mostly because our pit mom never talked. She sometimes warned one of the girls if she saw them popping or smoking drugs. The only times I saw her leave that chair was if a girl showed up drunk or some wayward customer found his way back to our safe zone, and she told him to get the hell out.

This was very odd, and I couldn't stop listening.

"He was mocked and laughed at, abused, and finally crucified, and all he could do was ask God to forgive those who did all of these brutal things to him." She stopped to lift her cigarette from the ashtray, flicked it, took a drag, and shook her head.

"Hey," she said, looking in my direction. I was sure I was about to be yelled at. "Everything's temporary here. You know that, right?"

I nodded, sprayed my Baby Soft fragrance, and finished with my lip liner. The dark-haired dancer took my hair and pulled it into a tiny ponytail.

"Your face is pretty, so leave it back," she said. "And thanks for the uniform." She laughed.

It would be years before I'd remember this conversation, but that night those words added to my ever-changing moral code. When I leaned down to strap my stilettos on, I realized I'd forgotten to repaint my chipped nails. What the hell, I thought. That is the last thing these lonely customers look at. Standing up, I caught a glimpse of my "uniformed" body in the mirror and said, "Steph, this is only temporary."

My song was starting, and it was time to slide and stretch around the pole, slither on the ground, and smile at those in need of affection.

It was time for work.

My brown-eyed girl, Mary

Mommy's got you, John

Cloud Nine Hopping

AFTER MY RETURN TO INTERURBAN City Express, I worked fewer and fewer nightclub shifts. Something inside me was causing me to make changes, in spite of my inability to take care of myself, sober or not. Some force was pushing me in a different direction.

On a hot August day I ran from my parked car to the restaurant to work the lunch shift and, barely making it in time to serve the already seated crowd, I took the last section.

"Hey, Steph, come wait on us," said Ron, a friend of Mark's. "When did you start working here again?"

I stopped at their table and saw him—Mark. He, of course, said nothing.

"I came back weeks ago. Good to see you all."

Ron went on, without Mark's blessing, I bet. "Steph, come with Mark to a party at my house this weekend."

I could see Kelly peering at me as if she were awaiting my answer, and I wondered if Mark even wanted me to go with him, but I didn't hesitate. "Okay, sounds good."

I was nervous he'd hate me or find out I wasn't really his type. But as this quiet man spent time with me, I discovered he was different from what I typically saw in men. I was taken with his quiet demeanor, and I came to realize his extreme quiet was a mask for someone who was very guarded. While in deep thought he'd smooth his goatee in a serious, reflective state of mind. I was beginning to figure out that this was his way to start conversations. With his dark brown eyes looking down, he'd try to say what was on his mind. Talking always seemed so painful for him and I never understood why.

After all I had been through and put others through, I had submitted to the idea that I absolutely did not know what love was. But honestly, I can tell you that I do know what it is. I have seen it in others. I have felt it in myself. Age not only gives us wisdom but also removes the rose-colored glasses, so we see things for what they really are. And love can have many definitions.

Mark had recently ended a twenty-year marriage, and I felt like he needed a life force, a friend. We spent day after day together, and we were rarely apart. My whole world was rapidly changing as I migrated toward what I thought would be a perfect life with him.

Fall was changing leaves, and life was changing me. Although I felt out of place, regardless of the refined, proper training Paul had forced on me, I went to see Mark at his elegant home anyway. Unaccustomed to having someone greet me at a guarded gatehouse, I just sat in my car waiting for instruction. The guard looked at me and until he motioned to roll my window down, I just looked back at him. "Who are you here to visit?" he asked. "Mark McAndrew," I told him. Walking into the tiny Hansel and Gretel-looking house, he wrote something down, picked up a phone, and then came back out as if I were his long lost friend. "Stephanie, go right in and have a good evening." "Thanks," was all I got out.

The homes towered so high, and the cars, so many in each driveway, were shiny and new. I'd been around refined people with Paul, but it was still different, and not flashy, really. Once I found Mark's home and went inside, I was greeted by his son Ben, who was even quieter and less unapproachable than Mark. Ben said, "Nice to meet you," and I've wondered ever since then: Was it really? Was he glad to have met me? Or was I a confirmation of his parents' relationship truly being over? As Mark and I made our way outside to have wine and time together, I felt overwhelmed with coming clean about my life. At least a portion of it at a time.

Finding out that Mark was in fact Catholic in upbringing, my grandma felt the need to set me straight on a few things. "Stephanie, now those Catholics don't divorce, so he is still married to that woman. They drink honey and a lot of red wine." And I thought being raised Baptist was tough! "They don't believe in birth control, and don't tell him about your abortion." I hadn't had the heart to share with my grandmother that I'd had two.

Mark was different, and I wanted to trust him. I began to half-assedly explain. "Mark, I have to tell you something," I said when we were sharing our life stories one night. "You will probably think I am an awful person, but I have to be honest. I had two abortions." I sat there waiting for him to tell me I was a horrible person, and for the first time in this new relationship, I was glad he didn't say anything. He simply smiled and we never talked about it again.

I was about to spill the tale of my entire history, come clean of all the mistakes I had made, all the things I had suffered. But I decided not to. I needed to learn when *not* to talk.

It would be nearly fifteen years before Mark realized that what I told him that night had happened only six weeks before we'd started dating. It was then, in the home we'd been in for fifteen years, that he understood how recent my scars—physical and psychological—really were.

Although some pain of Mark's divorce still lingered in their family, I thought—believed—that I could love it all away. For all of them.

Perhaps neither of us were well equipped to handle all that was happening. When a person who needs to be fixed finds another person with the same need, it's either a match made in heaven or a disaster waiting to cause a lot of hell. The thing is, neither of us knew which one was which. As I migrated toward Mark and his giant Catholic family and their gatherings, I finally felt at home. I made the effort to let my future overshadow my past with the hopes that my history would somehow simply vanish.

Mark found us an apartment close, so that when it was my visitation time, we'd have somewhere to go. Integrating Miranda into life with Mark and his kids would be difficult. Miranda and I feared being separated. When she visited, we slept in the same room, cuddling, as if to reaffirm that no one would ever fully take us apart.

I was beginning to see that God was guiding Miranda and me into a healthier environment and that the nightmares we'd both lived were disappearing. Life was becoming as normal as possible for all six of us. At least that was our goal.

Every little girl dreams that Prince Charming will show up on his white horse and save her from distress. My Prince Charming arrived, but he came in a white limo instead of on a horse. My friends of the neighborhood looked out their windows, watching this huge car try to turn around on a skinny street. Mark always had flair when he was showing his affection toward me.

In fact, Mark showed me such kindness, love, and generosity that I felt like I was living a Cinderella scenario—the portion of the story when she finds true love. No, there was no glass slipper, just soft penguin slippers that I got on Christmas morning. But this man was exactly what I needed, and even if I didn't know it, he needed me too. Our love was like eating an ice cream cone before it melted. It looked wonderful, but we felt we had to hurry or it would get messy.

When I dated Mark, my life became a tale of rags to riches, though I had to constantly defend myself against idiots who thought I had set out to replace my rags with the riches Mark had to offer. Of course I enjoyed the trips, expensive restaurants, and gifts that were his style, but it was our nights at the bowling alley and his drinking tequila shots with me and singing "YMCA" with my girlfriends that caught my heart. Mark and I had fun, he'd listen to me talk for hours, and, yes, I found out that he did know how to laugh. He would constantly say about me, "You can dress her up but you can't take her out." I still laugh about that one, and he still says it. I'm just happy that he took me out anyway.

While we were cloud nine hopping, we ignored the voices that were telling us to slow down and assess our situation. Christmas with Mark and his kids was like nothing I had ever seen, not since my Dad died. There was a tree, gifts, and the excitement of new possibilities, and their house was decorated as if they were trying to beat Clark Griswold's yard lighting in *Christmas Vacation*.

Life just seemed so, what's the word—normal.

On Christmas Eve, 1993, I had my first taste of Dom Perignon. As we shared the champagne, Mark and I watched the tree as if it would start dancing. Then surprisingly—yes, really, surprisingly—he was down on one knee, holding my hand and opening a giant card with a penguin on the front and the words "Will you marry me?" inside. He then opened a red box, and when I saw the huge diamond ring, all I could say was, "Is that thing real?"

He remained kneeling, waiting.

Finally I said yes. I had a few loose ends to tie up, and then I could just sweep my past under the rug in hopes that Mark wouldn't trip over it like Bobby had.

But then I got scared. Sometimes I think that even though I felt honored that Mark wanted me to be his wife, I still didn't feel worthy of it. I went into hiding for a few more nights, a few more strip club shifts, unable to tell him about my other jobs. I wanted to be free of my treatment bill, have enough child support to pay in case I didn't work much after we were married. Not that I had assets to bring to the table, but at the very least, I didn't want to add to his debt just by marrying him.

When I had his car one day, I accidentally came across a letter he'd written to his ex-wife. His sadness and love were poured onto the pages, and by the time I finished it, I was worried he really wasn't over her and that I was, in fact, the dreaded rebound girl. I talked it over with Marie at The Beginning and spent a few weeks coming up with all kinds of excuses. Pulling away from him and forgetting the whole thing seemed to be the best idea, but after I finally talked with Mark about it, things changed. I felt less afraid. I wasn't about to let fear or a feeling of unworthiness win and make me lose. After all, how can you not have sadness and love for someone you spent twenty years with? This was his history and it was now part of mine.

On my last night at La Rouge, I was loading my stuff into the car when I looked up at the January moon. I felt happy. I felt life finally working out for me. I also felt something else.

Planned Parenthood

"GET THAT DAMN PICKET SIGN out of my face!" I growled as I tried to get to the front door of the clinic. I was cold with terror as I walked to the front desk and asked to see someone for a pregnancy test. Calming myself, I realized something. Six months earlier I had a decision made for me for the second time; this time I was going to make my own decision. There was never any question. I was keeping my baby!

"Here, sweetheart," said the nicest lady. "Fill this out, and I will be with you shortly. It's going to be okay."

Trying to relax, I sat next to a much older woman with three small children running around and wondered if she was there for a pregnancy test or—I hoped—birth control pills. I smiled at the kids and started my paperwork.

Leaving the clinic, I stopped at a pay phone and called Mark's oldest daughter. Emily had just found out that she was pregnant, and I knew that even if we weren't close, she was the one to confide in.

Pulling my car into the lot of a gas station, I jiggled the rickety ignition key to get it out, and the car teetered to a stop. I shrugged off any insecurity that the Saab wouldn't start again. That uneasiness was minor compared to the insecurity I was about to have.

Lifting the sticky receiver and wishing I had one of those cool new cell phones that everyone had, I dropped a quarter into the metal box. My heart missed a beat as I heard Emily say, "Hello."

"Uh, Emily, it's Steph ... Stephanie." Like she didn't know who Steph was—the girl who had somehow jumped into her dad's life, either saving or destroying him. Emily was still unsure, I knew.

"I went to Planned Parenthood today and well ... you know?" Emily was silent, like her dad. I used to think it was always because she didn't like me, but I learned that the processing of words, thoughts, and feelings was something she didn't take lightly. She took her time to answer, also, just like her father.

"When will you tell Dad?" she asked.

"Oh, should I? I don't know," I said. "I am only six weeks along. Maybe I should wait." It was more of a question than a statement.

"He'll want to know, so I would say soon. Where are you?" she asked.

Standing there with the stench of old cigarettes and God knows what on the black receiver, I started crying, and I wanted to hide my sobs from Emily. She had always seemed so emotionally strong, and me, well, I'd cry if the drive-through girl screwed up my order, thinking she did it on purpose.

I couldn't believe that God would give a person like me a miracle like this, something I still didn't believe I deserved. "I'm in Edmond," I said, "but I have to get to my shift downtown at the restaurant. I'll see your dad tonight when he takes me to dinner." That was the extent of our conversation. I never knew what Emily did after we hung up, or what she thought.

Luck was on my side: The Saab started right away, but for a minute I just sat staring at my engagement ring. I turned it over in the crease of my hand to hide the huge diamond while I waited tables, for fear of not making tips because of it. Meanwhile, my mind was going through all the things Mark had done for me and imagining dinner later that night. When I told him the news, Mark would either react as I feared and call off the wedding, or he'd wait until the time was right and be the next one on my list who tried to deny me my baby. Our baby.

My rage was rising as I worked up a conversation in my head. I was not going to lose my baby! Not again! No, there was no God in Heaven who would allow it to happen one more time. No devil on Earth that I would not battle to prevent it! Breathing heavily, I put my hand on my belly—which wouldn't show my baby for quite a while—and vowed out loud, "You will be safe and always with me, I promise!"

After I parked and stuck the rolled-up three dollars into the slot of the metal collection box, I grabbed my black apron and bag and, as always, added more eyeliner. I was standing ten feet tall and proud of the decision I had made: No matter what, I would have this beautiful baby, and Miranda and I would love it, even if Mark did not want me anymore.

Walking into the restaurant, I went through my mental pros-and-cons list about the man who was supposed to be my husband within five months, and I said a prayer that he'd be happy about this new development.

"Hey, Steph," Kelly yelled from behind the line—restaurant lingo for the spot where food is picked up.

"Hey!" I yelled back.

"So how's the soon-to-be Mrs. McAndrew?"

Oh god, I hadn't even heard it said before. "Oh, uh . . . good. Yeah, good, and you?"

Quickly Kelly came out from the kitchen side of the line and said, "What's up? Come on, spill it."

Kelly always knew when my heart was full and my spirit was frightened. So I did, in fact, spill the news, and we talked while I tied my apron on, turned the headlight-size diamond around, and reapplied the eyeliner. She made me feel better as she reassured me—with no doubt whatsoever—that this man, Mark, was different. He was kind and good and real—the real deal. And I could finally stop hiding behind my perpetual black eye liner.

Please Don't Take My Baby—Again

AS I WORKED THROUGH MY shift, I tried to focus on the conversation I would have with Mark, rather than the aroma of the hamburger and fries on my customer's plate, which I wanted to wolf down. By the time I finished and clocked out, it was nearly 7 p.m. There was no time to drive back to my apartment, so I used the bathroom in the basement of the building to change into my skirt, top, and boots. For some reason, boots always give me a sense of security and confidence. I have always loved my boots!

I pulled into the underground parking lot of Junior's Restaurant, and Mark was just getting out of his car. He stepped on his cigarette butt, popped a mint into his mouth, and kissed me. I could tell he was processing feelings and thoughts like his oldest daughter. He seemed glad to see me. I prayed that would be the case after he found out that at forty, with three grown children, a new stepdaughter, a grandchild on the way, and a soon-to-be new wife, he'd also be a new dad again.

He held my hand and opened the door to Junior's, a jewel of a place where we celebrated just about every life event imaginable. As you entered, your eyes had to adjust to the darkness while you got a greeting from the proprietor.

"Mark, hello! And you brought your lovely bride-to-be. Good," said the elderly woman with a grand smile that set me at ease. My grandmother used to tell me, "Stephanie, be a good old woman. That is what God will see." I thought of this each time the woman welcomed us. The food at Junior's was equally enjoyable, whether just the two of us were dining or whether we were with a large table of family and friends. The restaurant served heaps of great fried chicken, biscuits, and the best wine ever, but it was the people I remember—beautiful waitresses in red leather miniskirts and red heels who shared their life stories (and my love for red shoes).

Before dinner, Mark and I drifted into the bar. I'd decided to wait until Mark had a few gin and tonics before dropping the information about his new child. But then the fear crept back in, and I began to lose my composure. I jumped up and bolted to the bathroom. At least I could cry without anyone noticing.

Out in the hallway, I looked up and there she was—the grandmotherly owner with her arms open wide for me to walk into. And I did. Without even hearing my news, she lifted my chin and said, "Honey, just tell him. Mark is a good man." How is it some women just know? There's some female radar that goes off to help our fellow sisters, I suppose.

After a few more minutes in the bathroom, my nerves calmed down. I knew Mark was not the monster I had once lived with. He was *not* that guy. He was different.

And he was waiting for me outside the ladies' room.

"Your steak is ready," Mark said, "and you haven't even made your snowman with the butter balls." That was just something silly I always did when we ate there: stacking the perfectly round, ice-cold butter balls into a snowman.

"Are you okay, Steph?" he asked.

I smiled, knowing that I would be okay, and that he—that we all—ultimately would be too. I sat down, placed the napkin in my lap, took a deep breath, and said, "Mark, instead of the that stair climber we were going to buy for my birthday, can we buy a baby bed?"

He put his warm hand on top of mine, and when the waitress came over to check on us, he said, "Well, it looks like Steph is eating for two. Better bring more bread."

Aloha

"MOM WANTS US OVER FOR lunch. It's my sister Theresa's birthday," Mark said without expression. I had no idea if I was in trouble or if this was just his morning-before-a-cigarette personality. Later that day, when we pulled into the drive, his mother, Ladene, met us at the front door, and I thought how beautiful she was. She pulled me in for the tightest hug I had ever had, a gesture that was uncharacteristic for her—with me anyway. I wouldn't know until later what her hugs meant. She was facing her own health issues but never let anyone know.

Ladene was a strong-willed soul who was the foundation of this family of seven kids. Her middle son was soon to be my husband. I'd hear stories of the tough woman and her control over the family. I respected her for that.

"Stephanie, you need to eat more," Ladene told me. "Feed that baby." That clued me in that Mark had told his parents our news. Of course, by the time I made it to the cramped kitchen after all the kids and their kids had filed through the food line, there wasn't a whole lot left. However, I could depend on a piece of Boston cream pie, Theresa's favorite dessert.

When Jack, Mark's dad, took me out to see the strawberry patch Ladene had planted in their backyard, he said something I had longed for since I was twelve years old: "Steph, you are one of my daughters now, and we love you." At last I had a dad again.

Before we left that day, Ladene pulled me into her tiny sewing room to make my already purchased wedding dress fit over my growing belly. By the time the wedding would happen, I'd be five months pregnant. We had planned to have a double wedding with Mark's oldest daughter, Emily, in Hawaii, where we'd fly forty-plus family members out for the huge event. It would become a custom at all family gatherings that everyone would be there—even Mark's ex-wife. The dynamics of our family were set. Perhaps it was odd, but we all knew how to make it work.

When we arrived in Hawaii, we didn't see Mark's mom until she surfaced for the ceremony. Rumor had it that she was sick, but I had no idea how sick. I will be forever grateful that despite her physical limitations, she was there for Mark. I am humbled by such a committed mother. She was there in her sickness and in health.

The Big Island looked different than it had in the brochure. I gazed at the ocean, confused by the fact that the beach was black and the sand was difficult to run my fingers through. Things aren't always what they seem, I realized; certainly they aren't what we think they will be, either. I always had pictures in my mind of what things ought to be like, but they were generally very different from reality. Listening to a TED talk once, I heard the line, "Expectation is disappointment in training."

I had just finished spraying an unusually large amount of hair spray on my baby-fine hair, thanks to the suggestion of one of my soon-to-be sisters-in-law, but it was clear that if I did not get away from the all the women who were getting ready in the ladies' locker room, I would implode.

I was having a huge panic attack, especially after one of the sisters mistakenly called me the name of Mark's first wife. I ran as I waved my hand at my brother's wife, who knew exactly what I was feeling—that I needed to get outside.

"You go, Sister," she said. "Get some air."

I was almost running when I found a vacant spot outdoors, and I sat down. Spreading my flowing gown on the rock seat overlooking the ocean, I took a deep breath while holding my moving belly and muttered a prayer: "Please, God. I don't want to hurt anymore. He has to be the one. I know he is the one. Oh, God, please let him be the one."

I removed my white satin shoes, which now had water stains from the mist that was also pasting my new hairdo to my head. When I looked up, I noticed a woman walking toward me who I hadn't seen for several days—Mark's mom.

Our families had mixed and matched all week, getting to know each other before the big day, but this lady had made herself scarce, and I had no idea why.

"Well, I thought I had fixed the dress to make you more comfortable," she said. "That baby takes up a lot of room in there, and we still have four months to go. But I'm afraid we can't fix that look in your eyes."

"Oh, I'm sorry," I said. "I'll fix my hair and get my act together. Promise."

"You know, Stephanie," she went on, "sometimes when we are the most afraid, it becomes clear that we need to really listen with our hearts. Have you?"

"I have," I said, "and I know that everything is happening the way it ought to be happening, but I am scared to death today."

"Good, honey. Being afraid means you are alive and have passion. You will be a stronger person because of it."

She hugged me, straightened her own dress, and forced herself weakly to her feet. Then she turned and said, "I'm sorry that one of Mark's sisters made that stupid remark about how your hair reminded her of his first wife's. Sometimes people speak before thinking, don't they?"

She left, and I cried. The next time I saw her was when the photographer was taking wedding pictures. She stood next to her son, my husband. God has many ways to grace us, and I felt it on our wedding day, Mark's birthday, in 1994.

As our baby girl grew inside of me, I'd spend a lot of time with Mark's mother. We'd read books about crossing over into what we referred to as "the other side," because neither of was comfortable with the word "death." Unable to say good-bye to my restaurant family, I was still waiting tables, struggling each day to tie my apron under my huge belly and knocking drinks off my tray while trying to serve guests. My Interurban City Express family was the one I finally left all the other jobs to be with. I belonged. Very soon I would say good-bye because we were moving to Texas. But at the time, I wanted to be at the hospital where Ladene was undergoing bouts of chemo.

I'd sit in a chair while Ladene dozed. Every once in a while, she'd reach over and put her hand on my belly. Sometimes the beginning of something is the end of something else. Eight months later Ladene was gone.

There is a theory—a belief or a feeling, perhaps—that when death is taking someone from us, that person's life force enters another who is coming. As Ladene left us, she promised she'd always be with our baby, and I know beyond any human comprehension that she is, in fact, every day.

Mark's daughter Betsy was driving around with me one day doing errands when she asked, "Steph, have you and Dad thought of a name to go with Grandma's name?" We had decided to use Kathryn as our baby girl's middle name.

"No, I keep getting confused," I said.

Betsy smiled and looked over at me and said just one word: "Mary." And Mary Kathryn was named.

Visiting Angels

AS WE WERE WATCHING THE cycle of life—with Ladene leaving this earth and Mary arriving—we'd see hummingbirds everywhere, it seemed. They circled all of us, but mostly they circled Mark.

Finally, October brought Mary to us, three months after Jeremy, Emily's firstborn son, arrived to make Mark a grandpa for the first time.

Four months later, we waited for Mark's mother to make her way into God's arms. We were staying in a hotel in Oklahoma City because Mark and I had recently moved to Texas. Mary was getting tired, and I decided to take her back and put her to bed. I tried to wait up for my husband to return from his mother's side, but I quickly fell asleep. I woke to a freezing cold room and hurried to cover Mary and close a vent. But there was no vent. And Mary was babbling, cooing, and carrying on as though she was laughing with someone. I checked the time, and when Mark came back, I told him about that strange moment and what time it happened. Mark had tears streaming down his tired face.

"Mark, I am so sorry, honey," I said.

"No, that's not it," he answered. "It's about what you just told me, Steph." He got up, walked to Mary's crib, and rubbed her head.

"That was the exact time my mother died," he said.

I was sure life in Texas would only get better. It did, even with all the hurdles of mixing families and personalities. It was a new beginning for us all.

After we moved, we saw the horrific calamity of the Oklahoma City bombing on the news. That day the world we were part of was shattered. I will forever bow my head and say a prayer for the victims' families but never think for a minute I can feel the pain they still feel every day. We watched the television as downtown OKC, which was so dear to us, was demolished. I saw the face of a man I had served lunch to daily on the screen; he was a victim of this bombing. I was grateful that Mark's schedule had changed and that he hadn't been there at the time.

Much later, when we walked around the memorial, my heart began to open to the idea of helping children, helping everyone.

Mark and I settled into another gated community that I just had to get used to. I was sure I would finally find the one true friend I'd longed for since high school, the kind of tell-all girlfriend who would bond with me for life. We joined a country club, although my only golf experience had been bumping my golf cart into Donald Trump in Aspen, Colorado, years ago. And as for tennis? Well, I love the skirts, but I've never played.

We had barely unpacked when Julie, the lady across the street, invited me to a luncheon.

"Just be yourself," she said, "and wear what you normally wear. Be comfortable, you know, country club casual."

That was the year I discovered Teva sandals, and I was happy that my once-pregnant, 190-pound body had returned to a size zero because of the new diet pills on the market. Thanks to these and my old habits, I could fit into my favorite cutoff jean shorts. I donned my comfy and casual lunch attire and ran across the street to hang with the girls. I was excited. Because I had had some great friends back home, I was convinced that my soon-to-be girlfriends would be equally easygoing and real. It's what I hoped for, anyway.

Well, the word "luncheon" should have registered in my head when Julie invited me. I should have known that I needed at least to ask around about how to dress and act for a "Texas luncheon."

Mark would always caution me, "There's a time and place, Steph." Slowly I was learning how to dress and act appropriately. Years later, Mark was reminded by Bernard, a colleague of his who knew me, "Whatever is in the back of Stephanie's head comes out the front of her mouth." I know Mark embraced that aspect of me, but I did attempt to learn how other people behaved. I'm very trainable. Once I walked through the door of this neighbor's house, I realized that my training was starting right then and there.

At least I'd put the tear-apart-and-bake cookies on a nice tray we'd received as a wedding gift, so I wasn't a total loser. I stood in the entryway with hopes too high and shorts too short. The neighbor was very nice and looked at me sympathetically. She smiled and coaxed me inside, where I glimpsed about twenty women wearing Chanel and dripping with jewelry. One small point of solace: I could keep up in the jewelry department, thanks to the eye my husband had for size and clarity and his generosity in placing a three-plus carat princess-cut on my finger when he proposed. Oh, turns out it *was* real.

But at that moment I felt so out of place. I would never fit in with these Texas women, I thought, let alone with anyone outside of a waitstaff break room or the pit room at a strip club—two places with real and loving people. Only a few lifelong friendships had happened for me in those environments, because I wasn't ready for them. I lived in a haze back then; I just needed better air to breathe.

I walked into the room where all the women were sitting and stopped to put my tray on the counter. A uniformed member of the waitstaff that was catering the luncheon took it. Standing in the kitchen entrance with one foot in my past and one in my future, I wasn't sure which way to go.

Then a sweet lady approached me, and I smiled and said, "Hi, how are you?"

"Oh, are you Julie's daughter's friend?"

I laughed. "No, but thank you." I was flattered that she thought I was that young.

"Oh, I'm sorry." she said. "You just don't have your uniform on yet."

I froze. I *was* standing on the inside of the kitchen with the staff, out of habit, I'm sure. But her words emphasized just how out of place I felt. I didn't say a word or grab my silver platter. I simply walked out.

Feeling a bit unsure of myself and lower than just about anything—including the neighbor's Yorkie dog, which I couldn't keep from crapping in my newly planted flower garden—I dried my eyes and did what every respectable woman would do. I went shopping.

From that day forward, I decided to find a way to fit in with that crowd and to do it bigger and better than any of these women could dream of. Now don't get me wrong. I've never been and will never be a snob, but my will to survive kicked in, and this time it was about saving my dignity. My dignity would max out a few of the credit cards my husband so lovingly provided and cause him not to see retirement for quite a few years.

The Universe
Is Unfolding as It Should

DURING THE TIME WE LIVED in Plano, Texas, my stepdaughter Betsy and her brother, Ben, lived with us in between the times when they went off for self-discovery. I often wondered what I did that made them feel it was time to leave. Probably the attack of my Post-it notes all over the house: "Shut the cabinet" or "No smoking in the house!" I could never discover a way to be Betsy's friend, and although she had her own mom, for some reason I kept trying to fill that role too. I felt that my stepdaughter needed me. I related to the things she was going through, and I thought we'd be close. There were days when we'd put Mary in her car seat and just drive around and talk about life.

It's difficult to talk about this portion of my story because it has no closure; maybe it isn't supposed to. I miss her. Our push-pull relationship just couldn't get a running start, it seemed.

The day we ventured to the army surplus store in east Plano, I found a plaque that was hidden in a junk pile. The words on it have stayed with me, and the plaque hangs in my home today. I see it, think of Betsy, and pray she is safe, empowered, and finding her way to peace. I'm hoping her life is all she dreams of. "Never give up on the things that make you who you really are," that's what I'd always tell her. This is the plaque we found together.

DESIDERATA
written by Max Ehrmann in the 1920s

Go placidly amid the noise and the haste,
and remember what peace there may be in silence.

As far as possible, without surrender,
be on good terms with all persons.
Speak your truth quietly and clearly;
and listen to others,
even to the dull and the ignorant;
they too have their story.
Avoid loud and aggressive persons;
they are vexatious to the spirit.

If you compare yourself with others,
you may become vain or bitter,
for always there will be greater and lesser persons than yourself.
Enjoy your achievements as well as your plans.
Keep interested in your own career, however humble;
it is a real possession in the changing fortunes of time.

Exercise caution in your business affairs,
for the world is full of trickery.
But let this not blind you to what virtue there is;
many persons strive for high ideals,
and everywhere life is full of heroism.
Be yourself. Especially do not feign affection.
Neither be cynical about love,
for in the face of all aridity and disenchantment,
it is as perennial as the grass.

Take kindly the counsel of the years,
gracefully surrendering the things of youth.
Nurture strength of spirit to shield you in sudden misfortune.
But do not distress yourself with dark imaginings.
Many fears are born of fatigue and loneliness.

Beyond a wholesome discipline,
be gentle with yourself.
You are a child of the universe
no less than the trees and the stars;
you have a right to be here.

And whether or not it is clear to you,
no doubt the universe is unfolding as it should.

Therefore be at peace with God,
whatever you conceive Him to be.
And whatever your labors and aspirations,
in the noisy confusion of life,
keep peace in your soul.

With all its sham, drudgery, and broken dreams,
it is still a beautiful world.
Be cheerful. Strive to be happy.

Thank you, Betsy, for that day, even if you don't remember it.

But You Seem So Perfect

───────

IT WAS TIME AGAIN TO try to get a few more pieces of my pieced-together college degree, so I headed to Quad C, a local community college, and found classes that I needed and that I liked. American Sign Language was one of them. I had never known anyone deaf until this class, but I wanted to learn every language in the world.

As class started, a beautiful woman in a British Airways uniform walked in and sat next to me. Jacqui from England was my first friend in Texas. Although life and time has separated us, we will always be close. She gave me the gift of listening to me when I needed it.

One day while Jac and I were sitting in the break area, practicing our hand movements while I sated my strange craving for salt-and-vinegar chips and Dr. Pepper, I noticed a sad girl off to my right. She was in our class, and it seemed she needed to talk. I wasn't sure if I should approach her, so I waited. A few days later I sat down with her at a break and asked, "Are you okay?"

"Please don't judge me," Jill cried into her folded arms. She had countless piercings, light-brown roots sneaking out under black-dyed hair, and onyx nail polish that suggested an edgy approach to life—an approach I have always liked. We sat at a table in the commons area, two strangers sharing dark secrets.

Crying and continuing to hide her face, she told me, "My boyfriend made me get an abortion last week, and I feel so sad." Looking up at me in shame, she added, "You look like you have a normal life, and you probably don't understand—"

"Try me," I said. Jill shared her pain, and I listened and cried with her. My own past enabled me to help her through that moment.

I never dreamed that the scars of my two abortions would someday benefit others. The early death of my dad, the lack of my mother's attention, the incest, the alcohol and drug abuse, the failed marriages, the loss of my custody of Miranda, the suicide attempt, the eating disorder, the stripping, the destructive choices, and the physical, sexual, emotional, and verbal abuses had all left me with a huge list of issues and wounds I thought I could never heal from. But I've witnessed it over and over—the healing that happens when I allow my traumas to help others. I am capable of rigorous honesty, and when I am honest, someone is helped and I am healed.

I still struggle to see worth in myself. When I look in the mirror, I often see an unstable girl. I wrestle with issues of love. Establishing and maintaining appropriate boundaries escapes me. I have trouble discerning truth, distinguishing motives, and interpreting behaviors. I always want to believe the best about the human race. I'm learning how to determine the appropriateness of conversations. Now, I call it my radar. It goes off to warn me. The difference is that I am finally hearing it.

Because of my struggles, others are drawn to me; they know they can share their deepest secrets without condemnation. I know how to be vulnerable. I know how to be real. My life was a mess—and still is a mess in many ways—but I don't try to hide it.

My outlook on life, coupled with my openness, offers comfort to those who are hurting. So I welcome the opportunity to share my pain with others. The truth has let me proclaim that life can be better, that despite the pain of the past, life can be good.

That is what happened that day. Instead of drowning in a sea of emotion, I was floating to safety, reaching back into my childhood and bringing the child in me home to the woman in me who could take care of her.

Labor of Love

OF ALL THE PEOPLE I wanted in my life, Nese was one I missed more than anyone, it seemed. I'd yo-yoed in and out of her life because I still hadn't divulged the truth about what I had gone through at the hands of her dad and brother. I couldn't. I'd spent half my life trying to protect her from it and praying to God she'd never experience what I knew DeDe and I had. I was still treating her like a toddler, I guess, as if she couldn't deal with the hard, cold facts.

After I finished my class on Friday, I put Mary in the car. I didn't want a weekend in Plano without Miranda. When I did have her, she'd fly in and out of DFW airport by herself at ten years old. How brave and strong Miranda became as a child was beyond comprehension. But she had to be that way. On that Friday, I drove us to Siloam Springs. I hadn't been there in years and probably would never have gone back there if Nese hadn't been living there. Even if my hiding after our time together confused the hell out of Nese, she still allowed my visits. It hurt her, though.

On our five-hour drive to Arkansas, I consumed four bags of salt-and-vinegar chips with beaucoup Dr. Pepper. Jamming to the tune of Veggie Tales with Mary, suddenly I felt ill. Mark and I had talked a few months before about not "worrying," another term for not taking birth control. I wanted to have a son so badly, and I knew that I would if we tried. Mark and I never really needed to try. Just like in that old wives' tale, I'd get pregnant if he just looked at me. Soon after I pulled into Nese's driveway, hugged her, and talked about her pregnancy, we decided to go get a test for me.

"There you have it!" said Nese, when I got the results. "Congrats! We are both having a baby!" In the fall of 1997, I found myself in a tiny building that was the McKinney hospital. After firing the doctor I had used in the first two trimesters of this pregnancy because his bedside manner was nonexistent, I found a wonderful doctor who helped us get John into the world.

During one discussion Mark and I had about the birthing process, I said, "I don't use epidurals." Mark looked worried but respected my decision. "Really, even if I beg for it, don't let them give it to me. I mean it!" He said, "Okay."

After twelve hours of labor, even though I had birthed my first two without epidurals, I was wishing I'd scheduled one as a backup plan, begging my doctor to give me one anyway. Mark was unsure if that meant I really did or I really didn't want one. He was mostly concerned I'd make him actually watch the birth from a bird's-eye view. That terrified him! Bless his heart. He couldn't have won any battle that day.

Once Emily finally arrived and sat three-year-old Jeremy down while she checked on me, the decision was finally made that regardless of the fact that I was already dilated eight centimeters, they ought to give me an epidural anyway. My doctor stumbled out, frustrated. I was happy Miranda was at home, waiting with Mary, and couldn't see this part of me. Jeremy quickly asked his mother, "Why is Steph dying?" The man with the drugs came in and quickly poked the epidural in my spine. Then John decided to show up, and I went numb. I'd say epidurals are highly overrated, but I didn't really follow protocol. So I didn't have the benefit. But there I was, watching my beautiful baby boy cry as Betsy cooed at him. And then he was in my arms. My son had arrived.

Heavenly Dish

MARK AND I TRAVELED A lot. Even though the luxury of private jets sounded like a sophisticated problem to have, I was tired, not to mention still lugging around my post-baby weight, and all the luxurious hotels in the world were still just hotels and not home.

But if I were traveling to a place where my convention friend Dish would be, I was happy. When you find yourself in a situation with a bunch of corporate wives, you have to kind of feel your way around the ones who will allow themselves to be real and the ones who sit next to you with a fake grin just because you're the boss's wife. My friend Dish was real.

She and the others I had "real" friendships with would sit for hours, drinking all sorts of concoctions that the lunchtime bartender would experiment with while the men were in meetings. Later, when I lost Dish to leukemia and I was asked to read a letter I had written to her at her funeral, I barely made it through. That day all I could see was the face of this friend who had stuck with me through so much. Dish and I had daily phone conversations through the years as we attached to one another over mutual understandings of what it was like to be a survivor of molestation and rape. We wondered if it would be possible to actually get that piece of ourselves back, and we discussed whether we could learn how to rebuild ourselves and our lives. To lose a portion of yourself seems irreversible, but it's not.

I had plans to rebuild myself, starting with my education and searching out a true expert in the field of sexual abuse to put the rest of my demons in the ground. She and I were going to grow old and strong. She was already weak though, but she hadn't known it until it was too late.

Hiding my lack of self-assurance in encounters with these

"sophisticated" people, I tried to learn about whatever they were discussing. If it was finance, I found a book on it and read it feverishly. I'd save the *Wall Street Journals* from our hotel stays and learn from them. If it was related to travel, I'd ask Mark if we could go to wherever it was I wanted to learn about at the time, and we'd see the place firsthand. If I didn't know what a sprinkler system was because I was used to a green garden hose connected to a sprayer, then I'd find out about it, too. Despite the failure of the educational system, I realized it was possible to learn anything I needed.

As for my children, when it came to creating a path of learning, well, you'd better bet I made it happen! I was not going to do what my mom did to me—waste brainpower, learning ability, and a potentially educated mind. Instead of harboring resentment at the neglect of my education, I made sure they would have what I did not. My children were not going to have to go to a vo-tech school to learn to properly read and write at the age of twenty-two.

I always made sure my children could and would learn everything they needed and a lot of what they wanted. I made sure that they absorbed their reading, writing, and arithmetic so no one could claim they were uneducated, especially themselves, but at the same time I set out to see that these kids of mine could go out into the world and humbly help others who needed guidance with their own education. Being smart was about more than answering trivia questions; being truly educated was about being well-rounded about the world, life, and mankind. And about themselves.

When I am gone, I know that my children will see that their children know the importance of empowerment in education, too. I've always taught them to give to the world what they can. Because I know each of my children intimately, I am certain they will be better than I about boundaries. As I heard recently, "Once you become a mother, you stop being the picture and start being the frame." I have never had trouble giving my kids center stage. Defining myself as "mom" is allowing their lights to outshine mine any day of the week.

What's Going On?

MAKING OUR PLANS TO BUILD a home in a town nearby called McKinney, Mark and I had even less time together. I was able to spend a lot of time with my friend Sandy, who relocated to Texas after we did. During lunch one day, I said with a very heavy heart, "But Sandy, I don't want to live in a compound, and this new home is getting bigger by the day."

"Tell Mark that you're not comfortable with it, Steph," Sandy has known me like no one else. I met Sandy at Interurban City Express while I was waiting tables. She walked in alone and sat in my section, and we started what would be a lifelong friendship. I hated that she knew the pain and loss of being forcefully separated from her children like I had been from Miranda.

When I was ready to tell Mark how I felt, our foreman ran off to Europe with a lot of our money, and Mark spent every extra weekend in McKinney scraping paint off the new windows.

So I kept my insecure mouth shut and was going to learn to live in yet a larger home and another gated community. The days of rathole apartments were gone. My new closet was as big as that apartment had been, literally. Life in this mansion was such a whirlwind that I could barely keep up, clocking in and out daily with the tasks of family, education, traveling with my husband. Not to mention having to prepare for Saturday night dates and thinking of strategies to keep him satisfied. When you have to use Post-it notes to remember to shave your legs, then things are possibly a bit too busy.

A deep-seated fear stirred in me constantly that if I took a breath, this whole fairytale would shatter like a mirror. Trust me: If you still have underlying issues that you've ignored, they will surface. Even if you have six kids, two grandkids, two St. Bernard dogs, and a ten thousand square foot home and yard to deal with. Funny thing about those hidden little secrets we have: They are very cunning, baffling, and patient, because they know the longer you wait to expose them, the stronger the force they have to destroy you.

I was probably okay with trying to forget where I came from, but eventually my past would surface, and each time it seemed more difficult to ignore. Sometimes that's exactly what we need to do. Ignore the demons in our head. I'd spent years trying to get out bits of information to Mark about my childhood, but was never fully heard. My life was somewhat settled now, and I didn't want to screw it up. The only remotely awkward things were the visits I had with my mom, who had once again given up being close to me. We would have a few get-togethers here and there, but it always took me weeks to find myself back in a place of peace afterward. I always seemed to be waiting for her to read my mind about my childhood and apologize for what had happened. But she never brought it up, and she never said she was sorry.

As I learned to be a mom myself, my increasing awareness of her total neglect for me as a child was like a snowball of turmoil inside me. As the pride in my children grew, I saw more clearly the lack of parenting I had had myself. And this only made me resent her more. Mom had spent my lifetime just trying to be rid of me.

Then my world started collapsing. Without warning, I was bulimic again and partying like it was 1987 again, but without the drugs! I found myself diving face-first into bottles of wine to numb something that I couldn't even explain. My body started physical combat against my soul. Or was it yelling at me to listen? I was never certain which.

I was seeing the effects of years of abuse, inflicted by myself and others, take hold of my body, which was falling apart piece by piece. Because Paul first suggested I get breast implants in 1988, I was dealing with the fact that they did come with an expiration date. Of course, many things like implants or explants that are said to be easy and routine are still hard on the body. By the time I hit age forty-four, I had already had my fair share of hospital stays. I'd thrown in a hysterectomy and back surgery after a rock climbing accident, but I vowed to be done, and I thought I was.

Wonderful blessings show up when we least expect them, and that is exactly what Maria was—like Mary Poppins but without the umbrella. She knocked so quietly at our mammoth wooden door, I almost missed that blessing. After having a few caregivers sit and talk and play with my baby boy, it was Maria he chose. As a one-year-old, he went peacefully to her arms, claiming, forever, that she was a part of us, our family. Never our housekeeper, never our nanny, never anyone but Maria. God brought her to us, and if it hadn't been for her, I think I would have quickly sold the house and happily moved back into an apartment, rats and all.

This small but very strong lady has never left my side, carrying on with an all-encompassing, unconditional love. I thought I'd hired her to help with the duties of running a home and taking care of children; I never imagined that she would also take care of me. Maria was the mom I never had, the friend I needed, someone who helped me love all of our children. She loved Mark and me as well. In my experience, it isn't always blood that runs thick. Love and forming a family have nothing to do with being related by blood. In a family we have to learn, listen, and get to know one another, related or not.

My Mosaic Family

I CALL THOSE WHO LOVE me and have allowed me to love them my mosaic family. This starting with Nese, whose commitment to our sisterhood has made her a large piece of the mosaic.

Then I met Peggy. As I glided—well, more like steamrolled—through life, I was accustomed to wiggling in and out of friendships, but she just kept up and watched from the sidelines. I began to notice that when someone was really getting close to me, I would recoil and go off alone. But Peggy never wavered. She waited for me to reemerge, the kind of woman who stood on a firm foundation ready to hold everyone up.

Then Pam arrived. On my morning runs I'd stop at a spot in an empty field in our neighborhood. I could feel that someone new was coming for me.

I knew that the family moving onto the site was probably focusing on their own future, but somehow I sensed that whoever the woman of the house was, she would make sure I was part of their plan. Now the kitchen of that home sits on top of that once-empty field. It's a place where a loving family cares for each other every day, a place where I have found refuge and protection. The refuge isn't really the home, though. It's Pam.

During these years, I struggled with bouts of manic depression, and from time to time, I'd hide from friends as well as family. My friends have understood this struggle and coaxed me through the tough times. They've helped me with my children and underlined the importance and the meaning of love. Friendships such as these provided strength and helped me forge a new self-respect. These women were tough and loving, and they taught me how to live within healthy boundaries in all my relationships. As moms with elementary-age children know, it's kind of a ritual to develop friendships in the carpool line waiting for our offspring to run out the school doors in the late afternoon.

Jen and I formed a bond when I pulled up next to her SUV daily and we chatted through our open windows. I have grown through the kindness and love she and her daughters, Rachel and Megan, have given me and my children. There are times in life when we cannot figure out, nor do we care at the time, what that bond between us and our friends actually is. We just know it's preordained, and we respect where it came from.

I want to teach all my children—girls and boy—the importance of a strong woman. There have been many in my life. Their voices were telling me something that I needed to hear, even if sometimes I just wasn't able to listen until I was ready.

After my stay in treatment, Marie encouraged me to write my story to help others; she believed in me. Cheryl, Bobby's sister, showed compassion when my life was shattered. It was proof of love without judgment. To this day, Bobby's mother, Carolyn, never forgets my birthday, reminding me yearly that even through it all, she thinks I'm still a blessing to her. God, I love that woman! When depression stalked me, Pam "talked me off the ledge." And if I make some stupid decision, my girlfriends will invariably call me on it. They've been busy through the years.

Maylee came into my life like a song, the kind that remains your favorite no matter how many times you hear it. It was pouring down rain the day the movers got us from Plano to McKinney, and I went in search of a quiet spot. That was back in the day when there was only one Starbucks in town. Nestled in the corner, trying to nurse my newborn son, after a customer—a man—complained that it was indecent to nurse in public, I noticed the couple the moment they came in. George and Maylee always make a wave when they enter because of their immense love for people and one another. Maylee walked over to sneak a peek at my now sleeping baby. She sat down beside me, and we began talking about the miracle and fear of birth. They had just discovered theirs would be a boy, Raine. I was marked with the love she so willingly delivered to people and I have been forever blessed.

These women care enough not to let me ruin my life. If it hadn't been for them, I wouldn't be able to tell my story. These girlfriends brought the gift of healing to my battered heart. These relationships provided the honesty, accountability, and comfort that I never experienced in the family I grew up in or in my romantic relationships with any man.

These women have seen me come from nothing to where I am today. They've never been afraid to give me a passionate kick in the ass—or as the kids at youth group call it, a "Jesus slap." I hear Sandy when she says, in no uncertain terms, "You have come from waiting tables and swinging around polls to this amazing, beautiful, strong creature that I see today. You have survived and fought everything and everyone, and there is no way in hell that you are going to give up on yourself, ever. Because you never have!"

On our walks Jen reminds me that by my strength she finds her own, and I feel honored.

Creating strong bonds like these is worth every effort it takes. Life is richer when we share it with like-minded girlfriends. But reaching out to other women begins with you. Show up at a neighbor's luncheon even if you don't own Chanel. Enroll in a college course, join a community group, spend time in church, volunteer your service. Open your heart and recognize the women like you who are also looking for a sister relationship. If all else fails, take a walk with a new friend, have a coffee, or just stand on an empty lot and pray for a friend.

A Time to Heal

———

"LET'S INVITE THOSE DEMONS IN, Stephanie," my new counselor said. My foundation of support needed to be built before I was ready to do that, and the groundwork was being laid for me to start working on the remains of my broken past. I was just beginning to find the strength to do it. My body sent warning signs, and I chose to listen. It's that rumbling of something in the air, but you just can't figure out what it is.

I was determined that my fear wasn't going to win. I was ready. I drove down Highway 75 every week for counseling from a woman who came highly recommended. Before we started, I spent weeks getting used to my new friend, Zoloft. It was essential that I take the medication to prepare for the work that was waiting for me. Only then was I able to enter the temple of doom, open the door to my nightmares, and differentiate between truth and illusion.

Months before this collapse, I began reading *The Artist's Way* by Julia Cameron. I took the twelve-week suggested program of journaling and spending time alone. It broke me, and then I confronted myself. I learned that what I had hoped was a bad dream—what I wanted to be something called "false memory syndrome"—was reality.

As the months went by and I met weekly with this professional, we'd sit and wait as long as needed for me to be able to say the things I had never been able to say. Even during all the weeks in addiction treatment, I hadn't been able to delve as deeply into my past as I was able to with her. During treatment at age twenty-five, I had been perfecting my skill at simply staying alive on a daily basis, working with people to help my dyslexia and reading skills, and learning about the effects of addiction. Here, I'd call each and every nightmarish person by name. We aired my secrets and my shames, and we figured out why I made the choices in life that I had. Since I was suffering from post-traumatic stress disorder (PTSD)—a severe anxiety disorder that arises after repeated psychological trauma—the counselor had to be very gentle as she exposed my past and then skillfully bring me back to my current reality before I headed out her front door again. I will be forever grateful.

Too Pretty

WORKING WITH THIS THERAPIST INTRODUCED a new concept, a switch from focusing on what had been done to me through life, to what I could do to help others heal from what had been done to them. The year I was a room mom in my daughter's first-grade class, I noticed a quiet child who played alone, sat alone at lunch, and sometimes seemed to vanish before our very eyes. Initially, I didn't pay attention, but one day, when I had playground duty, I saw her with a bunch of girls in her class. At first I was happy to see her playing with the other girls, but I quickly realized there was an argument going on.

"Don't call me pretty!" she yelled at the other girls. Her words reminded me of my own so many years ago. Shaking my head, I went over to her and said gently, "Honey, let's go sit and rest under that tree, okay?" I gave the other kids a look like, "I got this; run along and play." I planned to talk with the teacher about the incident the next day, but at home that night, I couldn't get the little girl off my mind.

The following day during class, while I helped the kids get out their craft supplies, I saw this same girl take her tiny, fat-handled scissors and begin cutting off her eyelashes, right there at her desk. As the young teacher looked on, surprised and concerned, I walked to the girl's desk and asked, "Sweetheart, why are you cutting your eyelashes off?" She pushed the pieces of lash around, looked up through her uneven bangs, and said, "I'm too pretty."

With tears burning my eyes, I didn't waste a minute. I hurried to the counselor's office in search of the woman who I knew could help. I was never officially able to find out what happened, but I did hear through the grapevine that something hadn't been right. I pray that she was removed from her living situation and that she is healthy and healing, that she is safe.

Perhaps I am one of those overzealous parents who grow anxious over things like an unchaperoned four-year-old walking alone in my neighborhood. Or a toddler playing in ocean waves without adult supervision.

I'm just saying that if you have radar about issues like child safety or possible abuse—or other horrific things like animal cruelty—you'd better speak up. We are all in this together! It's not butting in, and it's not about ego; these are matters of survival. Because that four-year-old I mentioned? He was alone and lost. And the mom of the child by the ocean was facedown, drunk and passed out.

Open your eyes. You might save a life.

Where I Came From

WHEN IT CAME TO MARK and me, life was always intense. Out of respect for my family and myself, I won't get into the details of why we separated except to say that sometimes after setting boundaries and following through with them, things just get complicated. Rocking the proverbial boat will cause some to fall overboard. There is nothing simple about this portion of my story. I was ready and willing to fight for a long time to make a stand against the things I would no longer be able to live with and that were breaking us. But eventually I wore out. When he was finally ready to listen, I didn't have anything left to say. Feelings of impending doom wouldn't stop haunting me—us. We separated, and then—undoubtedly this was the impending doom I'd felt so intensely—we divorced.

I stopped trying to explain to people why he and I were no longer married. As our marriage ended, I heard a few unasked-for opinions. One woman who had seen me at conventions approached me in a Starbucks and said, "I am so sorry to hear about your divorce."

"I'm sorry," I had to ask her. "Who are you?" She told me, "My husband works for your soon-to-be ex-husband." The way she said "soon-to-be" caused me to want to cram that sticky pastry down her throat and spill her coffee drink all over her Louis Vuitton pantsuit. "I have been to many conventions," she went on, "and have seen you many times. A few years ago I watched you walk into that large ballroom, and I thought you looked beautiful, but your eyes were sad."

Was it really so noticeable that not even my notorious black eyeliner and red lipstick could cover my pain then? As I said goodbye to the woman, she had the audacity to ask, "Dear, how will you make it now?"

It must have been apparent that I had abdicated my throne as Torch-mark's first lady, and I was totally fine with that.

Shaking my head and unable to mutter anything audible, I wondered what the hell she meant and why I hadn't just walked out. I looked at her and said, "I *am* making it, but I think our definitions of what I am making are different." She, of course, was referring to the level at which I was living in the material world. I guess she was wondering how I could possibly think of letting that go and living in what I call "the real world." It's debatable as to what the real world is exactly, but I can tell you what it means for me.

The incident reminded me of how one year at a business convention for Mark's work, he and I were making our way through the crowd, saying hello and shaking hands, and I heard a woman, a corporate wife, exchange words with the waitstaff. She was complaining about a staff member who had a piercing in her lip. As I got closer, I heard her say something derogatory about the girl's tattoos, too. Enough! It was time for *my* two cents.

When the woman saw me coming, she said, "Oh good, don't you think that if these kids are asked to serve at this plush dinner, they should be asked to remove body piercings and cover their tattoos?"

I looked at the girl in question, whose head was hanging down. I had been introduced as the "first lady of the corporation," a phrase I had always hated. This girl, who was in her late twenties, quickly began to apologize: "I am sorry, ma'am. Next time I'll do better with the dress code."

Before I knew it, the words were rolling out of my mouth. I was angry and I was going to say why. "Wow," I said, "I didn't realize that it was offensive. I am so glad that I covered the tattoos I have and chose a dress that wouldn't expose my belly button ring!" With my head held high, I went on: "Listen, Mrs. Goody Goody, you forget you are no better than these hardworking people. You're not the one who calls the shots here. And I am proud of my tattoos. When I was waiting tables and swinging around a pole for a couple of bucks so I could eat and pay child support, I had people like you stare me down, too. I probably would have told you to kiss my tattooed, pierced ass!" I wasn't one for scenes, but sometimes it's necessary.

Needless to say the lady huffed off. If only we could always be reminded that we all started from the same place in life—birth—and we will all finish in the same place—death. It's the time in between that counts.

Finding myself in exclusive places that some will never see began to feel mundane to me. I was losing the spark of life that I'd always had. Even in destitute times—living in a car and taking truck-stop showers or making my dining room table out of a huge cable spool—I could find and relish moments of laughter. For me, these were the real things in life. Even with the pain that absorbed me back then, I still knew where I had come from.

What's in a Name?

NOW THAT I FOUND MYSELF alone again, I was relieved at not feeling guilty for not enjoying the things that money could buy. And I was learning to become what my soul had longed for—an activist. Someone who could bring relief, not only with money but also by boarding plane after plane to find those in need, across the world and at home.

Now, please do not confuse me with someone who doesn't like nice things. If you tried to count the pairs of shoes in my closet, it would take you all day. I do love beautiful things. But every year Mark would ask me the same question: "What do you want for your birthday, anniversary, Christmas, and Valentines Day?" I'd repeatedly say the same thing: "I want a love letter." To no avail.

I no longer have to swing around a pole in order to get my child support paid, and I might now be able to help those who do it out of desperation to have *their* needs met. If I can convince one girl in our youth group that she doesn't have to take a job at Hooters if she doesn't feel good about it, then I will be happy. (Though I'm not knocking it. I actually liked working there.)

Mark and I used to spend time talking about the way in which people are categorized and why I, for one, have been placed in many of those categories. Maybe I just couldn't figure out which one was authentic. Or perhaps we just play a role for a specific period of time. I do know that if people are judgmental because they never had to experience anything like drug or alcohol addiction or never entered a tattoo parlor, strip club, or courtroom, they will find themselves humbled at some point in life. That's karma. Sometimes I still have reminders of the choices I made over and over again.

When Mark and I went to renew our passports for that ten-year anniversary trip to the Mediterranean, we walked into a small passport office, and I asked for the proper paperwork. The large woman behind the glass window never looked up as she handed me the forms and recited her litany of directions. I gave Mark his papers, sat down to fill out mine, and peered at the space that asked for any and all last names I might have had in my life.

This was going to be a challenge, since they had to be in chronological order and I even had to list the times when I returned to my maiden name after a divorce. It was quickly obvious that the tiny line was not going to give me nearly enough space to write all the names I had acquired over the past thirty years.

I returned to the window. "Excuse me, ma'am. I have a problem," I said. "I've run out of room to list all the last names that I've had." She looked up and said, "I've been here for fifteen years, and I've never heard that problem before." She turned to her coworker and said, "Sue, look at this. This lady doesn't have room for all her last names." Sometimes being reminded of your past is important. This time, though, being reminded that I'd been a hopeless romantic simply cost me a bit of humiliation. Surely a day would come when I'd finally be who I am suppose to be— and have the last name to show it.

My Tattooed Heart

ON MY LAST VALENTINE'S DAY date with Mark—my last Valentine's date, period—we went to dinner at our usual place in Dallas, Del Frisco's, and he asked, "What do you want more than anything in life, Steph?"

I answered, "Peace." I've searched my whole life for peace. Picasso's Dove of Peace was etched on my left wrist. It was a start.

Tattoos decorate my body and remind me how I want to live: Pegasus, my horse with wings, declares my freedom from my sad past life, the freedom to be with my daughter Miranda now whenever we want. This flying pony often makes me think of her, the daughter I'd fly anywhere on Earth to be with. Eventually I would have to fly to see her because she'd moved to live in another country—Bermuda.

The dove on my wrist reminds me of the peace of mind I now possess, the peace that entered my life when I had my daughter Mary. How Mary's entrance into my world actually saved me. My dove carries three olive branches, reminding me of the three children I have and how I will carry them through life.

To mark an anniversary of my dad's death, the day after Christmas in 1976, I flew to Mexico alone on Christmas night and had a dragon holding a peace sign inked on. With it, I felt my dad's presence and also that of my son, John, who has the courage of a dragon and a peaceful spirit. Through the recent years this symbol calls up for me the need to be as tough as I need to be, and to set boundaries but also have the gentle spirit that is so needed in our world.

It's a different exterior message than that I used to deem important. Those of us who use body art to proclaim some conviction we have understand it. Some people just think we're crazy or addicted to the

pain. Possibly it's that too. Years later I'd add one more tattoo: a blue butterfly. The butterfly's wings effect change as it soars through the world.
This is my hope, this is my passion, and this is my life's purpose.

Looking back, I see the futility of focusing on the exterior I used to
focus on. I'm not the sum total of my breasts, hair color, and tight butt
(which is less tight with age). I've turned my attention, instead, to tattoos
of the heart—imprinting enduring principles that define me as I age.
True beauty is expressed in honesty, discipline, and humility. Love, compassion, manners, and kindness are now what build my character, what
I teach my children, and what I will teach my grandchildren. I aspire to
surround myself with people who are authentic, and I want to be the
emotional equivalent of comfort food to those seeking relief. I want to
be a safe place for others.

My grandmother taught me so much and gave me the safety that
was possible given the circumstances. Watching her age I became acutely
aware of the way some of the younger generation treat the elderly.
Sometimes it's necessary to remind them that we all arrive at the same
place of old age if we're lucky, and aging gracefully is my hope. I haven't
been added to the mass-mailing list for AARP yet, although I did receive
a catalog targeting middle-aged women. In it I discovered items I hadn't
even thought of when I was worrying over my changing looks. Products
geared for panicky women whose bloom was fading caught my attention: chin wraps, wrinkle creams, and vagina-tightening gadgets. "What
the hell is that?" I caught myself saying out loud. The most humorous
offer came in the form of a lipstick-tube-look-alike intended to catch
urine if you couldn't make it to the bathroom in time. Now I can see the
need for something of that nature.

At forty-five, I succumbed to the Botox appeal once, with a really
bad side effect that made me look like Donald Duck. I've allowed doctors to alter my appearance from head to boob to toe and have suffered
the consequences. Seems like I was always trying to outrun old age, but
it kept up, nipping at my cracked heels.

For me, true beauty comes from the interior; it has to do with the
strength for me to be who I am, without succumbing to comparisons
with what an ideal body and face might look like. I could never be the

gal who, when asked, "Have you ever had any work done?" would lie and say, "Oh no, honey. It's genetic." I have plumped my lips once, and dealt with plumping my once nonexistent boobs. And as a result, I have a few surgical scars. At least the emotional scarring is lightening up. I would be lying if I said I never relapsed in my eating illness, because I have. I can't tell you I like aging, because I don't—but I keep spas in business because I am a product junkie now. Life is a process. I relapse and experience failure, but I return to a place of strength and the failures are fewer today than they were twenty years ago. I recognize the discipline I possess, the ability to keep going, the resilience to endure persistent assaults of growing older, and the willingness to accept myself as I am.

Meanwhile, my algebra teacher would be proud of me—or should be. But who knows if insensitive coaches who make inappropriate comments to young girls even think about those they once tormented. Twenty-five years after graduating from high school, I returned to the local community college to face my algebra demon. I passed with a B+ and rescued my dignity, thanks to Mary's ability to sit with mommy after she was out of elementary school and explain how numbers and letters go together in algebra and why it *is* important.

Finding out that I wasn't stupid was the most empowering thing I could do. Walking out of the college, I punched the air in a very self-assured way, saying, "Hey Coach, take that!"

Steph, You Can Do This

SO I WAS STARTING OVER again. More accurately, I was starting somewhere in the middle of my life. I was hit with an insecurity about walking into a gym. That horrible comparing thing we do as humans: My hair is straight and I wish it were curly, or I have green eyes but I've always wanted brown. But I forced myself to roll out of bed and head to the gym before I was too awake to talk myself out of it. Good ol' Nike coined the best phrase, right? "Just do it!"

One thing was certain: I needed help, and not just a friend to work out with. I needed someone who would find a strong part of me and at the same time would argue with the weak part of me. I found my help in the form of a man who not only trained my body but also spent endless hours working on my spirit. People who come into our lives unexpectedly change us the most, it seems, and Mitch was one of those people. He helped me lift physical weights as well as the weight I carried on my shoulders. In this world of sweat and no makeup, I had to dig deep inside for strength. Not just physical strength, but the kind we need to survive the rest of our lives. And so with each step I climbed and each breath I took, I gradually became stronger.

For the first time I gave up my illusion of perfection and performance. I pushed myself into a place that chipped away at my fake shell of identity. I found myself crying a lot, sweating profusely, and metaphorically turning myself inside out so I could see who I was truly supposed to be and remind myself how to continue this road to self-preservation.

Mitch showed me how to transform sabotaging habits into something I could gain self-esteem from, to use the anger instead of fighting it off with pity. Thanks to him, I never allowed the hate I had for myself to win. He became my friend, someone who taught me to find strength

I didn't even know I had, as well as a peace that comes from within. He may never know what he did for me, but I am blessed to have known him at a crucial time in my unraveling world.

I was sitting in Playa Del Carmen with my friend Marianna when she said, "Life is like a car ride, Steph."

Snickering, I said, "Yeah, like a hit-and-run!"

"No, loco chica," she went on. "It's like a car ride, a road trip. Some people get in your car and ride a short distance, and you let them out when they have arrived at their destination. Others ride with you longer, and some stay until the end of your journey."

Well, Mitch jumped in for the road trip during a very bumpy portion of my journey, at a time when I wasn't even sure which direction I was even going. I became focused and ready. Life really is a highway, and often the traffic wasn't going my way. Every time I said, "I'm sorry," when I was insulting my own strength, he'd make me drop and give him twenty pushups. The best shape I've ever been in was during the two years we trained for a huge event: life.

2009–present

Empowering orphans in Kenya with Mary

Undeniable strength of my now young man, John

Miranda and Mom, never apart

The House That Hope Built

DURING MY OWN LIFE CHANGE I was in Mexico a lot. It was always a bit comical how some thought I'd run away only to drink the local tequila and end up facedown on the beach in sorrow over the divorce Mark and I had gone through. Oh, I did throw back a few shooters, I'll be honest about that. But Mexico was a place where I found myself and further confirmed my purpose in life. When one experience places you where you really can cause change, no matter how small or big, it's when we discover the "it's not about me" mentality that things start adjusting in our thinking. Seriously in need of something empowering and fulfilling, I began to research what that might be. After months of searching the phrase "helping others" online and then more specifically "helping others in Mexico," I was led to a site for an orphanage in Bonfil, just outside of Cancun, called Casa Hogar Esperanza, "Foster Home of Hope." Photos linked it to an organization called Global Colors, now called Guerrilla Aid, founded by Barton Brooks, a person of incredible humility who will never take any credit for the life-changing work he does. He's taught me the power of a seven-dollar chicken and of throwing on a backpack and flying to places I had never seen before. To work with humanity and learn how to create safety for others. To empower women and children. Through the years, as I have spent endless hours talking and sharing, Barton has transferred strength to me as he does to so many. Thanks, my sweet friend and mentor!

Boarding a plane for Mexico, I started my new adventure. When I arrived in Cancun and picked up my baggage, I began asking where Bonfil was. For some odd reason no one knew. At the hotel the concierge overheard me. "I know Bonfil. It is my home."

Traveling alone is certainly one way to spread your wings, and jumping into a cab and heading to a bad part of town, off the tourist-beaten path, is another. Yet I was never scared. Though many things frightened me as a child, as an adult, I've come to realize that God doesn't mind working my guardian angels overtime. Neither do I.

I found Casa Hogar Esperanza, and after many trips back, I've come to know everyone by name and shoe size. Of course, it will take many lifetimes to abolish human trafficking, child slavery, and hunger. But with programs that are diligently maintained by some of the most incredible people I have ever met, it will happen. It has to happen. The day will come when there is no first, second, or third world, because there will be only one world, and we all live in it together. If an eight-year-old little girl in the Bay Area of California can make lemonade at her stand for over 200 days straight, never missing a day, and raise so many hundreds and thousands of dollars to end child slavery, then isn't it possible—even probable—that all human slavery can be abolished? The answer? YES!

There have been times, and I know others relate to this, when I could only contribute money but not time. Money is necessary, of course. But I challenge you to see where the money that you willingly give goes. Go see how it's used and feel that warmth in your heart. We all could use a dose of humility and real purpose in our lives from time to time.

As I returned again and again to Casa Hogar Esperanza, my mind opened up. I started to see puzzle pieces to my life that I had overlooked. Placing them where they belonged, I found where I belonged at the same time. During an afternoon in Bonfil, when I was sweeping the play area for the kids, I was picked up by a local friend and taken to a shaman. As incense burned, I closed my eyes and listened to this woman chanting. I could understand some of what she was saying but not all of it. When she finished, she looked at me and asked, "You know what you are supposed to do, don't you?"

Smiling, I hugged her and said, "Thank you. Yes, I do." My life's work was suddenly very clear. I had never felt more attached to the world than in that moment. My existence made sense, and I felt a sense of my own worth. At last I had found what we all search for—a sense of purpose. Purpose as a mom was a huge part of me—the most important part of me. It's just that I knew I could also find others to help. My purpose basically expanded. Moreover, my purpose was not confined to the town I lived in, but ranged across the globe. I transformed myself into an activist for the safety, well-being, and rehabilitation of everyone I could possibly help. I desperately wanted to find all those out there like me, those who felt afraid and unimportant, and tell them, "Speak up, I hear you. You do matter."

Bohemian Faith

WHAT DOES FAITH REALLY LOOK like to me? Maybe a monster truck, painted a sort of camouflage gray and white, roaring up and down the street that my kids and I took to and from school every day. It wasn't the typical SUV that I see daily in our neighborhood. The driver intrigued me, even though all I could see of him was a glimpse of long dreadlocks blowing through the open window as he zoomed by. This was Ed. He would help my children and me find our way to God's unconditional love. Ed was our youth pastor, our friend, and a source of guidance for kids and teens in a scary world. This man with his bohemian looks exuded the love of God and gathered his flock safely in. By his example, I could revel in the fact that we are all very different and that my own difference was a good thing. Who cared if I didn't fit in? What was I trying to fit into anyway?

Church was a place I went to on Mother's Day, Christmas, and maybe Easter. It was a place where I wasn't very comfortable. When I was young, church was a place where I was reminded every week what a loser I was. Now, even if I am still confused about quite a bit of what's in the Bible, I nevertheless see in it confirmation that God loves me just as I am. Wherever I am in my life. My spiritual well-being was my responsibility, and it was also my responsibility to guide my children toward this same well-being.

Finding my moral compass has been part of my journey. Instead of despising the religious confines that I felt I had been so screwed up by, I started at the beginning and have taken what I believe to be truth from the religions that feel right to my soul. I was able to sit weekly and hear words that didn't feel judgmental. I wanted to know who I really was. I was starting to have answers. Having studied different philosophies I was able to piece together my personal belief system, staying away from fundamental judgment. I've judged myself so harshly I didn't need any help. So I began to put my convictions into action. I volunteered my kids and myself for a mission trip to Juarez, Mexico, for a lesson in building cinder-block homes as well as building character. The people we worked with added to our family.

During our stay in Juarez, the kids and I adapted to brushing our teeth with small amounts of bottled water and tried to ignore the source of water used to wash our dishes, learning simply how precious clean water sources are. We knew this was an opportunity to make an impact on lives, to make a difference for people who didn't have the conveniences and comforts we enjoyed on a daily basis. Anyone who has done work like this understands that a first step—even if it's a baby step—casts us into the world and opens our eyes.

Personally I have felt the opposite of egotistical my entire life, but I've discovered feelings of pride and worthiness—and the personal power they give me—by teaching others that they are worthy, too. If you think you can change water by sticking your finger in it, try it. You can only change the lives of others when you devote a portion of your own to helping them; that is where you can make a real difference.

When I feel small in the scheme of the world, it reminds me that we are all truly in this together. It's one very real reason I speak up. I have had many people come up to me in the past few years to thank me. One said, "Steph, thank you for telling your story. I wish I could, but I can't reveal mine."

My reply? "Then my personal story is on your behalf." I respect those who cannot or simply choose not to speak. Many don't want to talk about their abuse, and that is perfectly fine. Maybe those people will find healing vicariously through me.

In Juarez, we'd start early in the morning and sweat through most of the afternoon. Mixing cement, hauling buckets of water, and carrying large cinder-blocks made the days exhausting, but we weren't tired. Lupe, one of the local mission workers, often flashed his three-toothed smile at me as he called out, "*Más agua*, Stephanie?" More water? Children waiting for their new home to be built would coax Mary, John,

Peggy's son Shane, and other young volunteers to join them in a game of soccer during breaks on the work site, and they tossed around the Frisbees we gave them. We'd watch as they used soapy plastic wands to blow bubbles.

One morning, as I dropped another cinder-block in the dirt and listened to Spanish banter bouncing off the block walls, I realized how far I had come from my early days—the times when my own needs consumed me, when my emptiness almost destroyed me. I was grateful that I could be here in Juarez to make a difference in others' lives, and I understood that our lives—mine, Mary's, and John's—were being transformed, too.

When we returned from our trip, our new pastor, David, pulled me aside. "Stephanie," he said, "would you be willing to share with the congregation about your trip to Juarez, about the changes in your life, and about what family means to you?"

Painful moments of my past flashed like a slide show through my head. My memories wanted to mock me, but I grabbed the opportunity to declare my freedom from shame, to proclaim freedom from the past, and to embrace grace. Words like "redemption" started having new meanings for me.

So did the word "testimony." When I was asked to give a testimony with regard to this mission experience and what my church family meant to me, I had to rethink what that meant. Growing up, testimony marked that fine line between bad and good. Giving testimony was supposed to be a confirmation that I would never be bad again.

But I knew that testimony now would have to be about the real me. The one who messed up and still fought demons and self-destructive thinking. Even if I was far from my old patterns, I was still me. We all have a testimony and can deliver that testimony however best fits us—in a church, at a coffee shop, or once in my case, sitting by a stranger in a bar. See, testimony doesn't have to have religious connotations. It is basically our life story up to the point of where we are.

Since I knew my unfiltered way of sharing might be an issue, I went to visit with Pastor David. "I would like to, yes," I told him, "but there is a lot about me you don't know." I told him that some people might

ridicule me for my history as well as for the book I was about to pub-
lish. Or they may just get uncomfortable about him choosing someone
with my sordid past. David looked right at me and said, "I've seen a lot
of people in my life," he replied, "who know how to run a church. But,
Stephanie, you know God, and that was what I saw in you when we first
met. That is why I asked you."

That day I felt God had blessed me, though I know some might not
like what I was going to tell. I was determined to tell the truth, no matter
how uncomfortable it got.

Even for me.

Panda Bear

APRIL 2010, JUST AFTER MIRANDA turned twenty-five, she called from Bermuda.

"I just wanted to tell you," she said, "that someone asked me at my birthday party, 'Who is your best friend?' You know what I said? I said, '*My mom!*'"

"I am honored, baby!" I said. "I love you, Miranda!"

It's amazing to me to think that twenty years earlier, I had stood in a break room at the treatment facility, on the phone with my daughter on her fifth birthday. I tried never to miss her birthdays. There is no way for me to go back and change the abandonment she suffered. When I bring this up, Miranda seems to pardon me. But as I was finishing this story, which started as her story, I can only be grateful for the grace that gave us a connection to one another. We were never apart.

I fought for her violently, quietly, and with everything I had. Back then I failed her dramatically. In spite of all of this, Miranda has turned out to be a strong, beautiful, and passionate woman, the kind of woman people aspire to be. I knew God would gift her with children. I knew she would one day soon be a mommy and one her children could trust to always be present, be involved and connected. Before her next birthday would come, she would in fact be a new mom. Henry had joined our family.

Life was getting fuller with every healing moment and every new addition. I had built a fortress of safety against a world of abuses, stacking brick after brick to create a strong, protective place around me and my children. Miranda was building her own fortress and learning how to activate her own power at the same time. I could release myself from the shame of what our past had done to us both and move forward and use it to help her. Knowledge is power, of course, but I found it in forgiving myself.

If old patterns were still knocking at my door and lessons were still being learned, at least I could be happy that my ability to learn them took place a bit quicker than they used to. And there were always lessons. Just when I thought I had all the answers about love, I'd found out I was very wrong. Dang it!

I still had another lesson to learn about truth.

Even Humpty Dumped Me

I HAD MOVED WITH MARY AND JOHN out of the compound and to a different house down the road. We were settling into our new environment and a new life. As I opened my steamer trunk and pulled out years of photos and journals to sift through, I was getting strong enough even to see photos of Mark and me and to know that our time together was part of the plan.

I worked at making our new home a peaceful spot where we could all heal, the kind of place where others could come and find their own peace, too. I have always wanted to offer that to other broken spirits like myself. My first candidate would be a man I hadn't seen in years. A message from him came through on my computer. He—let's call him D—asked if I remembered him. I did, but being newly separated and still very raw, I needed to think before I responded.

I grabbed my coffee, looked at the family pictures around me, and decided I was ready to move on. I knew that Mark was dating, so I felt justified, I guess. I got my laptop, said a prayer, and replied that, yes, indeed, I remembered him.

I'd first met this man some years before when he strung Christmas lights on our house. Our interactions and conversations were only an annual thing: I would hire him at the holidays, and we'd exchange pleasantries about family life over hot chocolate. I'd noticed his eyes the first day he arrived at my front door. They were a piercing blue and hinted that much was going on behind them.

I've often been intrigued by other people's eyes and what they must have seen. The intensity of his left a mark on me. Now I wonder why I couldn't read what they *really* meant, but I felt that a bond was rekindled when he entered my world one more time.

Sometimes we fill our days with things we have to do, never sensing an invisible tie that brings people together. This is one of those times for me. The forces that pulled us together, however, were not the forces I thought they were. I would be terribly deceived. Not only by him but, worse, by myself!

His message offered simple friendship, but my reaction to the email told me that if I opened myself to this person, there would be much more than friendship. When I replied to him, he said we were going through the same thing, although I was a few steps ahead of him, meaning I was separated already. I believed we'd be able to relate to the common pain of our marriages and possibly find some answers we were both looking for. I had no idea what I was getting into. D claimed he had a strong faith, and that was appealing to me. At this point in my journey I might have fallen for anyone who showed up with the so-called good moral qualities that Grandma wanted for me.

Making plans to meet for coffee took some time to arrange. Then finally he came to my home. He was so reluctant that his truck seemed to edge very slowly around the corner. I watched him walk hesitatingly up to the front door. When I opened it, the first words out of his mouth were, "I really don't want to be here."

"Okay, why are you, then?" I asked.

He said his world had been shattered. In his tattered jeans and a gray pullover, he slowly stepped inside and gave me a hug. Three hours later, having talked about every topic that came to mind, we left to get a bite to eat. I was amazed at how comfortable I felt sitting in the passenger's seat of his truck.

It had been years since I sat near a man other than Mark. It felt strange, but I was willing to try moving on.

Weeks turned into months and then into a year. I ignored the warning signs that Pam and Peggy pointed out to me. I ignored my friends altogether. I didn't pay attention to the fact that Mary was uneasy about the thought of this man with her mom. Then Miranda's reaction started to wake me up for a moment, as she suggested that I was, in fact, making the same wrong choices I had made before in love. The things she tried to make me see and hear hurt badly, because they were true. But, still, I let this man convince me otherwise. I will stand strong behind my opinion that if someone has to hide something they are doing then it's most likely wrong—for everyone involved.

I always have to experience something for myself before I can learn from it. So even though my daughters, friends, and everyone else tried to tell me to break off my relationship with Mr. Blue Eyes, I wasn't ready, I guess. Until circumstances forced me to.

I had just had another surgery, and I wasn't getting out much, so on an early weekend morning, when I had planned to rest all day, D showed up for coffee. Letting him in, I asked, "Are you hungry?"

"No, thanks. It's Saturday," he said, "and even if things are bad at home, I still show up and make breakfast for my kids." He had been in the process of moving into a different house that I had helped him get ready, though it was unclear when he'd actually move in. He had borrowed enough money from me to finish and furnish it; all that was missing was his courage.

We were drinking coffee and laughing about something I'd said, when we heard a knock at the door.

Suddenly he jumped to his feet as though his ass were on fire.

"It's her!" he said.

"It's who?"

"My wife!"

Ever have an "Aha!" moment? Well, I suddenly had one that I wished I had had much earlier. I suddenly realized, "Oh, good Lord, this guy is still very much married." I guess it's safe to say I wasn't the sharpest tool in the shed when it came to guys. Girls, if you are seeing someone who refers to another woman as "his wife," then it's probably a good idea that you are not the girlfriend, don't you agree?

So what did benefit-of-the-doubt Steph do? I had him open the door and let her in. I was sure that we all just needed to have a little chat. I went to my bathroom to get dressed. I needed to use the bathroom, so I shut my bedroom door, the double doors to my bathroom, and the single door to the toilet.

Then I heard a crash and yelling. I assumed the unhappy couple was fighting. I was glad that John had gone for a sleepover, but I was worried that Mary would wake up.

The crashing came closer and closer, as I stood, pulled up my shorts, and was about to head out to mediate the situation. But the situation had made its way to me. Someone was kicking in the toilet door, then kicking me in the ribs, and pushing me back down onto the commode.

"Are you sleeping with my husband?" his wife screamed at me.

Isn't the truth supposed to set you free? I gave it a whirl. "Yes."

Well, that obviously wasn't the smartest thing to come out of my mouth. She kicked me again. Finally D surfaced—which took a while, I might add—and pulled her off me, and we all three somehow got to the living room to discuss matters. He was telling her to calm down, not at all concerned with my well-being. Not to mention that my surgical scars had split open from the kick and I now had a newly replaced boob lodged in my armpit.

As D was trying to console his wife, several things hit me: Number one, he was still very much with his wife with no intentions of moving out, which was the first real problem. Number two, he'd lied about a trip we'd recently taken. Lied to both of us. But those weren't the only things that hit me. When she asked me if he had been with me on this trip, I did it again. Told the truth.

"Yes, he was," I said. She flew over the couch, grabbed a handful of my hair, and hit me again! *Damn, Steph! Shut up and start lying,* I began thinking to myself.

When he finally got her out the door, he acted as if he was planning to stay. I quickly blurted out, "Oh, no. You are leaving too, big guy!" I didn't ever want to see him again.

Making sure they were gone, I locked up and decided that since Mary was asleep and fifteen years old, I could quickly drive to Pam's and ask her to come back home with me. I was in shock, or else it would have occurred to me to call her and not leave. Pam opened the door, and with no questions asked, she yelled out to her husband, "I'll be back!" She told me, "Get in the car, you need a doctor." Was it the scratches on my neck, the pulled hair and torn T-shirt, or the fact that I was holding my boob, trying to keep it in place? We drove back home first to find Mary still asleep, and then we went quickly to the emergency room. D called my cell while we were there, and Pam answered and told him to leave me the hell alone. I sat there brokenhearted, and the X-ray confirmed I also sat there with two broken ribs.

Monday, it was back to Dr. Booby to repair the boob damage. If only he could have repaired my emotional wounds.

Even though D was a fireman, I'd have to say that if I were on fire and he were the only one answering the call, I'd prefer to just burn to death.

It has always been a problem for me to think that I can change people, to make them see that life would be better if we all stopped lying about the things we spend so much time and energy lying about. I did that myself. Why was it that I had to constantly seek out men who used me?

With my heart broken again and my pride completely gone, I started to get sick a lot. I wore Pam out, as she took me in and out of emergency rooms while I fought against high fevers and horrible stomach pain. Plus, I couldn't eat—at all—an affliction that I was intimately familiar with. Mary and I were supposed to leave for a mission trip to Kenya, and though doctors kept telling me that a trip to Africa was not going to happen, somehow I thought I'd be fine. I begged the travel health clinic to fill me up with whatever medicine it would take to keep me alive while I was so far from home, because I was determined to go. And we did.

Zoe's Children

———

CURLED UP IN AN UNCOMFORTABLE position on a hard couch,
waiting out a six-hour layover in London after an eight-hour flight from
Nairobi, I was trying to sleep. Mary had plumped up her new Kenyan
bag, making a makeshift pillow for me.

"Mom," she said, smiling, "I can't believe we really went to Africa."

"I know, baby, we did, and it will change us forever."

Our trip to Kenya was part of a mission called Zoe Ministry. We met
our group of twelve in London en route to Kenya, and now we were all
departing to head home to our different states.

I've continued to find fulfillment through giving, listening, and acts
of service. Marilyn Monroe gave me guidance into womanhood, and
out of honor to her I'd continue to learn what she hadn't—boundaries. Ernest Hemingway, of course, guided me to writing. I know the
intensity of writing to stay alive and fighting inner turmoil, a battle he
eventually lost. I added one more to my list of deceased mentors, Mother
Teresa. Growing up, Grandma would talk about this woman, and in her
description a martyr was a powerful thing to be. How could one claim
that this blessed being suffered loneliness because she gave her life to
God's work? I'm not worthy of the grace I have been given. It isn't the
opposite of empowerment to know that I am not. It empowers me with
humility and the complete and utter knowledge that I am here simply
to be a channel for that grace to touch others. Things of this world are
not ours to hoard and keep merely for our own satisfaction. Neither are
things such as grace and forgiveness. Even if I choose to remove someone from my life, it doesn't mean that I haven't forgiven. I have.

When I found out through the youth pastor, Ed, about the opportunity to go to Kenya, I was eager to hear more. My son, John, and I went

to meet a wonderful man named Reegan, who spoke about the conditions of his own childhood in Kenya and how he got started with Zoe. Hearing him, I felt desperate to go and help. But I was really in awe at the way Reegan showed such pride and strength. It was his number one thing to create safety and prosperity for the children of Africa who knew firsthand, as he did, the fear of being alone.

Because John was very young and I was unsure what he'd see in Kenya, I felt it best to only take Mary.

The journey to Kenya connected Mary and me to even more of the world, further confirming my passions. Mary and I—and the ten others, led by Zoe's leader, Greg—spent two weeks in Maua, a village in Kenya, where we learned about Zoe's orphan-empowerment program. Visiting sites where children had been left in horrible conditions of poverty gave my heart new focus. When the beat-up van came to a stop, we got out and gathered around a hut where three children lived and cared for one another because their parents had died. I was so overcome with love that I felt the need to embrace each one of the children. They were at first limp and unreceptive, but within seconds, one squeezed me, then another, and then the other. As for the tears I tried to hold back, they were tears of joy because the children knew we were there to help, and most importantly, they knew they were not alone anymore.

Waking in the middle of the night to a strong burning smell, I opened the window to the building we were locked in and watched people around a metal can trying to stay warm. African nights are cold. Two people were fighting, and then one fell to the ground. Another couple was yelling at each other and a few children were playing and laughing. Sitting there, I was struck by the question of why I am who I am. Why I wasn't put in this place with these circumstances. Then it was even more clear. My purpose—my ability to cause whatever change I could—was what I'd focus on. As my eight year-old mentor Vivienne says, "if one person can make a difference, then why can't I?" Waking a few hours later to the aroma of breakfast, I brushed my teeth with a small supply of bottled water and put my hair up in the baseball cap I'd brought. Mary greeted me at my door and smiled her beautiful smile. We were ready for a full day's work building a home and tarring a roof.

As with every meal I ate there, I felt guilty. I and the other volunteers were eating three meals a day when most of the population ate one meal every third day, if that. But Reegan taught me not to think, at home or in Kenya, that I shouldn't eat this food because of my guilt over the starving children. "Stephanie," he said, "do not feel badly about having food. Just be grateful and feel blessed when you have it." It has been one very crucial healing point for me with the struggle of my eating illness. Eat only what I need, and by all means, don't throw it up!

We were having a conversation about my health and why I couldn't eat in the first place, when I said, "Reegan, my body seems to reject food."

His soft smile always made me feel like I was in the presence of Jesus himself. "Stephanie, it is because you see food as your enemy, because of the way you have been raised to see mostly gluttony. We see it as life-sustaining and only eat that which keeps us alive, nothing more."

"I feel badly that I have food but don't want it."

Reegan got up to fill his plate with small amounts of rice and chicken. Putting his hand over mine, he said, "Then just eat it for the children you wish you *could* feed." And so I did. I was going to eat vicariously for all those children and adults we saw digging through the trash in the early morning for a meal. Ingenuity and survival were what defined the starving people of Africa. Grace and pride is what defines their character.

All through life I've heard, "If not for the grace of God there go I." But not until that day did I fully comprehend the meaning of that phrase. Instead of feeling bewildered at why I wasn't someone who lived in this place and in these conditions, I decided that it had to be, because I felt and saw what needed to be done. I would go home and find the needs in my own homeland as well. I realized that if I have been given a gift, then it is essential I share it.

During the evenings in Kenya, after a tiring day of work on the site we were building, our group leader asked what our "God moment" was. Greg had us pick a moment in our day in which we saw the hand of God working. Describing it in detail to the rest of our team was a nightly ritual.

For me, that moment came during a meal that we shared with the staff of the Maua Methodist Hospital. We were covered head to toe in paint, dirt, and tar from the work site. One of the hospital people announced that after introductions we would enjoy our meal. So we all sat up and put our forks down, ready to go through the mantra of where we lived and how this experience was touching us individually.

To our surprise, it was the local men and women who introduced themselves to us. Each of them worked daily to save lives and improve the health and well-being of the people of Kenya. But they actually took time out to meet the twelve of us and honor our presence. The hospital director went on about how they were our servants and put us on a pedestal, as he thanked us for being in their country. That is where the God moment started for me that day.

I could see that one of the men on our team looked almost angry. He seemed very uncomfortable at the way this hospital director and his colleagues were thanking us for coming so far and doing so much for the people of Maua. Thanking us was fine, and we appreciated that, but I fully understood the feeling that I assumed was building inside my friend Jon. When the intros were almost over, and we, too, had a chance to speak, Jon got to his feet and expressed a very different emotion.

He made it clear that *we* were the blessed ones, that being welcomed as if we were entitled to something was not warranted. Instead, he tried to make everyone in that room understand that we were servants to the needs of the people there. We were called by a power greater than any of us—by God—to do what we could do to make a tiny difference. His words washed over me. In fact, they reflected what I had been thinking, and I was grateful for his thoughts. Jon's tears made a huge impact on the people there, and I watched as each Kenyan and the others from all over the world sat up a bit straighter thanks to Jon's recognition and grace. I felt the same pride. We knew we were the blessed ones there.

One of the lighter and even comical moments traveling the dirt roads was when our team went to church one Sunday. Having to go potty really bad, I headed toward the woods. Once I found a private—or so I thought—spot I started to hike up my skirt. Standing there off in the distance was probably the oldest woman I'd ever seen. She walked my direction, shaking her head as I was rethinking my skirt hike. She motioned at the same time and pulled me to the hut that I knew held the toilet. I use the term "toilet" loosely here. I can now tell you from experience that even if taught by an elderly village lady how to position yourself on the squat and potty, you might pee on yourself and her, too, and then the only thing to do is walk away together, laughing. Despite the language barriers of this world, we all have a common bond, and sometimes laughter is the best way to reinforce it.

A Girl Named Peata

THE NEXT DAY WE SET off down more bumpy roads to visit a village called Tharaka. I thought it was going to be a day spent hearing stories of victories about healthy livestock and supple gardens that produced with little problem. The day turned out to be much more than I expected because of a girl named Peata.

During our time in Kenya it was customary to visit the orphans' homes and see their overall success with crops and livestock. As we walked along the paths, we were told that if the children had healthy livestock and produced crops, then they were deemed wealthy by the villages they had come from.

Peata was one of the orphans in Zoe's empowerment program who'd overcome horrific circumstances. Hers was such a powerful story of redemption that she was chosen for our group to visit that day. Arriving at her hut, we found shade and sat down to listen to the journey this teenager had been on and learned about the strength she had summoned in order to survive. As she spoke, her own little girl held tightly to her mother's skirt, adding her own luminous presence.

Peata told us of the night that she made the choice to give her body away for 500 Kenya schillings, around six or seven US dollars. Then she started to describe the farm she successfully took care of every day. Going from one emotion to the next, Peata lowered her head, kicking the dirt as she then told us that she had also been raped. In her young mind, there seemed to be a difference in giving her body away for the survival of her family and in the attack that had happened to her. She began crying and told us that the little girl, her daughter, was the product of that rape. I was shocked and enraged. She loved that little girl, who was so beautiful and loving and who seemed to be attached to her young mother with a grip that no one would be able pry apart. My heart ached with the common bond I felt with this girl I'd just met.

During the long ride back from Tharaka, I decided to let my mind take me back to the age of thirteen and the times I had been forced and coerced to have sex. Having listened to her, I felt that if I could let each image from my past bubble up, even my confusion as a toddler after having been molested, that I would finally be able to rid myself of this shame. For some reason I felt that I had a message from God that it was time to bring those experiences to the forefront of my mind. I could either toss them to the wind and forget about them, or use them to start growing my own strength. I could use my story for the greater good.

I was not risking myself for food. I never fought or scratched or screamed. I just froze completely because I never knew that I had the right to say no. I was never taught to fight back—or that I was worth the fight in the first place.

But Greg was right, and as God's words flowed through him and to me that night, I opened myself to tears. I came to understand that redemption meant I could receive a gift of beauty even from a bad situation. As I held the hand of my daughter, who was the same age as the Kenyan girls who were having babies and raising families, I felt pure love wash over me. I felt the grace that confirmed that my children would not have to suffer at the hands of someone else for their own survival. Their knowledge about the world—good and bad—would protect them, and they would learn to protect others.

When I left for Africa, I had been full of worries: Why didn't my mother say good-bye and wish Mary and me a safe trip? Why had I yet to get over the pain of my divorce from Mark? How would I make everyone happy and still run my life the way I believed I should? Why hadn't I been able to protect myself and not allow people to use or abuse me? When would the day finally come when I would love myself? At least until that day came, I could at the very least learn to like myself.

Things were going to be different. I could breathe and allow myself to rest and plan my next course of action with a newfound power. Watching the plane skip across the clouds while we made our final descent into Dallas, I thought to myself, "Steph, your life has a plan now, something you've never really had." The only thing I needed to fight off was the high fever that was rising in my body. I was sure it was just jet lag and fatigue. It didn't faze me though, because when I heard the airplane's wheels hit the runway, and I listened to the rain falling the afternoon of our return, I felt washed and clean.

For My Children's Sake

———

BECAUSE OF MY OWN EXPERIENCE with the lack of parental involvement in my education, I've been careful to provide them with a framework for success—a consistent routine, a schedule, rest, and opportunities to relax. Their educational achievements will ensure survival beyond school; my kids won't have to resort to street smarts and bullshit to survive. I promised that my children wouldn't have to hide something like not being able to read or write correctly like their mom did.

I want my kids to have more than educational tools, however. I want them equipped emotionally to step out into the real world. Assurance of unconditional love is the only way to impart that to them. As their mom, I have passed on to them a belief in themselves. My children possess the ability to say no and enforce it, and to be vulnerable and strong at the same time. I am thankful that I hold the honored position of their mother—I get to love them.

Providing a stable home environment isn't something that came naturally for me. I had no role models. When I was little, I probably would have said that a good home on a good day included a mom and a dad together and involved in my life. Concerned. Interested. Caring. Alive and there. I'd have wished for my Utopia.

I'm in a different place today. While my kids are still the most important people in my life, I'm now more equipped to be the woman I need to be, and I don't expect my emotional needs to be met by anyone else. Not until that person is good for me.

Since I'd missed out on the kind of relationship I wanted with my parents, I made sure my kids had the things I longed for when I was growing up, and I don't mean a dream dollhouse or a fancy new car for their sweet-sixteen birthday. I longed for safety and security. A listening ear, a warm blanket, and nights when I could close my eyes and sleep without fear. To be heard. My kids know what it means to be treated with dignity and respect and to have their opinions valued. I'm not much of a cook, but we do have fun in the kitchen at times, especially if Mary is baking at Christmas time or Miranda is making her famous spaghetti sauce. We have meals together, even when we're not at home.

I told my three children that I'm their dictionary when life needs to be defined. I'm not the law and certainly not the judge. Only God sits on that throne. But I have been entrusted with their lives, and I have a privileged job as their mother. No matter how I got here and no matter the mistakes I've made in trying to do my job, it is still my responsibility to be here for them. Recognizing the esteemed role that I play in their lives, I hope they never regret placing their trust in me. After all, trust is more difficult to win than love.

Baby's Got Blue Eyes

MIRANDA, YOU TAUGHT ME FORGIVENESS.
The most amazing thing happened the day I was with you in your new home on the beautiful island of Bermuda. Morning rain was falling and you were up, making your way quietly into the kitchen, to start brewing my strong coffee.

As the night sounds of the tree frogs ended and the sun rose, I lay in a cool room wrapped with blankets that looked like the blankets I used to wrap you in as a baby, only larger. I was thinking about a sad day when I found one of those tiny blankets but didn't have you to wrap in it. Now, though, I was feeling only the peace that most certainly surpasses all human understanding. In the home you made with your loving husband, Chris, I was sure that the next season of our lives has only blessings ahead.

Rolling to my side and stretching, I rose to find you quietly sitting on your cream-colored sofa with your two tiny puppies curled around you.

I was happy to have the full attention of my daughter for the day, and I hugged you as you served me coffee. How proud I am that we proved through the years that nothing could keep us apart.

You are a gracious woman with the wisdom of someone much older, and as you stood there, I could already see in a mystical way what your life would be like in the future. Right then and there I prayed for the blessings I so desperately want for you. Your beauty is much deeper than the obvious physical beauty you were blessed with. Your deep laugh can rock the surface of the coldest heart. Knowing and honoring yourself and the depth of who you are is what will sustain you in life and create true happiness.

"Mom," you said, "I think I will write a book someday titled *All the Things My Mother Taught Me.*" I laughed and said, "What not to do, right?"

You turned and looked at me, and suddenly I saw the two-year-old girl I had put through so much. I had unknowingly destroyed her childhood with my demons, and I felt a huge wash of sadness. Trying to realize that it was also through the mistakes of others was difficult. I decided a long time ago that all that occurred was strictly my doing.

"Miranda," I said, "I love you so much, and I am so proud of who you are."

"Mom," you answered, "it is because of you and our relationship that I am as strong as I am today."

Miranda, you and I have survived much more than most—a lifetime of bad choices and situations, an ocean of separation, and even having you ripped from my arms as a child. Because of our "winners never quit and quitters never win" attitudes, we never gave up. We never allowed defeat to weaken us or keep us apart. And we never will. The battle is over and through God's grace we won.

So as this book comes to an end, I can look back and find humility in forgiveness. I see how our history has made us both who we are, but most importantly I see how it has made you the kind of person who can adapt to others and see the truth in them. I am grateful to be part of you and your world. And I'm especially grateful that the night I sat in the pink tent and believed that you would be better off without this unfit mother, that I was not successful in ending my life.

I love you, Miranda, from the depths of who I am.

My Brown-Eyed Girl

MARY, YOU SAVED ME.

Having had so much disappointment and pain in my life, I believed that I wouldn't have any more children. I had felt like such a dismal failure as a mom that I succumbed to the thinking that I didn't deserve another baby. But when I look at you, I am astounded at how much God loves me.

The beauty of your strength is humbling. The way you conduct yourself as a young lady is a testament to your values. Knowing where your strength comes from is a foundation that will not waver even in the face of the storms of life.

You have allowed me to grow up alongside you, to mother you, and to be my authentic self with you. I pray that you have benefited from my overwhelming passion to make your life better than what I had. You have made me a better version of myself as well.

I want you to know that in life, it's okay to be both vulnerable and trusting. No matter the outcome, you give as only you can. I understand that the reasons I have had to endure all the ridicule, bad choices, and pain inflicted by others—as well as the bad choices I've made myself—is that God knew I would be able to create safety for you. I was made stronger because of it. Having the assurance that you would never be harmed by the wicked people in the world allows me to look back into my life and say I would do it all again.

Your beauty stops people in their tracks because they feel your personal power.

At first sight, your bold smile captured me. At that moment I thought of the day a year earlier when I stood in an empty parking lot of a place I worked. A wind of change, if you will. That day I had an intense feeling that something was about to happen that would save me, and it did. Your birth began to heal me.

You taught me to realize a strength that I didn't know I had. You gave me purpose and power so that I could be all I needed for you, all of you.

You will know what it is like to love and be loved, because you have had that from me and from those who cherish and surround you. You will know that sacred connection to others and the love that God is preparing you for.

You have seen pain, and you have seen disappointment, but it does not scare you, because you believe in a greater good and your faith in mankind.

I want you to feel grace, to have mercy and tolerance, to be humble. To feel so sure of yourself that you can hold your head up with honor and at the same time recognize your talents as a gift.

My pride goes deep. I feel proud of the person you are today and the way you have grown into your own identity. I respect and care for you far more than you will ever imagine, my daughter. It's true that by receiving love, we gather more from within to give to others.

I love you, Mary, go love the world.

The Boy with the Angelic Eyes

———————

JOHN, YOU NEEDED ME.

I am so proud to know you, son. It is difficult to find the right balance between love and hovering, which I am always accused of doing. But my mission has been to raise a strong man with a tough exterior and the ability to hear the needs of the world as well.

With your birth, I felt complete and able to forgive myself for all the losses of motherhood I had suffered. A missing piece that once found made me whole. I knew the world would welcome you. People love you, John.

The winter after you were born I was walking in historic downtown McKinney, Texas, and I stopped in front of a frame shop. As I reached down to cover you with your blue baby blanket, I noticed a photo in the window. I had been to the shop months before, and now looking back at me was a framed photo of you. The owner had asked to keep it for a while, because everyone loved that picture and wondered who this little boy was. With pride I said, "That boy is mine."

You're my child to teach, to guide, and then to let go into the world to find your place. Be a gentleman, son. Be one who understands the delicate balance of life. Give freely, but with boundaries. I pray I've provided a place for you to grow and learn, a place where judgment doesn't exist and you know your worth.

I understand that we create our futures by the choices we make, good or bad, and I do believe we *are* our choices. Take the time to stand still and listen to your heart and make the right choice for yourself. If it's a healthy one, then everyone you love, including yourself, will benefit. If it's not, and you have to learn lessons through painful experiences, well, welcome to the human race, baby. We have all been there. You are strong and allow life to train you, never be cynical about hope.

The power of affection is what I chose to empower you with. I will guide you. I know I am a girl raising a boy, and sometimes I may not do such a good job. But even if I have to Google how to teach you to shave, I don't mind. Be an honest man, son. That is the key to happiness.

I love you, John. Always listen for opportunities to show love.

Letting Go

IN RWANDA, ZOE'S EMPOWERMENT PROGRAM once again strengthened my commitment both to my life's meaning and to what I wanted my children to learn: kindheartedness and tenacity. That experience intensified my determination not to give up despite harsh circumstances, even when I felt some uneasiness, as if something was shifting in the universe.

Our last night in Kigali, Rwanda, I was unable to sleep, and I went knocking on Peg's hotel door, hoping she was still awake. "Peg, can I just stay in here and try to sleep?" I asked her. I felt strange, a feeling of worry and dread of impending doom.

"I have that same feeling," Peg told me. It might have been underlying concern about being in this city. We had spent hours trying to get one of the women in our group safely back into a taxi after we decided to go out after dark. I usually don't fear things like that, but I have to admit I was a bit concerned this time. Sometimes feelings don't make sense; they are just feelings. Mine, though, usually show me at some point what they were all about.

As I closed my eyes, I kept thinking about how I needed to get to Missouri to see my grandma, to take her a wood carving of Jesus that one of the orphans had made, and to tell her about everything I had experienced in Africa. She loved talking about missions, and I desperately wanted to share my experiences on the trip. In the middle of the night I woke up with an overpowering sense of some presence, but I shrugged off the feeling and chalked it up to my malaria medication, which sometimes caused weird dreams.

As the sun rose, a few members of our group wanted to go for a walk and take some more pictures. We set off to see where *Hotel Rwanda* had been filmed, and along the way I stopped to photograph a sign for my grandma. On it, an arrow pointed to a restaurant tucked away down a narrow road. The sign read: "Heaven This Way." I knew she'd love that. "Hey, Peg. Look! I can tell grandma I found it," I said, laughing, as we caught up to the group.

Everywhere I went that morning, a white butterfly followed me. I even pointed it out to Peggy, who had noticed it too.

Finally, our days in Rwanda were over. We got our duffle bags and headed to the airport, where I grabbed a coffee and tried my cell phone. There was a message from Miranda, asking me to call. Because of the huge time difference between Rwanda and Bermuda, I was worried I wouldn't reach her before we made our next connection. But she answered right away, "Mom!"

"Baby, what is it? Is everyone okay?"

Miranda was crying. "Mom, Grandma Smith died yesterday." As she told me when it happened, I was reminded of the night that Mary's grandma had come to her as a visiting angel so many years ago. The last time I had spoken to my grandma before I left Texas, she assured me we'd see each other soon. We did, but she was in the form of a white butterfly.

I have been told time and again that acceptance is the key to all my problems. Forgiveness is essential to letting go; suffering is essential to learning lessons.

In my opinion, everyone ought to read Hermann Hesse's novel *Siddhartha*, the account of Buddha's life—even if you don't subscribe to a belief system that allows you to learn lessons from other religions, philosophies, or just my crazy story, I recommend that you read about a man who learned life's meanings through suffering. He even brought it upon himself. I'd like to believe that since he hadn't attained enlightenment through everything going his way, we had a kind of common bond. You have to know bad before you know good.

As I finish this, it's my birthday. I am forty-eight. My dogs are curled up next to me on the floor of my office, where I have been living and reliving my life in these pages. There's music in the background, and I am at the end of this story. The framed picture of Ernest Hemingway on my desk reminds me that I can do this. There's also a picture of my brother wrapping his arms around me.

And there are pictures of my children: Miranda, at two years old, placing her teddy bear in her pink baby carriage. It was taken in my tiny rathole apartment the year I lost custody of her. She's smiling, because we are together that day. There's a picture of Mary wrapped in my arms with that intense smile and her hand reaching out to touch mine, always reassuring me she isn't going anywhere. A photo taken of John crushed against me, with both my arms around him, conveys the safety and love I have for him.

Dad's picture is from a time I thought would never end, but did—quite abruptly.

Even Marilyn Monroe—Norma Jean, since I prefer the authentic her—sits looking back at me with some kind of haunting "thank you" for telling a story with similarities to her own.

With all the people who have come into my life, I wonder what it would be like for them if I weren't here any longer. The ones who had to go through my stuff, would they ask each other, "Why did Mom have this Thumbelina doll sitting here all the time?" "Why does she have a picture of each of us with a note by it saying, 'I will keep you safe'?" "Where did this old bear that sits by her dad's photo come from?" And, "Is this Grandma Smith's old scarf?"

There would be a lot of questions. But the beauty of it is that because I have told you my story, you would have all the answers to the one big question: Who was Mom?

One thing I promise for sure: I would be sleeping.

Henry and Nana

Epilogue

HAVING MOVED INTO MY NEW life, I am excited to share all that I have experienced through my travels globally, locally, as well as right out my back door, where I can often find one of the newest and most exciting additions to my life—Henry, my grandson.

Discovering that your mosaic family continues to build with those placed gently in your world, I have accumulated so much love.

Making a stand with a nine-year-old soul sister, Vivienne, has boosted my movement into such a monumental space that daily I close my eyes in prayer, so grateful for the grace. Ending child slavery in her lifetime is a foreseeable possibility.

As I do my part in the eradication of human trafficking and domestic violence across the globe, I know that I won't see this hope come to fruition in my lifetime, but in my lifetime I will fight against it to the best of my ability.

For today, I head outside with my dogs and let the gravity of love keep me firmly planted to why I am here.

Closing my eyes, I sit with the sun shining down on me and feel empowered by the strength of its rays.

References

ACTIVISM FOR EMPOWERMENT FOUNDATION

stephanieannhenry.com

MISSION: Activism for Empowerment is dedicated to keeping the public informed about and involved with such issues as illiteracy, eating disorders, sexual abuse and domestic violence.

GENESIS WOMEN'S SHELTER DALLAS

genesisshelter.org

MISSION: To end the epidemic of domestic violence against women and children by stopping individual victimization and reducing the devastating impact of family violence through safety, shelter, and expert services to battered women and their children. We are committed to preventing violence by raising the level of community awareness regarding the pervasiveness and effects of domestic violence. If you need a safe place, call the Genesis Hotline: 214-946-HELP (4357). Help is free and confidential.

CASA OF COLLIN COUNTY

casaofcollincounty.org

MISSION: Mission CASA of Collin County promotes and protects the best interests of children who have been abused or neglected by training volunteer advocates to improve the child's quality of life and serves as their voice within the court system to ensure they are placed in a safe, permanent and loving home.

THE NATIONAL CENTER FOR MISSING & EXPLOITED CHILDREN

missingkids.com

MISSION: Established in 1984, the National Center for Missing & Exploited Children is the leading nonprofit organization in the US working with law enforcement, families, and the professionals who serve them on issues related to missing and sexually exploited children.

GUERRILLA AID – FOUNDER BARTON BROOKS

guerrillaaid.com

MISSION: Guerrilla Aid is a style of volunteerism—simply go somewhere and do something, while teaching others to do the same.

S.C.A.R.S., SAVING CHILDREN AND REVEALING SECRETS – FOUNDER/EXECUTIVE DIRECTOR DEBI RAY-RIVERS

scarsbermuda.com

MISSION: To reduce the risk of child sexual abuse and to be an advocate and voice for children who have been sexually molested and their affected family.

ZOE

ZOEhelps.org

MISSION: It is an all too common sight across Africa: children caring for children because their parents have died of HIV/AIDS, disease, war, famine, and other causes. They face lives of loneliness, hardship, and hunger. Many of the children end up begging for food, living on the streets, or worse. ZOE works to break this cycle of poverty and give these children hope. ZOE goes into communities where the orphans are already living, and brings them together in supportive groups. ZOE provides the resources and training they need to pull themselves out of poverty in just three years.

PROYECTO ABRIGO PROJECT SHELTER

proyectoabrigo.org

MISSION: For over seventeen years, Proyecto Abrigo has worked to make a difference in thousands of lives in Juarez, Mexico, and throughout the US.

MY SPA WATER – AUTHOR PAM WENZEL

myspawater.com

MISSION: Since introducing her Spa Water Collection in 2010, Pam has established a personal mission to educate others on the many key benefits of consistent water consumption. Via her speaking, travels, (like the one she shares below), and Spa Water products, Pam has made it her main goal to encourage others to adopt and maintain a healthy hydration ritual and overcome poor drinking habits and soda/sugary beverage addictions.

MAKE A STAND LEMON-AID – FOUNDERS VIVIENNE HARR AND ERIC HARR

makeastand.com

MISSION: Our mission is twofold: End child slavery in our lifetime, one bottle at a time, and empower kids with the belief that anyone can change the world with a little "heart work."

LOVE LIFE FOUNDATION – FOUNDER MAYLEE THOMAS-FULLER

lovelifefoundation.com

MISSION: To further expose the plight of abused children in our community by promoting awareness in our neighbors, family, and friends, encouraging their generosity and inspiring them to become involved. To break the cycle of child abuse by promoting and supporting those agencies that provide valuable aid, refuge, and hope to these innocent children.

Acknowledgments

———————

TO PAM, MY DEAREST FRIEND and business partner. Driving down the Dallas North Tollway, you looked over at me and said, "Girl-friend, this story—your story—has to be told." Through the many brutal hours of my research and documenting, you have been a constant guiding light, always directing me toward the goal—speaking up. I cannot thank you enough for sharing life with me and for the endless hours of talking through the night that got me to the other side of pain. You got me to power and to peace.

TO DARREN, AN ARTIST and my personal friend. When you discovered the look in my eyes that was undoubtedly the best option for the most important part of this book—the cover—I was able to "see" the dream. Thank you for capturing what I felt and reassuring me that I was supposed to put it down in writing. Thank you for helping everyone who reads this book to see themselves in it, and to have what I pray is truly a spiritual experience in their own healing.

TO JAY, MY SENIOR EDITOR at Greenleaf Book Group. You were the one who could truly hear my voice when I told my story. Your undeniable expertise took these words that I had written so many years ago, after many long workdays, and formed them into a clear message. Only you could translate my deepest thoughts onto paper. Thank you so much for the hand-holding to comfort me in telling the tale exactly how it happened and giving me the courage to not be silenced any longer.

TO KRIS, THE MANAGING EDITOR at Greenleaf Book Group. You always asked the right questions to keep me on schedule, help me meet deadlines, and cover every detail in the production of this book.

Your ability to know how to fit author and editor together is a gift. Thank you for your time, energy, and direction in the completion of this book.

TO BRYAN, MY PROJECT MANAGER at Greenleaf Book Group. It goes without saying what you have done to keep this well-oiled machine in working order. It was nearly an impossible task to keep "Steph" on schedule. I will be forever grateful for your professional way of getting us all to the end of the work but the beginning of the journey.

TO JESSE GRACE, EDITOR. Thank you for the time that we spent working together with pages literally spread all over the floor and for helping me to place the story in perfect order. If you hadn't shared your time with me that night in Seattle going through the exact details, I am not sure I would have arrived at the place I did in publishing this work.

TO JAYME DURANT, EDITOR. Thank you for the months of deep conversation and taking the time to read and reread the manuscript to help me through the beginning stages of the book. You're a gift, and I appreciate your time and energy spent on the project.

About the Author

A writer, mother, lover of life, speaker, and activist, Stephanie Henry has overcome tremendous adversity, which has in turn birthed a passion to help women and children rise from pain to power. Stephanie believes "passion is something born from loss" and embraces hers wholly. Born October 8, 1964, in Blackwell, Oklahoma, Stephanie was an I-35 nomad until she found home in McKinney, Texas, in 1997. Like many other women who've suffered adverse life experiences, Stephanie is a survivor.